REMAKING
AUSTRALIA

Remaking Australia

The state, the market and Australia's future

Hugh V. Emy

ALLEN & UNWIN

First published 1993
Allen & Unwin Pty Ltd
9 Atchison Street, St Leonards, NSW 2065 Australia

National Library of Australia
Cataloguing-in-Publication entry:

Emy, Hugh V. (Hugh Vincent), 1944– .
  Remaking Australia: The State, the market and Australia's future

  Bibliography.
  Includes index.
  ISBN 1 86373 450 3.

  1. Australia—Politics and government—1944– . 2. Australia—
  Social policy—1990– . 3. Australia—Economic conditions—1990– .
  4. Australia—Economic policy—1990– . I. Title.

320.994

Set in 10/11¼ Plantin Light by DOCUPRO, Sydney
Printed by Australian Print Group, Maryborough, Vic.

Contents

Preface   vi

1 The challenge for Labor   1
2 The background   12
3 Structural problems   43
4 Labor and structural reform   76
5 The Liberal alternative   108
6 The industry policy debate   129
7 The impact of globalisation   161
8 The social market model   196

Notes   222
Bibliography   245
Index   253

Preface

The struggle to modernise Australia's economy, to place it on a different developmental trajectory capable of surviving in the next century, is still only half-complete. Despite Labor's victory at the last election, it is not clear that it has the policies or ideas to bring restructuring to a successful conclusion. It is clear, however, that nobody else, including the Opposition, has a credible alternative program to offer. This is worrying because it is equally clear that Australia's economy remains in a highly vulnerable condition. In fact, with unemployment around the million mark, uncertain growth, a persistent deficit on the current account and a large foreign debt, there is no longer any margin for error. There are also serious problems of poverty and inequality.

At the time of writing (April 1993) many people clearly feel that Labor's previous commitment to free market policies should be modified. Mr Keating appeared to promise this at the election by invoking social democratic values, but how much substance was there to his remarks? The general economic situation severely constrained the government's capacity to change its general policy direction. It also feared, not unnaturally, to say or do anything which would call in question its primary commitment to the goals of structural reform. And, it was all very well to say that the government should change its policy mix, or distance itself from 'economic rationalism', but what did this mean in practice? The government's critics did not all speak with one voice: many of them were much clearer about what they opposed than what they were for. If the government wished to head in a different direction during its fifth term in office, it required a fresh conceptual map.

These are the issues, and the situation, with which this book is concerned. It explains, as clearly as possible, the contemporary debates about structural reform. It provides a sense of the background—why structural reform was and is an imperative— together with a balanced critique of the free market approach used extensively thus far. It tries to reconcile the central aims of the economic reformers with the chief points made by their critics. It argues that the time has arrived to replace the free market agenda with the model of the social market. The latter provides a way of rethinking the most important, residual question in the debate about how reform should proceed, namely, what is the role of the state vis-a-vis the market economy?

Chapters 6, 7 and 8 present reasons for relying rather less on market forces (and free market theory) alone as the catalyst of structural reform, and a little more on the state to steer or plan the overall process of reconstruction and modernisation. Bringing the state back in has some practical benefits for discussions of industry policy or the impact of globalisation on Australia. It makes possible incremental policy adjustments which the mindset of neo-classical political economy tends to rule out. Arguably, the idea of the social market provides Labor with the kind of conceptual map it now requires if it is serious about moving in a social democratic direction. It opens up options and pathways which were previously in danger of foreclosure, while also preserving the commitment to creating a more open, productive and competitive economy. It follows on from what Labor has been trying to achieve, it is credible in both intellectual and electoral terms, and it provides a way forward by showing how some of the more intractable pieces of the existing policy jigsaw can be rearranged to make a different pattern.

Overall, this is an essay in contemporary politics and political economy which blends the intellectual and political dimensions of debate in a style which is, I hope, as accessible to as many people as possible. It is also an essay in political education: it tries to provide citizens with information and a sense of perspective so that they may make better sense of the policies and social forces which are changing their lives, often, it seems, for the worse.

My thanks are due to Monash University for providing me with the opportunity to write this book; to Mark Tredinnick of Allen & Unwin for waiting patiently for a manuscript which proved more difficult to write than I expected; to Chris Wilding and Pauline Dwyer for their invaluable assistance in producing the manuscript; and to my long-suffering wife, Susan Schwartz, for facilitating the creative process in so many ways.

To every complex problem there is a simple solution and it is always wrong.

H. L. Mencken

When you hear an argument based on 'economic fundamentals', you would be wise to place a hand firmly over your wallet and keep it there until the perpetrator has moved on.

Robert Reich

Most people hunger after spirituality, even if that hunger remains unconscious . . . the sense of real purpose—the life force—could be expelled from a society whose leaders are obsessed by money, muscle and machinery.

Patrick White

The Owl of Minerva flies only at dusk.

G. W. Hegel

1

The challenge
for Labor

When Australians voted on March 13
1993, a Liberal victory seemed the most likely outcome, even
though opinion polls during the campaign had showed the Liberal
lead diminishing steadily so that on the morning of the election
the outcome was virtually too close to call. Labor had been in
office ten years and a number of ministers had plainly come to
the end of their tether. Registered unemployment stood at 11.2
per cent of the workforce, or one million people. Despite the
first signs of economic recovery, voters were well aware that
Labor had engineered the country's most severe recession since
the 1930s. Labor with 77 seats enjoyed an overall majority of
only 7 in the House of Representatives. The Liberal–National
Party Opposition required a swing of just 0.9 per cent to win
government.

In the event, Labor was returned with a majority of 13 seats,
its fifth successive federal victory. Despite a loss of 5 seats in
South Australia and Western Australia, the party acquired sufficient seats in the other states to secure victory. There was a
national swing of 1.9 per cent in the two-party preferred vote
to Labor. More notably, Labor's share of the primary vote, which

had fallen in every election since 1983, increased from a mere 39.4 per cent in 1990 to 45.46 per cent, back to the level of 1987.

For Labor, it was indeed a victory snatched from the jaws of defeat. For Mr Keating, it was 'the sweetest victory, a victory for the true believers, the people who in difficult times have kept the faith'. The result was very much a vindication of his political judgment and his campaign tactics; above all, it was a tribute to his own formidable skills, both shrewd and raw, as a political fighter.[1] However, it was debatable whether Labor's victory was due more to the political errors of its opponents than to its own merits.

Labor won because over the last two weeks of the campaign it was more successful in dictating the terms of political debate. Mr Keating especially turned the election into a referendum on the Goods and Services Tax (GST) and, running true to form, the electorate rejected it. Labor won because it played successfully on the fears of a conservative electorate. The Liberals, said Mr Keating, would create a fiercely competitive, dog-eat-dog society: their policies would compound existing inequities and exacerbate social conflict. Labor cared more for community values, for fairness and social justice. Labor would protect the Australian way of life. By appealing to traditional social values, reinforced by an appeal to nationalist sentiment, the Prime Minister apparently persuaded voters to overlook the fact that it had been Labor in the 1980s which had led the assault on the institutions, culture and practices on which the traditional order had been based since Federation. Similarly, Labor emphasised the far-reaching and unknown quality of the Opposition's economic agenda, especially its proposals for radical tax and labour market reforms. The fact that Labor itself had been advocating free market ideas, including labour market deregulation, was obscured. Labor positioned itself successfully as the moderate party of the centre, the party to be trusted with the all-important task of economic management, despite its record of one million unemployed.

Labor won because it better exposed its opponents' deficiencies and deflected attention from its own. It exploited whatever advantage it could find and in this respect waged a ruthless but brutally effective campaign which caused great resentment among senior Liberals.[2] However, although Labor fought a skilful rearguard, blocking campaign, the campaign was by no means a wholly negative one. Labor fought for the right to continue with its own policies—and here there were significant differences between the parties. A vote for Labor was a vote for retaining Medicare intact, for consolidating existing reforms in higher education, and for a more generous approach to social policy (although that point is certainly arguable). It was certainly a vote for a more consensual (or quasi-corporatist) approach to structural reform in general, and a more conciliatory approach to micro-economic and labour market reform in particular. It was also a vote for a rather more cautious approach to tariff reform, rather less emphasis on privatisation and for retaining a larger, if unspecified, role for government.

Given the nature of modern electoral competition, it is quite likely that the election was decided by differences in tone and style, in images and sentiments, as much as by substantive differences in policy. In this area, Labor had the edge: its pragmatism was more attractive than the Opposition's dogmatism, or 'ideological fixations', a phrase which the Prime Minister reiterated. Labor also grasped that the time had come to provide economic rationalism with a human face. Mr Keating clearly realised this during 1992, and although his speeches from early 1993 were mainly rhetorical exercises rather than attempts to restate in any detail the content and direction of Labor policies, nevertheless they were of some symbolic importance to both the Labor faithful and the electorate.

In January 1993, Mr Keating announced that he would fight the election as a traditional, middle-of-the-road Labor leader committed to extending what he called 'social democracy'. Thereafter he seized every opportunity to define Labor as the party of equity and fairness, and to portray the Coalition as elitist, inequitable and obsessed by its desire to unleash unfettered market forces. He sought to identify Coalition policies with those of Jeff Kennett in Victoria, and with the effects of Thatcherism in Britain. He disputed Carolyn Hewson's publicised belief that egalitarianism in Australia had brought mediocrity. Such people 'cannot imagine that we can have excellence in a system which is fair. I cannot imagine having it in a system which is not fair . . . Equity and excellence are not incompatible concepts'.[3] Where the Coalition feared, apparently, 'that the poor will drag us down', Mr Keating emphasised that fairness and efficiency were not mutually exclusive values: a social democratic society was one which tried to balance the two, and which tried to foster social cooperation and community development as well as a more competitive economy. Although Mr Keating did not address the question of *how* this balance might be struck, quite possibly he said just enough to differentiate the ALP from the more austere face of economic liberalism, and to re-kindle some hope among the true believers that Labor might yet reclaim its mission for social reform.

In other areas, too, Labor had a positive message to convey. Mr Keating argued with some passion that the nation should have a head of state and a flag which were distinctly Australian, which confirmed Australia's status as an independent sovereign state, and which were not reminders of the country's colonial origins. This tapped a swelling vein of nationalist sentiment: opinion polls suggested a growing number of voters found Australia's residual constitutional links with Britain anachronistic if not meaningless. Labor also offered more explicit support for multicultural values and, whatever its deficiencies in the eyes of committed environmentalists, it was still more receptive to their concerns than the Coalition. Mr Keating had also committed Labor to a formal reconciliation with the Aboriginal people by means of a peace treaty. Labor recognised that the Mabo decision, which overthrew the doctrine of *terra nullius*, might well lead in the direction of giving the Aboriginal nation a territorial base of its own. Finally, while both parties favoured closer ties with Asia, Labor advocated a greater political and cultural rapprochement with Asian countries, not just more extensive trading links.

With such issues, and in its greater support for the Arts, Labor revived its claim to be the genuinely progressive party in Australian politics. Indeed, it was at a concert given to launch ALP policy for the Arts that Mr Keating (with the aid of his speech writer, Don Watson) found the words which did project the kind of difference which Labor certainly believed existed between the parties. Australian voters, he said, could choose between, in Manning Clark's terms, the enlargers or the punishers: 'It is only the enlargers who push out the boundaries of this country. . . And of course the Labor Party is the party of the enlargers in Australia. We dream big dreams. We have a sense of a compassionate, creative society.'

He called on Australians to participate in building this society, multicultural and independent. In contrast, the federal Coalition were the punishers, 'narrow, hard people who never want people to lift their gaze, who preach that there's no gain without pain'.[4] It was the Labor party which had 'the bigger view of the place' and 'could do the big things'. Perhaps just enough voters believed him—even though there was a palpable gap between the hopes and goals expressed by Mr Keating and the policies required to implement them.

Following the election, however, that problem was obscured by the more immediate problems confronting the Liberals. Defeat seemingly confirmed what many had said previously: *Fightback!* was too large and complex a policy document for the electorate to grasp. The GST, even in its revised form (see Chapter 5) was politically unsaleable: evidently, too many people absorbed the message that it would leave them worse off. Too few grasped the package of compensatory measures intended to offset its impact on living standards. Liberal proposals for labour market reform, a faster rate of micro-economic reform, further reductions in tariffs, and for further reducing and redirecting government spending had a similar result: their adverse effect on particular interests or electorates was easier to assess than their possible longer-term benefit for society as a whole.

The Liberals were over-identified with an ambitious program for economic reform which did not pay sufficient attention to the social problems which ten years of restructuring, plus the effects of recession, had already created. Faced with the reality of one million unemployed, and the problems this created for many communities, there were a good many voters who were opposed to a greater emphasis on restructuring, to further appeals to reconstruct the economy on even more efficient lines. The Liberals, in fact, were speaking a language whose resonance and credibility among the electorate were already in decline. They were over-identified with a type of economic rationalism whose legitimacy had come under increasing criticism since 1990. They were perceived as ideologues when the Australian electorate was already beginning to return to its usual preference for more cautious, middle-of-the-road positions.

With the benefit of hindsight, one can say that (most) Liberal leaders were not sufficiently sensitive to the degree to which electoral opinion in the eighteen months prior to the election was already receding in its support for thorough-going market reforms: a good deal of Labor's unpopularity was due to that fact, to a resentment that Labor was not doing enough to assist the victims of structural change and recession. The Liberals were not sufficiently skilled to provide their reform agenda with a human face. They misread the mood of the electorate and offered what seemed to be a high-risk strategy for recovery at a time when the electorate had had enough of risks and pain, and wanted more reassurance—and a rather different social vision. The result confirmed that too few voters believed in the kind of economic revolution Dr Hewson promised.

Defeat left the Liberal party teetering on the brink of intellectual bankruptcy. Its lack of both options and a clear intellectual direction was demonstrated by the re-election of Dr Hewson as party leader concurrently with the decision to jettison *Fightback!* and the GST; and by emerging divisions within the party as to how far it should align itself with the movement for an Australian republic, and commit itself more fully to a multi-cultural society. Despite the advice proffered by senior figures in the party that it should adopt a more pragmatic approach to winning power, and/or re-invent the combination of middle-of-the-road liberalism and paternal conservatism which marked the Menzies era, the Liberals appeared reluctant to come to terms with the real message of five successive election defeats: there was something wrong with the party's social philosophy, with the kind of liberalism which now dominated the senior ranks of the parliamentary party. The latter's radicalism in economic matters did not reflect what many in the community, including some Young Liberals, now regarded as socially progressive politics. In addition, the party's free market rhetoric did not sit easily with the way states and corporations were actually behaving in the new global economy. The party also appeared out of touch with the rising nationalist strain in Australian society.

What the party required was a serious exercise in ideological self-examination to think out how far its neo-classical perspective on the proper relationship between state and market was appropriate in the face of globalisation, rising social inequalities and concern for the environment. It needed to think out more carefully where it stood in relation to nationalism, republicanism, multiculturalism and social policy; it needed to develop a more sophisticated attitude towards the concept of sustainable development. In all such areas, the initiative belonged with the ALP, at least at the level of electoral competition. Having practised a form of ideological exclusion for several years, which had narrowed the party's intellectual appeal, the Liberals needed to think about reversing this process, trying to attract a greater diversity of support at the grassroots level. Unless they could do this, or until they could produce leaders with a broader range of social values and better communication skills, it was hard to see just how the Liberals would regain power. In fact, unless they could devise a version of liberalism which possessed more depth and breadth than the neo-classical one, their chances not only of remaining in opposition but of becoming an increasingly marginal force in Australian politics, appeared uncomfortably high.

The election result certainly made the Liberals the primary targets for criticism because they lost an election which was theirs for the winning. However, one can go further: what this election really demonstrated was an intellectual vacuum at the core of Australian politics. Neither party offered the electorate what it most wanted to hear: a clear idea of just how the country was going to overcome its increasingly serious economic problems, by what means and when. Neither offered a developed social vision nor a national strategy for reform. A vote for either party was really a vote in the dark, a vote cast in hope, or against something worse, rather than a vote for a party which knew precisely what it was about and where it was going. The implications of this vacuum are discussed further in Chapter 2.

The election also revealed the ideological tensions latent in Labor's own position. Indeed, had Labor lost, it might well have experienced even more ideological feuding than the Liberals very likely will. Winning bought Labor the time and the opportunity to rejig its approach to structural reform in the manner Mr Keating was suggesting. However, while the euphoria of victory overshadowed the two main problems which had beset the party since 1987 at least, the victory in itself did nothing to resolve them.

The first problem was that of identity: what kind of party was it and what did it stand for? In the past, the party's avowed mission had been to create a fairer and more equal society, to civilise capitalism and ensure that the latter's productive energies were used to benefit society as a whole. Some within the party had seen its role as equalising the overall distribution of income and resources to benefit organised labour or, more broadly, the working people of Australia. Others thought the party's role was to use state power to qualify and redesign the way the capitalist productive system worked and by so doing to bring about a qualitatively superior kind of society, one which was more egalitarian (or less hierarchical) and which encouraged the creative talents of all its members.

In the 1980s, the party's social mission, its rationale as a party of *social* reform, was obscured by its pursuit of economic restructuring. Although Mr Keating in particular argued convincingly that restructuring was fundamental to preserving the future security of Australian industries, jobs and living standards, especially those of the working class, the more the party in government emphasised the need to create a more open, productive and competitive market economy, the more it seemed to be retreating from—and even reneging on—the party's original reformist ideals. The touchstone of this argument was the government's use of free market ideas and market forces (in short, 'economic rationalism') to engineer a more productive society. The more the government relied on what was seen to be the chief supporting ideology of modern capitalism, the more it seemed to distance itself from values like fairness and social equality.

So, when Mr Keating signalled a retreat from the free market ideology that had dominated the political agenda until very recently, the true believers were much relieved. At Labor's election celebration party, Mr Keating proclaimed 'we truly have the option of . . . becoming one of the great social democratic parties . . . for the great purpose of establishing a great Australian social democracy'.[5] Labor, he said, would now give greater emphasis to promoting social equity and distributive justice. He (and other ministers) foreshadowed a determined effort to tackle unemployment by giving a high priority to growth and increased government spending, even at the cost of a much larger federal budget deficit (forecast to be $16 billion in 1992–93); plus a somewhat greater role for government to intervene in the economy to deal with market failures. The overall aim was 'a society which works simultaneously to generate wealth and alleviate poverty'.

The outstanding challenge for Labor in the 1990s was how to resurrect its social ideals and how to marry these with the program for structural reform which had dominated its agenda in the 1980s and to which it was still strongly committed. This was easier said than done. The puzzle which has perplexed moderate democratic parties of the left in all countries this century is precisely how to reconcile the moral and social ideals which inspired social democracy with a genuine commitment to the wealth-creating mechanisms of the market economy. Labor was still committed to a program of economic liberalisation; the question was how and where to strike the balance between what still remained of economic rationalism and its revived concern with social justice.[6] Finding this balance was fairly crucial to its re-election prospects—and to Mr Keating's place in history.[7]

This point leads directly to the second underlying problem: how best to pursue structural reform, and how to maintain the momentum of reform which was still not fast enough for many business groups? Here the government faced a real dilemma. It was relatively easy to signal a retreat from free market policies. In fact, almost from the moment Mr Keating became Prime Minister, the government had been backing away from the free market rhetoric it had employed after 1987; throughout 1992 it had been moving, quietly, in a more interventionist direction (see mainly Chapter 6). Yet, while many in the party (and the community) welcomed this policy shift, for the government (and its advisers) repositioning itself vis-a-vis the market was a much more difficult exercise than appeared at first sight; it involved a substantial shift in intellectual perspective as well as a series of policy shifts which were not entirely incremental.

For one thing, any marked shift in policy could easily be represented as a U-turn, a surrender to special interests, a charge more likely to upset the foreign exchange markets than the electorate but serious nonetheless. For another, however much particular ministers might have wanted to change the policy emphasis, the government did not actually have available to it a coherent, conceptually-based alternative to the framework provided by neo-classical economics on which it had been relying for the past five years. Lacking such an alternative, at least one which had credible intellectual backing, the government was reluctant to move too far or too fast from its prepared positions and arguments, fearing it would still be vulnerable to attacks from the financial press if not the Opposition. Moreover, the government still agreed with mainstream opinion that the program of economic liberalisation remained *substantially* the best policy route for Australia to follow.

The other great unresolved question facing Labor, therefore, was what would or could succeed economic rationalism as the intellectual framework for pursuing further structural reform and economic modernisation? It was much easier to criticise free market ideology, to say that Labor should retreat from the language of market forces, competition, corporatisation, privatisation (etc.) than to spell out an alternative economic strategy which was consistent with the thrust of existing policy; viable given Australia's existing, rather vulnerable, economic situation (Chapter 3) and acceptable to the currency markets.

Moreover, criticisms of economic rationalism came from different political quarters and reflected different agendas. The government and its advisers were concerned that calls for more government spending, more intervention or a slowdown in tariff cuts contained the potential to divert or subvert the process of structural reform. The reform agenda was still at an early stage: reformers feared a revival of the earlier handout mentality. Anyone familiar with the strength of the previous rent-seeking culture (Chapter 3) would admit they had a point. The election also seemed to demonstrate that the electorate's patience with structural reform was shrinking: the government could not afford to change its rhetoric or its policies in a way which would, however unwittingly, undermine the community's will to press on with a process still only half completed.

The ALP's dilemma was how to modify its free market stance sufficiently to appease critics within the party and community without endangering the fundamental goals of restructuring: to create a more viable economy which could survive in the kind of global economy which had now emerged. In a real sense, most of its critics (except the Opposition) were now concerned to make a similar point: the emphasis on the unfettered market and a small state had gone too far; it was time for the state to be brought back in to 'the main game'.

The strongest industrial economies, those most successful in global competition, were those where the state played a carefully designed strategic role aimed both at fostering the internal competitiveness and productivity of the domestic economy, while assisting its more efficient (and strategic) industries to acquire and consolidate a competitive advantage in the global economy—

especially in those areas of manufacturing whose products were increasingly central to the viability of high-tech economies and the living standards of their citizens. What was emerging in 1991–92 was a strong suggestion that the state in Australia could and should do more to sustain the competitive advantage of Australian firms by developing a more discriminating and strategic industry policy than had existed hitherto.

Prior to the election at least, this suggestion had been resisted by most of the government's principal economic advisers (and by most of the financial press) who remained wedded, on the whole, to a neo-classical free market perspective. In their view, to embark on policies of greater intervention and assistance was to step onto a slippery slope. In principle, the most competitive firms were those which did not rely on various kinds of government assistance, but which prospered by their own efforts. Once again, free market reformers feared that to bring the state back in as a significant player in the process of structural reform, or to give in to the growing calls for a more definite industry policy, was to encourage—among manufacturers especially—the kind of cosy, dependent relationships with the state which had been such a feature of the era of protectionism. The only way to create a more efficient and competitive manufacturing sector, in Australia especially, was to make it crystal clear to firms that they could not expect the state to fight their battles for them. Proponents of an industry policy replied that this was a complete misreading of their own proposals, and a complete misunderstanding of the kind of symbiotic relationships between states and firms which increasingly characterised trade in the global economy (Chapters 6 and 7).

In this area, then, the ALP faced an awkward double challenge: if it wished to retreat from its free market agenda, and if it thought there was something to be gained by involving the state more directly in the whole process of social and economic reconstruction, could it 'bring the state back in', to industry policy say, on a *de jure* rather than a *de facto* or ad hoc basis, without repeating past errors, and without sending the wrong signals to special interests or the currency markets? If it accepted that its task was not simply structural reform but nation-building, and that the state had to play a more active role in steering the process of change and deciding what kind of society should emerge, then how to redraw the respective spheres of state and market? In particular, if the ALP was not, after all, going to go all the way with the free market, then what kind of market economy did it see itself creating? In other words, once the Labor party began to think that the emphasis on the market (or 'economic rationalism') had gone too far, it faced a major intellectual problem: not only how to bring the state back in, but how to reconceptualise—and to rework in policy terms—the relationship between 'the market' and 'the state', another enduring puzzle of the twentieth century. Resolving this puzzle was also crucial to re-establishing its own credentials as a social democratic party. If it wished to expand the state's responsibilities for social policy and welfare, and reclaim concepts like collective responsibility and the social wage, then it had to rethink both the proper size and province of government, and how far a market economy could (or should) be left to run itself.

The challenges facing Labor were indeed quite formidable: to clarify what it stood for and to re-establish its credentials as a social democratic party; to define more clearly the social vision which would inform its policies in the 1990s; to find a viable balance between its own selfconscious social mission and its structural reform agenda; to move in a social democratic direction without compromising its economic goals. The conceptual thread linking all these problems was how to redefine the balance between state and market. To these one could add many particular challenges: notably, of reducing unemployment, dealing with environmental deterioration, the aspirations of Aborigines, of women, of constitutional reformers and republicans; consolidating Australia's improving relations with Asia, or further implementing labour market and micro-economic reform. Many if not all of these formed part of one overwhelming challenge which was, in Paul Kelly's suggestive language, to determine what new amalgam of values, institutions and policies would replace the components of the Australian Settlement which finally disintegrated in the 1980s.[8]

2
The
background

Fate of a nation

For a century or more Australians have enjoyed and taken for granted the status and benefits of a 'developed' society—in material terms, at least. In the past decade we have had to come to terms with the uncomfortable realisation that in certain respects—notably our prolonged over-reliance on commodity exports, the lack of a strong, export-oriented manufacturing sector and the hitherto low level of formal educational qualifications—Australia has more the profile of a developing society (and is so regarded by many in Japan). For 40 years after 1945, Australia was protected by high tariff walls from the impact of dynamic changes in the world economy. Other countries industrialised, and adapted successfully to the accelerating pace of change in the global economy, while Australia stood still. Now the country faces a forced march to catch up, to adapt, to build the kind of economic base which will support the consumer and leisure-oriented lifestyles prized by Australians. Failure means the probable loss of those lifestyles by increasing numbers of people.

The 1990s will very likely determine whether Australia continues to enjoy the living standards of a developed first world society, or sinks further towards the bottom of the league table of industrial and industrialising countries. Between, roughly, 1960 and the late 1980s, Australia fell from fourth to sixteenth position in terms of Gross Domestic Product (GDP) per capita, in a list of 26 such countries.[1] Warnings of 'banana republic' status may well be an exaggeration but, without a sustained growth rate of at least 3 per cent per annum, and preferably higher, throughout the 1990s, Australia will not reduce the current level of unemployment substantially and will sink deeper into debt. It runs the risk of falling into the ranks of the poorer countries in the OECD (Organisation for Economic Cooperation and Development), such as Ireland, Portugal, Greece and Turkey. It may also be overtaken by a number of more dynamic economies in South and East Asia, a point which has repercussions for our economic and political independence in the future.

There should be no doubt, therefore, about the gravity of the situation. The point is, too, that having grappled with the task of economic modernisation for nearly ten years, Australia has recorded only mixed success. There are promising signs that some reforms are producing their desired effects. There are other signs that, economically and socially, Australia is drifting into a situation from which a full, long-term recovery will become increasingly difficult. A more productive economy is emerging but the intensifying rate of global economic change—i.e. the impact of 'globalisation'—threatens to overwhelm the country before the process of restructuring can be completed successfully. Overall, despite the gains to date, Australia's fate as a developed nation hangs in the balance.

Australia is sometimes compared with Argentina, a nation which until the 1930s also enjoyed high living standards, and an economic history and structure not unlike Australia's. In the 1930s, Argentina failed to adapt to changing economic circumstances. Economic decline then catalysed a sequence of class struggles and unstable regimes which has plagued the country ever since. While one should not draw too close a parallel between the two countries, nevertheless one relevant lesson from Argentina 'is how quickly the process of decline can set in and, once started, how difficult it is to reverse'.[2] One of the few safe generalisations (or truisms) from history is that no society lasts indefinitely (with the possible exception of China): societies mutate or disappear, their fortunes rise and fall. Or as Kipling put it: 'Cities and Thrones and Powers stand in Time's eye, Almost as long as flowers, which daily die.'

There is nothing guaranteed about Australia's survival as a first world society. Societies can go backwards as well as forwards. Survival depends on bringing the current process of restructuring to a successful conclusion, but that in turn depends only partly on finding the right policy mix. It also depends on skills and factors which are much more elusive: the quality of political leadership; the strength of the will to reform among Australians; sustaining community support for often painful reform. In all areas there is cause for concern. Australia is, in a telling phrase, 'on the hinge of history'[3], but too few Australians appreciate this.

The importance of restructuring

There is no doubt that by the early 1980s, if not before, the Australian economy required a fundamental overhaul (see also Chapter 3). It was simply not producing sufficient wealth to keep Australians in the style to which most had become accustomed. The main reasons for this were: Australia's main export industries, agriculture and mining, were no longer generating sufficient income to pay for the imports of manufactures which Australian consumers and business had begun to demand in increasing quantities (this point was underlined dramatically by the collapse of prices in world commodity markets in 1984–85) and endemic inefficiencies in many Australian industries, and in the public utilities which supplied them, had reached a point where even high levels of protection could no longer guarantee their survival in the face of foreign competition. Moreover, a large proportion of Australia's relatively scarce supplies of capital and labour were locked up in inefficient industries when they might be used to better effect elsewhere. There was growing cross-party recognition that, especially in the light of global changes, the Australian economy was not capable as it stood of protecting living standards in the next century. The longer-term future of many Australian industries, especially those most highly protected, was doubtful, as were the jobs of those who worked in them. Australia also needed to find additional, and more secure, sources of export income.

There was thus a strong and compelling case for economic modernisation, for 'restructuring'. This went beyond merely rejigging the economy: it meant creating a new kind of 'production structure'[4], one no longer based so heavily on the export of primary commodities (agriculture and mining); one with a much greater capacity to produce value-added goods, whether from resource processing industries or from a revitalised manufacturing sector; and one with much higher levels of productivity in all sectors and institutions. Among all mainstream policy-shaping groups there was, between roughly 1975 and 1985, a growing recognition that Australia's traditional economic structure, its trajectory of development since 1901, had come to the end of its useful life. Australia as a small trading economy had no choice but to construct a more diversified export base. That in turn meant pursuing a greater degree of integration with the world economy, and equipping Australian industries—and the entire infrastructure which supplied and supported them—to compete in global markets. It also meant changing long-established attitudes towards work and rewards.

The fundamental intent behind restructuring is to place Australia's economy (and society) on a different trajectory, one capable of surviving in the kind of global economy which has emerged in recent years: an intensely competitive one, where the most lucrative sources of wealth stem from trade in value-added goods, especially complex manufactures, and from the sale of high-value service goods, notably financial, design and engineering, and educational services. It is also one where the balance of world economic power is swinging away from America towards Asia and to some extent Europe—and where survival as a first world society depends increasingly on maintaining strong trading and technological links with at least one of the three leading zones of economic strength: South and East Asia, Europe, or North America.

In the current policy debate, those points should be kept in mind. Restructuring remains wholly necessary, a defensive response to events—and a quickening rate of change—occurring at the global level which Australia, because of its reliance on trade, could no longer afford to ignore. Restructuring is an attempt to improve the viability of Australia's economy and society in the face of globalisation (see further below). One may dislike globalisation and all that it brings with it, but one still has to cope with it. Today there is a rising and important debate about how restructuring should proceed, but there is no doubt it must proceed. Because we have a small and currently very vulnerable economy, we have to come to terms with globalisation. Opting out, or trying to recreate the conditions which existed prior to the 1980s, is simply not an option.

In the 1980s there was both general agreement on the main problems and a sometimes surprising degree of agreement on broad policy directions. Labor as well as Liberal agreed that the root cause of Australia's problems was the long dependence on tariff protection. This had locked up resources in inefficient industries, insulated Australia from changes in the world economy, and created habits and attitudes inimical to growth and development. Protection had created both 'a handout mentality' and 'a rent-seeking culture' (discussed in Chapter 3). Australians generally, in public and private sector organisations, managers as well as unionists, did not realise how far they had already fallen behind levels of productivity, competitiveness and technological achievement in other countries. The broad answer was to move from a protected to a more open economy. During the 1980s, both major parties, virtually all major business leaders and a majority of union leaders, especially the leadership of the ACTU, accepted that creating a stronger economy meant creating a more competitive market economy. This did not happen all at once— the Labor government did not commit itself fully to free market ideas until 1987—and there were important differences of emphasis: Labor for long resisted the idea of labour market deregulation (see also Chapter 4). Nevertheless, there was general agreement that the most efficient type of economy was a market economy in which open competition between buyers and sellers (or, simply, the operation of the price mechanism) determined the allocation of resources between competing uses.

Quite why free market ideas—or the theory and practice of neo-classical liberal political economy—achieved the prominence they did in the 1980s, in Anglo-American cultures especially, calls for explanations that go beyond this book. In Australia, however, one major reason for their initial popularity and implementation was that they provided ideal weapons for a loose coalition of like-minded people in the central bureaucracy, in the financial media, in sections of business (notably mining) and in both parties who, during the previous ten years had grown convinced that Australia's future could only be secured by breaking with protectionism. The strength of this feeling, and indeed its essential core of truth, should not be under-estimated. The drive for a market economy, and the ensuing faith in market forces which has come to dominate the political right especially, reflects a long bottled-up frustration with the excesses and inefficiencies of Australian statism, the cronyism and the near-tribal insularities endemic to some parts of Australian society. Free market ideas—or what is now referred to summarily and pejoratively as economic rationalism—provided the intellectual explosives with which to mine the tariff walls and overwhelm 'the special interests' benefiting from the whole culture of protectionism. This complicates the current debate because although one can accept that in the 1980s the program of economic liberalisation provided the necessary impetus to reform, that program was also supported and urged on by people whose goals went beyond economic reform, for whom restructuring formed part of an ideologically-inspired attempt to reconstruct Australian society on terms and values very different to those previously existing.

Greater support for the market and economic liberalisation represented both a sensible policy departure for Australia in the 1980s and an assault on values, institutions and, indeed, on a way of life which a number of people, mainly but not entirely on the right, thought anachronistic. It is hard to separate the two, hard to distinguish between using market forces to promote greater economic efficiency, and using the ideology of the market as the high road to constructing a much more thrusting, hard-nosed, competitive and individualistic society. Left-wing critics of market capitalism say that in practice the two cannot be separated, and they are not entirely wrong. But trying to distinguish the two, trying to discern and define a 'proper' role for the market, is crucial to the current policy debate in Australia.

The causes of Australia's fundamental economic problems are structural, i.e. they are not just the fault of governments: they are embedded in the way certain institutions work, in the way Australians think and behave, and in the location of the Australian economy within the world economy. These causes were and are sufficiently deep-rooted to require radical (i.e. root and branch) therapy, and free market theory provided this. It provided the crucial means of switching Australia's developmental trajectory from one set of tracks to another. Now it is a matter of deciding how far we should take the emphasis on the market (or, as left-wing sceptics might say, how to get the genie back in the bottle).

In the 1980s and until quite recently the reform process was supported and facilitated by a significant consensus among the principal groups involved. Substantial agreement emerged on the following five points:

1. Tariffs must be reduced. Australian manufacturers especially should be exposed to a greater degree of overseas competition. This would force firms to raise their own productivity and develop rational response strategies in order to survive. Inefficient firms would fail, thereby releasing resources for the more efficient. Competitive firms would pressure their suppliers to become more competitive, thereby creating a kind of chain effect throughout the economy. All firms should, ideally, search out export opportunities and become more outward-looking.

2. This strategy was reinforced by financial deregulation, i.e. floating the dollar and removing nearly all government controls on the way financial markets operated. It was hoped this would improve the supply of (cheaper) capital to the more

efficient Australian firms, and lower the cost of financial services to Australian consumers. With tariff reductions, this was a key part of the policy to integrate the Australian with the global economy. To date, it has been one of the least impressive reforms, although it may still be argued that it was a necessary and, indeed, an inevitable response to globalisation.[5]

3. It was further reinforced by competition policy, aimed at breaking down monopolies in both the public and the private sectors, and exposing all Australian firms and organisations to some form of price competition. This aim was expressed first as support for 'deregulation', or opening up hitherto closed sections of the economy to market forces. This in turn gave way to a greater emphasis on micro-economic reform after 1987 (Chapter 4).

4. It was also generally agreed that Australians in all areas had relied too much on government and should be encouraged to become more self-reliant. The public sector should be reduced in size, ostensibly to release resources for private sector growth. The federal government should reduce all forms of assistance to industry groups to force them to promote the efficiency of their own operations. Welfare spending should be targeted even more specifically at those in real need. All governments should prune drastically the number of rules and regulations which hampered business and discouraged business investment.

5. There was general agreement that labour productivity must increase substantially. By 1988 there was broad support for workplace reform, to be achieved through award restructuring and implementing the principle of structural efficiency. This in turn led to growing support for the idea of deregulating the labour market. Labor and the ACTU, having originally resisted this idea, by 1991–92 were supporting their own version of enterprise bargaining.

Australia's current economic plight should not detract from the scale of the changes which have occurred. These and others are discussed later in this book, but it is instructive to skim the list.

• In 1983, Australia (along with New Zealand) was the most highly protected economy in the world. The Labor government is now committed to reducing the tariff on cars from 35 per cent in 1992 to 15 per cent by 2000; on TCF (Textiles, Clothing, Footwear) to 25 per cent (maximum) by 2000 and on general manufacturing to 5 per cent by 1996.

- In 1983, those who attacked centralised wage fixation were regarded as heretics. Now both parties advocate enterprise bargaining, decentralisation and extensive award restructuring, although in different forms.
- The size of total public sector outlays in Australia fell from a peak of 42.7 per cent of GDP in 1985–86 to under 36 per cent by the end of the 1980s. Commonwealth budget outlays, which peaked at 30 per cent of GDP in 1984–85, were cut back to 23.5 per cent (or the level of 1973) by 1990–91 (but are now rising again in the aftermath of recession). Australia's historic reliance on the public sector to provide most of the social infrastructure has given way to cross-party support for the merits of corporatisation, contracting-out and privatisation.
- Until the mid-1980s, 75–80 per cent of Australia's export income derived from commodity-based exports. This pattern has begun to change. Between 1981–82 and 1991–92, total manufactures rose from 19.6 per cent of total exports to 27.3 per cent (almost equivalent to recession-hit total rural exports, 28.8 per cent). Exports of complex manufactures rose from $2.5 billion to $10.2 billion, or 18.6 per cent of total exports. Exports of services also grew from approximately 15 to 20 per cent of total exports during the 1980s.
- In 1950, half of Australia's exports went to Britain alone. By 1990, that figure was under 4 per cent. Exports to Western Europe have fallen from 35 per cent in 1962–63 to 16.6 per cent in 1988. Exports to North America have remained constant at about 12 per cent. Meanwhile, Japan now takes 30 per cent of our merchandise exports and other east Asian countries take just over 20 per cent. So east Asia takes over half our exports and supplies nearly half our imports.
- In 1980 Australia was very much an under-educated society. The 1981 Census showed that just on half the adult population had left school between the ages of 13 and 15. Seventy-one per cent of adults had no formal post-school qualifications. By 1985 that figure had fallen to 65 per cent and to 59 per cent by 1991. In 1980, approximately 1 in 3 students went on to Year 12. By 1992, the national retention rate was 70 per cent, and in Victoria 86 per cent. The numbers proceeding to university increased from 348 000 in 1983 to approximately 530 000 in 1992. There may soon be a similar expansion in TAFE.

In a very real sense, therefore, Australia is now on a different developmental trajectory and the Labor government deserves credit for confronting the problems and helping to bring about the transformation which has occurred. Nevertheless, in April

1993 Australia's underlying economic position can only be described as precarious, a situation for which the Labor government, having engineered the recession, must bear its share of the blame. Despite its election victory, and Mr Keating's new rhetoric, there is no certainty that Labor (or anyone else) knows what combination of policies are now required to drive the reform process to a successful conclusion. As Chapter 1 noted, the election result may also be taken as revealing the electorate's growing disenchantment with reform and restructuring. This situation is serious because community support is essential to maintaining the momentum of reform. Moreover, Australia's economic position is critical because there is no longer any margin for error (Chapter 3). Dealing with the current account deficit and the foreign debt, and creating jobs, depend upon sustained growth throughout the 1990s. Any slackening of momentum, any halt to growth, could have disastrous consequences for Australia. One might add that some of the calls for slowing down or modifying Labor's existing policies are not entirely consistent with the goal of creating a stronger trading economy.

The primary residual question on the political agenda is how far to take the market emphasis which has driven policy between, especially, 1987 and early 1992. Can one sustain the pace of reform without relying quite so heavily on free market ideas? Should the (federal) government play a greater role in steering the process of social and economic reconstruction? If it did, what would the respective spheres of state and market look like? What kind of synthesis might best unite community support for reform with the still-painful process of restructuring?

Arguments about restructuring

In 1991–92 there were already signs that the consensus which had supported restructuring during the 1980s was unravelling. The Opposition criticised the slow pace of micro-economic and labour market reform and argued that a stronger dose of free market policies was required to speed up the reform process and to get the economy moving again. However, the disagreement between the parties was only one aspect of a complicated field of debate. Between the two elections of March 1990 and March 1993 dissent from government policy was expressed in four main quarters: by leaders of business opinion, often via the Business Council of Australia; by manufacturing groups; by a variety of community-based organisations, notably ACOSS (Australian Council of Social Services) and several churches; and by 'traditional' social democrats within the Labor party. The problem was that each of the four had different substantive points to make: the debate about what should be done was increasingly confusing. (If one threw in the environmental lobby's concern for sustainable development, the views of traditional conservatives, and those of unions and managers in particular industries, one swiftly reproduced the Tower of Babel—which is what the government heard.)

Business, especially big business, leaders commended the broad thrust of structural reform, and welcomed tariff reductions and deregulation in the cause of creating a more productive, outward-looking economy. However, they were far more concerned than the government (or Treasury) with Australia's inability to eliminate the current account deficit and the inexorable increase in net foreign debt. To many business leaders (and to traditional conservatives, and to economic liberals like Des Moore and John Stone in the Institute of Public Affairs) the latter constituted a clear and present danger which should be addressed more urgently. Its continued increase raised the spectre of Australia being caught in a debt trap (Chapter 3).[6] It also made Australia vulnerable to punitive reactions on the currency markets which could conceivably devalue the dollar substantially, thereby increasing the overall cost of servicing the debt (nearly 60 per cent of which is denominated in foreign currencies), in turn forcing further borrowing.

The situation caused many business leaders to doubt whether the government had really grasped either the gravity or the urgency of Australia's position.[7] Whatever had been achieved, more remained to be done. Unless the economic position was secured, all other community aspirations—for welfare, for the environment—remained in jeopardy. The Business Council especially criticised the government for placing too much faith in a rigid program of tariff cuts without ensuring that aspects of reform crucial to reducing business costs (micro-economic, infrastructure and workplace reform) proceeded according to the same timetable. In its view, the government had not paid sufficient heed to coordinating the separate aspects of the reform process.[8] It had proceeded in a piecemeal or hotchpotch manner. It needed to set targets and dates, to provide more of a strategic vision to guide reformers in different sectors, and to galvanise the community. The government had failed to take sufficient account of the way its own taxes and regulations hampered business. It was dilatory in addressing obstacles to business investment, notably the lack of an accelerated tax depreciation scheme for larger investments. (This was established by *One Nation* in February 1992.) Neither had it really addressed the problem of Australia's very low rate of savings, the absence of a strong enough rate of domestic capital formation to help provide the huge amounts of money required to fund infrastructure reform and the expansion of the resource processing sector, which was especially capital and technology-intensive.

Some of these criticisms applied also to the Opposition's program. Would the Liberals be able to reduce business costs in line with their zero tariff timetable? Did the Opposition fully understand the operational realities facing business in the global economy, or the reasons why many businesses were moving offshore? Business leaders often welcomed the Liberals' proposed tax changes, including the GST, but were doubtful about the likely effect of the Opposition model of enterprise bargaining upon workplace reform. In 1992, they clearly entertained real doubts as to whether either party could maintain the momentum of structural reform in the 1990s.[9]

The manufacturers shared many of these concerns but had others of their own, which sometimes brought them into conflict with other business leaders, notably in the mining industry. Manufacturers and miners agreed on the importance of a lower dollar to assist exports, but disagreed violently on the speed of tariff reform and the liberalisation program. Many manufacturers (but not all) were rather less keen on a cracking pace of tariff reform because lower tariffs released real and immediate competitive pressures which, because other costs did not come down nearly so fast, very quickly forced manufacturers either out of business or offshore. Manufacturers stressed they needed time to adapt, time to reach international best practice in organisation and productivity, precisely because Australian firms were often so far behind the operational efficiency of those overseas. They also needed time to retool with new technology. While for the most part they accepted the need to export, they also thought, given Australia's high propensity to import (and 95 per cent of Australian imports are manufactured goods) that there was some point in preventing viable and efficient Australian firms in key industries from disappearing through sudden exposure to fierce overseas competition—especially when such competition was often aimed at forcing the domestic firm out of its own market.[10]

The manufacturers, therefore, were less than keen on adhering to a rigid program of tariff cuts declared in advance. They were too well aware of the difficulties of penetrating overseas markets in the face of quota restrictions, visible and invisible trade barriers, imposed by foreign governments to protect their own markets. The manufacturing lobby thought Australia should not divest itself of tariff protection completely: that amounted to unilateral economic disarmament[11] in the face of competitor nations which had no intention of behaving similarly. There was some point in following the example of other countries which protected growing firms in key sectors until they were strong enough to stand alone. Those associated with the Australian Manufacturing Council called for 'a middle way' between old-style protection and free trade and zero tariffs (Chapter 6).[12] The touchstone of this dispute was the car industry. Its leaders protested vehemently that tariffs of 15 per cent by 2000 threatened the viability of the entire industry: zero tariffs would be catastrophic. In a sharp and public dispute with Dr Hewson and Ian McLachlan in the spring of 1992, car industry leaders affirmed that some level of tariff protection was a prerequisite for further investment in the industry. Their stand drew a sharp rebuke from other business leaders, who were fearful that the momentum for structural reform would be stalled: if one industry claimed exception, why not others?[13]

The manufacturers considered that bodies such as Treasury and the Industry Commission, which had been influential in setting the reform agenda, did not appreciate sufficiently the role and significance of manufacturing in the national economy. They thought some, at least, of the government's principal advisers harboured a strong prejudice against manufacturing industry, because of its past sins.[14] Many government economists seemed curiously indifferent to the changing composition of world trade, notably the declining share of commodities and the steady rise in the share of manufactured goods, especially of ETMs (Elaborately Transformed Manufactures). The manufacturers thought policy prescriptions coming from the central bureaucracy which centred on the drive for free trade reflected ideas about the nature of trade and the theory of comparative advantage (the theoretical cornerstone of free trade) which now required important modifications to fit them to the circumstances of globalisation and the rising centrality of high-tech knowledge-intensive industries. Whereas the Australian government wished to reduce industry assistance and to confine its interventions in the market to specific cases of market failure, other countries were finding that governments could and should intervene to help create or consolidate a competitive advantage for domestic firms (Chapter 7).

The manufacturers were clear that if the government wanted a revitalised, export-oriented manufacturing sector, it had to do more to facilitate its emergence. They agreed by and large with the importance of creating a more competitive economy. They drew a distinction, however, between stage one and stage two of the process. In the 1980s, the first stage of reform was concerned to remove barriers to competition, including tariffs, and create the preconditions for a more competitive economy to emerge. In the 1990s, the next stage was to actually build such an economy, one that was durable and could survive global pressures. It was not obvious that simply creating the boundary conditions for a more competitive economy would actually see the emergence and/or consolidation of a greater range of industries which could compete globally. As *The Global Challenge* pointed out, there was little sign of new industries emerging in the wake of tariff cuts—but plenty of cases of firms collapsing or moving offshore.[15] The manufacturers doubted (to put it mildly) whether a policy of leaving outcomes wholly to the market would produce the desired effects: new firms would not sprout up like mushrooms overnight. They required a certain amount of nurturing. It was up to government and industry (or industry councils) together to work out strategies for assisting the development of key sectors, to identify promising areas where Australia either had an embryonic comparative advantage, or might acquire one. It was also up to government to encourage industries which could contribute to import-replacement: a single-minded emphasis on exports alone was misplaced, given Australia's residual balance of payments problem.

The manufacturers had a point. By the early 1990s it was becoming clearer that Australia had to adapt to two external realities, not one. It certainly had to restructure an economy that was in danger of being marginalised by developments in the international economy. This was the initial challenge of modernisation—coming to terms with the cumulative impact of structural change in the world economy; with the fact that the lucky country had run out of luck: the kind of economy that had worked reasonably well for so long could not secure living standards in the next century. Economic liberalisation was the correct response to this first challenge.

However, even as Australia belatedly tried to adapt, a second challenge emerged very rapidly in the 1980s, that of globalisation. This term refers to the rising significance of high-tech manufacturing industries in world trade and the increasing competition between both states and firms for privileged access to all kinds of global markets, but especially those for ETMs. It also refers to the fact that the sources of competitive advantage in a number of modern industries differ from those previously seen as central by economic theory. These points are discussed further in Chapter 7. The general point here is that 'globalisation' signifies the impact of qualitative changes in and to the world trading economy, which conceivably herald the emergence of a new kind of global economy, new forms of competition, and even a new mode of production in (and linking) advanced capitalist societies. Although there are substantial disagreements over the theoretical implications of globalisation, there is growing recognition that it is causing significant changes in the trading strategies of both firms and states, and these in turn are further undermining the rules of the post-war liberal trading system and the hopes and ideals embodied in the General Agreement on Tariffs and Trade (GATT).[16] The problem for Australia is that in the pursuit of economic modernisation it committed itself strongly to the ideals and the policies of free trade and economic liberalisation, at the very moment when powerful forces in the global economy were impelling most if not all other major trading states away from those ideals and policies, even while still paying lip-service to them. By the early 1990s, Australian policy-makers found them-selves pursuing free market policies intended to cope with one set of substantial structural problems, while the nature and pace of structural change in the world economy demanded new policy responses which were often hard to reconcile with the values and perspectives held by those who had galvanised the first stage of reform. Those who strongly believed that economic liberalisation was the best policy route for Australia found it difficult to adopt fresh policies which seemed to contain vestigial elements of protectionist thinking.

The manufacturers, meanwhile, were saying that although free market policies might be necessary, they were not sufficient to produce a stronger manufacturing sector. They wanted a definite industry policy which involved a more strategic role for govern-ment (or more forward planning and targeting of opportunities), selective forms of assistance including a more pragmatic approach to tariffs, and greater attention to the strategies for economic development used successfully by countries like Germany or Japan. In the light of government blunders in Victoria and Western Australia, this was not a popular approach: it seemed markets could pick winners better than governments. However, by 1992 the case for an industry policy presented one of the strongest challenges to the mainframe of government policy. It was an argument for bringing the state back in, for some degree of intervention, when neo-classical policy had been aimed very firmly at getting government out of the economy as far as possible. The manufacturers argued (though not always clearly) that they were after a different kind of intervention, a more balanced relationship between state and market; they were not seeking a return to the bad old days, but a middle way between protectionism and pure free trade.[17] They were nevertheless castigated as 'closet protectionists' and 'rent-seekers' by most of the financial writers, and by the Industry Commission. However, what they were arguing for touched important chords among other community groups and the ACTU, increasingly concerned with rising unemployment and the scorched earth effects of free trade policies. In 1992 the federal government was clearly more receptive to these critics, and had begun to move in a more interventionist direction, mainly for electoral reasons, but without a very clear sense of just where it was going.

Can society cope with restructuring?

While both business and the manufacturers focused on the viability of the economic base, others were growing more concerned with the damaging side effects of structural change upon society. The election of the independent Labor candidate, Phil Cleary, in the Victorian seat of Wills in April 1992 (re-elected in March 1993) symbolised rising community dissatisfaction. The question remains how far the recession has de-legitimised the whole thrust of structural reform itself, causing an unknown number of people to think that so much suffering is just not worth it—an understandable but mistaken reaction. The point is, again, that there is no way back. The only way out of the swamp is to press on with restructuring to create the conditions for sustained growth.

The recession accentuated and dramatised changes already under way. It turned the shake-out of labour—occurring through the pursuit of higher productivity, flatter, leaner management systems and cost-cutting via contracting-out—into an avalanche. It underlined both the erosion of jobs for the young and unskilled through technological change, and the renewed importance of education and training (Chapter 4). The experience of the relief and charity agencies confirmed the growing numbers of people unable, mainly through lack of a job, to fend for themselves. Although the recession halted the upwards trend in housing prices, it still appeared that many in the rising generations might find themselves priced out of the owner-occupied market. The general recession came on top of a rural recession induced by another collapse in commodity prices, causing widespread anguish and suffering in rural communities and many country towns.

By the end of 1992 the registered unemployed numbered 11.4 per cent of the workforce, or just on one million people. Both the economic and the social costs began to appear unacceptably high. Unemployment contributed to physical and mental illness, family breakdown and increased crime, all of which imposed substantial real costs on the community.[18] It also contributed to the widening gap between those at the top of the social pyramid and those at the bottom: income inequalities appeared to be increasing steadily in Australia (Chapter 8) and talk of two nations had some substance. Although unemployment fell marginally in the first quarter of 1993, it became clear that the rate would not fall much below 6 or 7 per cent for the rest of the decade. The number of those unemployed for a year or more, already over 350 000, might well reach half a million. Another alarming fact was the view of many labour market economists that a growth rate of 3.5 per cent was insufficient: to bring unemployment down substantially required growth of 6–7 per cent a year.[19] There were grave doubts whether such a rate was sustainable, given Australia's balance of payments constraint and the sluggish state of the world economy. Both before and after the election, spokespersons from ACOSS, the churches and the unions emphasised two main points:

1. Policies for structural reform must give more importance to generating employment opportunities. It was no use dismantling inefficient industries unless there were positive strategies for creating alternative sources of employment. This underlined the manufacturers' point about the need to build up new or existing industries, and for governments to take more positive action to persuade some firms at least not to move offshore.

2. Given existing social problems and those which might appear in the 1990s, Australia had to provide more assistance and compensation for the victims of structural change and recession. Australia already had one of the leanest welfare systems in the OECD.[20] It should pay more attention to the example of such countries as Sweden and Germany which sought to cushion and legitimise the impact of structural change by providing generous (or humane) levels of welfare assistance and retraining allowances for displaced workers.[21] Such support was essential to minimising social dislocation. Governments also had to find more money for the social infrastructure which supported the halt, the lame, the sick and the handicapped, because these facilities were under great strain at state level. Given the scale of the problems, their resolution could not be left to market forces. Welfare and religious groups took strong exception to initial Coalition proposals to in effect withdraw the right to the dole after nine months, and to wind down and privatise large parts of the welfare apparatus (Chapter 5). The Catholic Social Welfare Commission and others opposed the imposition of the GST on food and clothing. The churches and welfare groups found the Coalition's strict emphasis on individual responsibility and self-reliance both unrealistic and, to varying degrees, morally obnoxious.

This, too, was a call to bring the state back in to uphold the principle of collective responsibility. The problems of unemployment, poverty and homelessness were problems for the community to address, using the resources of the community. They could not and should not be left to individuals to cope with alone. Clearly, the transition to a stronger economy would take time: governments had to be more conscious of the need to hold communities together during this time: prolonged unemployment was a social cancer, producing hopelessness or even violence among those affected. Such tendencies had to be resisted or they would negate the goal of a stronger society. The government was sympathetic, but worried where the money was coming from. The Opposition, wedded to a view of society as essentially a collection of self-interested individuals, appeared to view such sentiments as inherently left-wing and wimpish.

During 1992, a significant fault-line appeared to be opening up over answers to the question 'should the government (or state) play a greater role in steering or managing the overall process of social and economic change, or should it stand back and leave results to market forces?' Growing numbers of people, for different reasons, were beginning to think that reliance on market forces had gone far enough. The manufacturers, with support from both left and right, favoured a policy of selective interventionism. Community groups were saying that treating restructuring as an economic exercise pure and simple was not enough: society was a moral association as well as an economic unit. Economic reforms and policies had to be consistent with the moral values on which society was based, such as human dignity, principles of equity and 'fair shares', civil order and the rule of law. It was not only a question of building a more productive economy, but of building a fairer society too. It was no use having a rip-roaring economy if the benefits went unequally to a few: the results produced by market forces had to be regarded as fair and equitable by the majority. Economic efficiency had to be qualified by a concern for social justice.

By 1992 there was a widespread perception in the community that Australia was adrift on a sea of troubles. Opinion polls reflected high levels of bewilderment and anxiety about what was happening to Australia, and growing pessimism about eventual outcomes. They also reflected growing disillusionment with politicians and the political process.[22] Although the Australian electorate usually regards its politicians as, at best, a necessary evil, the negative responses revealed by the polls in 1992 were serious for two reasons. First, they confirmed again that the public had an imperfect understanding of, and mixed views about, the structural reform agenda. Not only was consensus unravelling, but the public was more confused and more sceptical about where the politicians collectively were leading them: many seemed to think it was into the wilderness. This was worrying given that Australia was scarcely halfway towards its overall goals.

Second, the polls confirmed the gap which had opened up between the politicians and the electorate. This gap also reflected the degree to which both main parties had become distanced from both their traditional supporters and their previous ideological stances. Several commentators remarked on the degree to which both parties had exhausted their ideological and moral capital: what they stood for in the 1990s was less and less connected to the experience and values of many of the people who had hitherto supported them.[23] This made it harder for such people to find their political bearings, harder to make judgments on the parties' policies and performance. It also seemed that restructuring was proceeding in something of a moral vacuum: it was driven by an economic agenda aimed at improving efficiency and productivity—which were imperative—yet many of the side-effects seemed socially if not morally undesirable.

The debate about economic rationalism

It was all very well for Mr Keating to declare himself in favour of a social democratic society, but reconciling social democratic values with the kind of principles found in free market liberalism—on which the government's approach to structural reform had previously relied—was no easy matter. It meant reconciling a belief in the virtues of competitive markets with principles of equity (and minimum wages); striking a balance between competition and cooperation, synthesising individualist values with those of collective responsibility and community development. After the election, as it acknowledged the need to tackle unemployment, Labor's major problem was to work out quite how and how far to retreat from free market nostrums; and, in so far as it was willing to retreat, in what direction was it actually going? Or, more directly, what could succeed economic rationalism?

The great strength of the pure free market position was that it gave simple (or over-simple) answers to complex issues, notably to the central question of how to structure state and market. Very schematically, state and market were conceptualised as implicitly antagonistic to one another: the size and activities of the state were usually presented as an obstacle to the efficient development of the market. Expanding the latter not only meant cutting back the scope or role of government: it also meant conceptualising the state in a wholly supporting role vis-a-vis the market. It was there to provide the kind of order required by the market. In the eyes of the purists, the 'proper' state was a minimal state, one which guaranteed the efficient operation of 'free markets' and which intervened only to correct instances of 'market failure'. More than this was 'interference'. Free markets worked best when let alone. The price mechanism was a better regulator of social and economic intercourse than governments.

In Australia this position rose slowly to prominence by the middle-1980s as the antidote to the various infections thought to be poisoning the economy and the body politic. Though controversial (more so than its proponents acknowledged, because of the social theory which lay behind it[24]) it was initially, in many respects, an apposite response to Australia's problems. Protectionism had encouraged a raft of restrictive trade and work practices. Australia was a bureaucratised, rule-governed society. Not only was the public sector growing steadily in size, at state and federal levels, but its efficiency was very questionable. There was much evidence of government failure. Resource allocation, especially investment and tariff decisions, routinely reflected political influence ahead of economically rational criteria. For more than ten years Treasury and the Industry Assistance Commission had waged a mostly lone struggle against what they saw as the gross mismanagement of increasingly scarce national resources. They argued in particular that economic decision-making in the public sector, especially investment decisions, should be based on criteria similar to those which prevailed in the private sector: that the public sector should be subjected to a greater degree of market discipline.[25]

The 1980s represented the victory of the 'economic rationalists', those who wished to base public sector decision-making on more defensible economic criteria, and reduce the scope for politically-motivated rorts and deals; who wanted to curtail the excesses and the developmental tendencies which they genuinely believed had brought Australia virtually to the brink of national disaster. In their eyes, invoking economic rationalism—or a belief in the superiority of the market and the price mechanism—was a healthy reaction to statism, paternalism and protectionism, an attempt to re-invigorate both civil society and the private sector. Their arguments were reinforced by growing awareness of Australia's underlying economic fragility, a situation hitherto concealed by natural resource endowments and an over-valued dollar. (They were also reinforced by other changes in the climate of ideas.[26])

In the course of fighting for a greater degree of economic rationality, there is no doubt that leading personnel in Treasury and the IAC developed a very strong mindset in favour of neo-classical market principles and the supporting ideology of small government, economic individualism and regard for the superior virtues of the private sector which lay behind them. Consequently, what began as an argument for a more rational approach to decision-making soon broadened into a much more extensive program for social and institutional reconstruction. By 1990 or thereabouts there were growing fears that this approach was turning into an economic juggernaut without brakes: the mindset created by fierce adherence to its tenets—especially the faith in the market as a nearly self-sufficient vehicle for human progress—was getting out of hand. Economic rationalists were coming up with policy prescriptions which threatened to turn Australia into a wasteland. However, there was also a danger that the reaction to economic rationalism gathering pace[27] might itself go too far. There was (and still is) a risk that one extreme thesis might provoke its own antithesis; the resulting confrontation could force the debate over what should be done into an impasse, preventing the development of more appropriate policies.

There are, perhaps, four main criticisms of the perspective labelled economic rationalism.

1. It reifies the whole concept of 'the market'; i.e. it imputes to something that is in the first place an intellectual abstraction a greater degree of concreteness (or physical existence) than it really possesses. An economic rationalist is someone who focuses too much on the logical properties of abstract models which portray the key components and relationships of free markets (how they are thought to be constructed and how they are meant to work) and too little on the complexities of actual people and markets in the real world. Economic rationalists do not tend to study the market *in* society: they are too keen to abstract markets from both society and history.

   One may well agree that free markets are invaluable for organising the economic life of large, highly differentiated societies which have reached a fairly sophisticated level of technological development. 'The market' appears to be the best method for organising the production system in such a society so as to maximise the chances of supplying a majority of the people with the widest possible range of services and products. One may also agree that the price mechanism embodies a certain natural logic. Critics of economic rationalism argue, however, that markets are the unwitting result of collective human endeavours, cultural artefacts, the outcome of particular historical and social processes: there is no natural (or inherent) tendency for free markets to appear. Moreover, the emergence after 1750 of entire societies organised on free market principles occurred concurrently with the change from agrarian to industrial societies and the shift to commodity production as distinct from predominantly subsistence economies.[28] This marked a revolutionary—and most often violent—transformation in human social evolution whose implications we are still trying to understand.

Therefore, the claims of many modern economists to possess a privileged kind of exact or scientific knowledge about the way markets work, and of what must be done to increase the sum of human welfare, should be resisted. Certainly, Economics can provide one potentially useful form of knowledge about markets, but insights from other disciplines should also be included. The free market is neither an abstract model nor a mechanistic thing to be manipulated in the way some neo-classical economists suppose. It is embedded in society, politics and culture and its social dynamics are inherently complex. The problem with economic rationalists is that by stripping the market down to its barest essentials, abstracting it from society, they endow it with a misleading simplicity. By so doing, and by over-simplifying the social dynamics of market societies, they run the risk of recommending policies which may not contribute to the long-run viability of society as a whole.[29]

2. Arising from this point, economic rationalism embodies a narrowly economistic view of society which downplays other social and moral values. It therefore gives too little weight to the social evil of unemployment and is implicitly hostile to increasing the level of compensation available to those disadvantaged by structural change. It is too inclined to individualist rather than collectivist solutions when dealing with structural problems in the community.[30]

3. It favours a narrowly technical and quantitative approach to decision-making in which the means of policy—the way in which decisions are made, which factors are deemed relevant—determine actual policy goals, rather than the other way about. It represents a form of decision-making by numbers, attaching numerical weights to all 'relevant' activities, and downplaying the significance or value of what cannot be so quantified. Whatever the intrinsic validity of the calculations, there is (a) room for doubt over how the base figures and operational assumptions were derived and concern about what cannot be weighted; (b) among those affected by the emerging policies, a strong sense that the reality as defined by the numbers grows steadily more distant from their own working experience, or life. This generates strong criticisms of the

overly abstract and seemingly artificial nature of the policy advice generated by economic rationalists.

4. Together, these points further suggest that the reaction against the state and interventionism has gone too far. Certainly, using market forces and competition policy to correct government failures was appropriate initially, but the experience of virtually all other market-based societies, except America and Britain (and even there, attitudes are changing), suggests that the state is conceptualised more correctly as a partner rather than an opponent of the market. Most other market societies do *not* regard the market as a self-sufficient, self-regulating entity, do *not* regard selective intervention (including specific forms of industry assistance) as inimical to the 'natural order' of the market, and do *not* have such a narrow view of market failure. In the great majority of successful OECD societies, the state retains a clear residual responsibility to oversee economic development, and to ensure that the market develops in a manner consistent with long-term national security. This point also suggests that Australia has been paying rather too much attention to the wrong models of how to restructure, i.e. America and Britain. Clearly, there is more than one type of market economy, more than one way to restructure, and it is time to pay more attention to the strategies for economic development and nation-building used by more successful societies in Europe and Asia.

Consequently, one might agree that by 1991–92 the free market pendulum had swung too far. What had begun as a legitimate attempt to extract maximum value from the public dollar had turned into an assault on most forms of public spending, almost irrespective of its social value or purpose. What began as an argument in favour of increasing individual freedom had turned into an attack on virtually all forms of collective social responsibility. What began with a greater emphasis upon efficiency had produced a type of decision-making, or calculus, which seemed to be out of kilter with the realities facing particular industries and organisations—and which, in its technocratic guise, was not altogether consistent with commitment to human dignity. Given the social problems facing Australia, especially unemployment, there was an urgent case for broadening the conception of restructuring, and reinstating moral and social values alongside necessary economic principles. This was, of course, easier said than done.

However, by the early 1990s Australia was moving in a direction which was diverging increasingly from international practice. In other market societies, some form of managed capitalism appeared more prevalent than the kind of laissez-faire, minimal state model which had been gaining ground in Australia in the 1980s. Countries like Germany and Japan certainly valued the market as the most efficient system for allocating resources, but unlike neo-classical liberals they did not regard the market as a self-sufficient institution. They did not have the same belief in market autonomy, or think that more market necessarily meant less government. There was also a growing sense overseas that the quality of government mattered as much as or more than size, and the clever state could and should make a substantial contribution to improving the competitive advantage of domestic firms.[31] Such countries were experimenting with forms of intervention intended to improve the export competitiveness of their own firms (Chapter 7). By such standards Australia was going down the wrong path by treating state and market, or government and business, as opponents rather than partners. While the attempt to expand the scope of market outcomes was and is important, there was a danger that Australia, under the influence of Anglo-Saxon liberal political economy, was simply recycling an old-fashioned and rather simplistic form of market theory, one which relied too much on stereotypical views of state and market, better suited to the nineteenth rather than the late twentieth century. To come to terms with globalisation, one had to go beyond Adam Smith.

To say this was to argue primarily against free market fundamentalists (i.e. economic rationalists) who, coming from one particular tradition of liberal thought, claimed there was only one way to proceed, one way to restructure—whose position was really 'the market *über alles*'. That was the ideological face of free market liberalism. There are in fact alternative ways to pursue free market ideas. One should add, however, that the doubts which neo-classical economists still entertained about generalised calls for intervention were not groundless. The latter entails costs and risks, much depends on the quality of government (always a cause for doubt) and one must come back to the earlier point: there is still no alternative conceptual model available to provide more precise guidance on just how to redraw the lines between state and market. Failing that, it is always possible that despite the best of intentions more interventionist policies may produce worse results.

If one rejects the case for 'maximum market, minimum state' because it is too simple, it is not easy to say what a 'strategic' role for government actually entails. Once one goes beyond responding to defined market failures, then just how far and in what ways should governments intervene in the economy? What are the limits to intervention? Is one talking about a more overt

form of industry policy, or a greater degree of forward planning—even some form of French-style *dirigisme*? (i.e. a more
explicit role for the state in economic planning) If this is the
path, can one be sure it will not revive old habits? One requires
a good conceptual map to sort out these issues.

Currently we have some people for whom faith in the market
is still an absolute principle, an article of faith. We have others,
from both left and right, with solid criticisms to make of
economic rationalism, but whose own ideas could endanger the
program for restructuring. Some on the left remain hostile to
free market capitalism per se. Their opposition to economic
rationalism is simply part of this hostility. Some conservatives
on the right appear not unwilling to recreate a combination of
paternalism and protectionism. Neither is consistent with the
thrust of reform in the 1980s. The challenge now is to find a
synthesis which can create a new consensus for reform. This will
be difficult because it means navigating between two polar,
ideologically-conflicting positions, belief in the market v. belief
in the state, and as Barry Jones put it, Australians 'seem unable
to hold more than one big idea at a time'.[32] 'Economic
rationalism' may not hold 100 per cent of the answers, but it is
still rather more than half right. Australia's current prospects
depend on working out just how far its tenets apply and where
they must be modified. For restructuring to proceed, some form
of intellectual and political compromise is essential.

The market in perspective

In recent years, policy development in Australia has been constrained by an overly narrow conception of markets and by a
strange lack of interest in how other more successful market
economies actually work. Sometimes comparative data seems to
have been manipulated to make it fit within preconceived neo-
classical ideas of how free markets should work. This has to
stop: there are plenty of practical policy ideas available in other
market systems. What has been lacking so far is the will to
explore the practice of market economies in other, sometimes
less familiar, societies. Similarly, Australia now has to take more
account of the forces driving nation-states to intervene in both
their own and the international economy to defend both the
viability of domestic industries and the balance of class and
political forces on which the stability of their own regimes
depends. One has to devise policies which acknowledge that states
too determine economic outcomes, not just market forces. In
1992, and during the election campaign, there were increasing

signs that the government was prepared to respond more positively to the criticisms it encountered in 1991–92.

Business in general, some manufacturers in particular, stressed
the need for a faster but more programmatic approach to reform,
with a more systematic relationship between tariff reform and
other reforms aimed at reducing business costs. From late 1991,
they pressed the government to consider measures—notably tax
incentives and infrastructure reforms—to maximise the attractions
to firms of investing in Australia. They wanted longer-term
strategies to stimulate domestic capital formation and to channel
investment into building up Australia's productive assets. Some
at least favoured greater emphasis on sectoral planning because
different industries had different needs and different experiences
of the effects of globalisation. Business generally favoured a
strategic vision, or a strategy statement, modelled on the kind of
development plans utilised by several Asian countries. This would
chart the main corridors and means of Australia's future economic
development, and provide a way of coordinating the efforts of
different sectors. Business, in other words, wanted a more
concerted and strategic approach to industry and economic
development, as did the unions.[33] In effect, this was a suitably
constrained call for a mild form of planning.

Previously, the prevailing faith in market solutions had blocked
this call for a strategic vision by privileging the mindset which
said 'let the market decide' or 'the government should not pretend
to know better than the market'. The unaided market would
produce outcomes superior to those achievable by governments.
Although this was a useful warning against the opposing belief
that 'governments know best', it produced a somewhat mechanistic approach to reform. Policy became too much a matter of
creating the 'correct' initial conditions and then standing back
and waiting for things to happen. The hope was that once the
former had been achieved, the reform process could be left to
steer itself: the desired effects would happen by themselves. By
1992, however, it was not clear that this approach was working,
and very doubtful whether it could work in time to achieve stable
growth and eliminate the deficit. Currently there is no margin
left for policy errors. There is, therefore, some point in arguing
that the success of restructuring should not be left wholly to
market forces allied to a faith in the profit motive. The experience
of financial deregulation suggests the pursuit of short-term reward
(and short-termism is an acknowledged feature of many Australian entrepreneurs) can displace more productive, long-term
investment. The government, therefore, should provide both more
direction and a clearer timetable, in short a plan, to ensure that

structural reform does proceed, consistently and expeditiously, in the desired direction.

Any call, however, for some measure of strategic planning not only goes against the prevailing mindset; it also goes against the long-established views of Treasury in particular which has, since the 1960s, resisted all calls for any kind of planning for development, and has not infrequently clashed with business on this issue.[34] Two points might be made in reply. First, the reaction to more extreme forms of command-style planning has obscured the point that most OECD countries have found it necessary from time to time to engage in some form of indicative or strategic planning, especially to steer their economies through awkward patches of transition or restructuring. A perfectly respectable case for moderate, non-statist, non-prescriptive forms of planning exists.[35] In many OECD countries, recourse to planning has represented no more than an attempt to improve the certainty and efficiency of market outcomes, the degree of coordination between private and public sectors, or to stabilise potential conflicts between economic and social systems. Planning is usually seen as a necessary contribution to the joint development of durable market systems and fair and cohesive societies. As one German economist put it, 'the market as much as possible and planning as much as necessary'.[36] One should add that the type and duration of planning depends very much on circumstances: one can choose how much or how far to plan according to the relative strength or fragility of the market.

Second, it was the lack of interest in strategic planning which helped to produce Australia's vulnerable position in the 1980s. Australia has never developed any specialised institutional capacity for either strategic or sectoral planning, or (with the possible exception of the AIDC[37]) for linking business, labour and the banks at either national or sub-national levels. There have been attempts to remedy this in the 1980s by establishing bodies like EPAC and the AMC[38], and by the use of industry plans, but EPAC and the AMC have been effectively marginalised by the main economic departments. The experience of Germany and Japan especially suggests that one of the keys to building a durable market economy is knowing how to develop institutions and procedures to promote partnership and collaboration between the public sector and private firms, and especially between banks, industry and government agencies.[39] Australia, one feels, has to develop a similar cross-sector institutionalised steering and planning capacity to give reform a greater degree of coherence and direction.

Business calls for a strategic vision paralleled community calls for a clearer social vision for Australia, for reform to be driven by values other than just efficiency. The electorate clearly wanted policies to generate employment, to mitigate rising inequalities, to assist damaged communities and to reinstate some explicit concern for equality, dignity and human welfare on the central agenda. This, too, must be interpreted as a call for the government to retain an active, strategic role in reconciling the potentially conflicting requirements of economic reform and social cohesion. Again, two points follow. First, we are at the stage where we need a greater sense of national endeavour, a greater collective commitment to reform, if reform is to succeed.[40] Maintaining broad-based community support is vital. Here, too, overseas experience is instructive. It is clear from the literature that the countries which have built the strongest economies have done so on the basis of communitarian value systems, not individualistic.[41] At the least they have tried to balance principles of individual and collective social responsibility and reduce antagonisms between public and private sectors. Some, like Germany and Japan, have made a point of mobilising collective support for agreed national values as the cornerstone of economic development. There is a strong implication that the brand of individualistic capitalism favoured by countries like Britain, America and Australia is now less viable than the models of 'communitarian capitalism' found in countries like Germany or Japan, or the type of corporatist and managed capitalism found in a number of European societies (Chapter 8).[42]

Second, given Australia's social problems, the state must retain an important residual responsibility to see that the market develops in a way which is consistent with those fundamental moral values which also help to legitimate society: the state cannot be indifferent to the results or behaviour which the market promotes. These have to be evaluated against other criteria. Economic intensification in an industrial market system is likely to produce adverse social and environmental effects which have to be corrected in the long-term interests of the market itself.[43] The more rapid the pace of social and technological change, the more uncertainties it creates, the more one needs to keep a watchful eye on the effects. One should not simply 'let it rip'. All this suggests that a strategy of shrinking the state, dismantling one's institutional capacity, and placing one's faith in the efficacy (or superior rationality) of market outcomes, may not be a sufficient strategy. Even though one values the benefits of competition, one has to retain some capacity to steer or manage the market in its own best interests. This point is also reflected in overseas experience where there is rather less faith in the invisible hand, the 'natural' coincidence of private and public interest, and rather more in the capacity and responsibility of human agents to determine the values which markets should serve.

Having won the election, the challenge for Labor was to get the market back in perspective. This meant, first, drawing a sharper line between its own program to create a more productive society and an export-oriented manufacturing sector, and the Opposition's greater ideological commitment to creating a wholly free market society (and to free trade). This was not too difficult: Labor, and Mr Keating, were clearly receptive to arguments that 'the free market' was not and should not be seen as a substantially autonomous institution: it should not be left to run itself. Australia had reached a point where the social costs of restructuring, and the need to shore up community support for further reform, implied that the state had to be brought back into the picture to provide a greater degree of structural support for the market itself. Or, the state had to retain or reclaim an active responsibility to see that it developed in a way which was fully compatible with the long-term viability of the nation as a whole. This implied that the state might give a higher priority to spending on infrastructure reform—especially to provide employment—on education and training, and on various forms of structural assistance to help communities in difficulties.

Labor had been retreating marginally from its free market commitments during 1992. In espousing 'social democracy' Mr Keating now signalled that the government accepted that free market policies could not by themselves rescue Australia from its burgeoning problems. The market could not guarantee an equitable distribution of income; it could not by itself ensure that resources would flow into those areas required to consolidate Australia's long-run economic security; it was often blind to cultural and moral values which were just as important to community development. It was time, therefore, to reconcile the virtues thought to lie in free (or open) markets with social and moral values to be articulated through the state. The call to social democracy thus implied that the state should play a more pronounced or visible steering role in guiding and coordinating the two major processes of economic modernisation and social reconstruction. At this point, however, Mr Keating's commitment to social democracy appeared to reach its limits. He seemed happier with the idea of the state compensating for the errors and deficiencies of the market in a confined area of social policy, and less keen on an expanded steering role for the state in the area of economic development.

Conceivably this reflected the fact that the government and its immediate advisers were still preoccupied with the challenge of the 1980s: to modernise the economy by exposing it to international competition, forcing inefficient sectors to become more productive in order to survive. The government had not altogether come to terms with the changes occurring in the global economy itself, with the steady breakdown of the kind of international trading economy with which it still imagined itself to be dealing. Consequently, the government was reluctant to move more explicitly in the direction of 'managed capitalism' or the 'developmental state', even though most other OECD countries had either accepted, or were in the process of accepting, that states now had to play both a more proactive role in sustaining the competitive advantage of domestic industries and a greater role in strategic planning, deciding how national resources might best be used to foster the nation's long-run development and security in the face of intensifying global competition for resources and markets. There was some support in official circles for the idea of a national strategic plan.[44] However, the language used by Mr Keating in April 1993 to re-state Labor's commitment to structural reform was very similar to that used previously. In part that was quite understandable: his first objective was to reassure business and the currency markets that references to social democracy did *not* mean any retreat from the reform agenda: Labor was still committed to the program of economic liberalisation. However, the emphasis Mr Keating placed on creating a more competitive economy, including a further step away from centralised wage fixation towards enterprise bargaining (Chapter 4), and his evident keenness to scotch any suggestion of a more interventionist role for the state in industry policy, left two question marks dangling over just what he meant by espousing social democracy.

First, did it just mean placing a human face on reform by, for example, accepting the state's necessary role in reducing unemployment, or its role in compensating people against the unintended consequences of restructuring? Did he really intend that the state should now acquire a positive responsibility to steer and coordinate the overall process of reconstruction in line with consciously declared values? Social democracy usually means investing the state with a residual collective responsibility to define the way in which national economic development should proceed, giving it a steering role in relationship to the market itself. Was Mr Keating prepared to go that far? Or was he still in fact a closet supporter of the free market agenda which implied a subordinate role for the state?

Second, had he grasped that in order to integrate Australia with the kind of global economy now rapidly emerging the state would have to play a more active role than that acknowledged by those who had originally designed the program of economic liberalisation? Again, was he really prepared to bring the state back in to the main game as an important strategic player? The issue was really whether Mr Keating was using the term 'social democracy' for political effect: did he intend a more substantial revision of the relationship between, and the relative importance of, state and market, as the term itself signified?

Just after the election, it was still too soon to say, although it did appear that Mr Keating needed to take one or two steps more towards a greater role for government if his wish for a social democratic society was to be fulfilled. As it was, he appeared to have one and a half feet still planted in his previous agenda. One should add at once that no doubt one principal reason for this was the lack of any developed conceptual alternative to the neo-classical position. Critics of the latter, especially on the left, were too willing to reject or put at risk the agenda for structural reform which Mr Keating quite naturally was intent on bringing to a successful conclusion. In the circumstances it was very much a matter of feeling his way towards a different policy mix. However, one could say that, in so far as Labor and the Prime Minister did wish to invent such a mix—or were seriously interested in developing a new intellectual synthesis on which to base policy—this meant being able to explain why a stronger state was a prerequisite, not an obstacle, to building a stronger and more durable market economy. For this they required a fresh conceptual perspective: a different way of organising the pieces of the jigsaw. The shift in perspective required was not a large one in most respects, but it did mean relying a little less on the efficacy of market forces, and moving a little more towards a strategic role for the state. With this in mind, Chapter 8 will suggest that we put less emphasis on the free market economy, and think more in terms of a social market economy. This retains the central role of competitive markets but stresses that these have to work within a given social and political context. This apparently small shift does help to place the debate on different theoretical premises by emphasising the essential complementarity of state and market. It also emphasises the importance of communitarian value systems, in line with overseas examples.

Restructuring cannot succeed without consensus—or at least the absence of major conflicts. Thus we have to develop a policy framework which both parties and the major interests can substantially support. This will call for some degree of compromise on both sides. The political left has already had to accept the centrality of the market: it is here to stay. The political right, and those neo-classical economists who support its individualist values, will now need to make some concessions on the state and intervention. Neither side can afford to drive its preferred values to extremes if it sincerely wants restructuring to succeed. The attraction of the social market is that it does provide a model which, albeit with a different emphasis, both sides of politics may support. In the current electoral and intellectual climate, it provides one means of avoiding otherwise paralysing disputes and confrontations. It provides a way to realign the pieces of the jigsaw to yield a different picture of what is still possible—though only just.

3
Structural problems

Lucky no more

When *The Lucky Country* appeared in 1964, many people took the title at face value. Tucked away in the South Seas, rich in natural resources, with generally high living standards, Australia seemed a very lucky country indeed. Donald Horne's book, however, was the first real warning. Australia's prosperity was not permanent: it rested on circumstances which were already changing. Unless Australians took account of the quickening pace of economic and technological change abroad, they would not enjoy their prosperity indefinitely.

There was much to admire in the national character of Australians and their achievements, but behind the facade of innocent happiness Horne found less impressive traits: provincialism and insularity, a lack of thought for tomorrow and a lack of interest in formal education. Australians were too eager to exploit Nature's bounty in a crude and shortsighted way for the sake of acquiring immediate riches. They gave too little thought to the economic future. In this and other books Horne portrayed Australians as people with large hearts but small souls, materialistic, too fond of muddling through, too tolerant of the second rate (except in sport) and rather inclined to put difficult choices in the too-hard basket. In the next fifteen years, Horne's critique received a good deal of support.[1]

In the 1970s further warnings came from professional economists, who pointed to the structural problems in the economy nearly all caused, directly or indirectly, by the country's long reliance on high tariffs. No less than five major official reports recommended in the 1970s that Australia restructure its industries to make them more competitive and to diversify exports.[2] Despite the warnings, Australia did not react in a concerted way until the Labor government which came to power on 5 March 1983 made economic reconstruction a central priority. By then delay had cost the country dearly. Towards the end of the nineteenth century Australians enjoyed one of the highest standards of living in the world, perhaps the highest. In 1890, for example, Australian Gross Domestic Product (GDP) per capita was nearly half as much again as the figure for America. By 1987, however, Australian GDP per capita was just 65 per cent of the American figure.[3] As late as 1960 Australia still ranked fourth among OECD countries in income per head; this had dropped to sixteenth position (out of 24) by 1987. This slide occurred despite Australia recording, between 1950 and 1974, the longest period of sustained growth in its history, averaging 5 per cent a year. Some of the benefits were absorbed by high population growth, mainly the result of immigration, but the real point was that even while the Australian economy grew, other economies were growing faster. Moreover, while Australia continued to rely heavily on the export of foodstuffs and raw materials, other countries set out to create economies based on export-oriented manufacturing industries. In the kind of international economy which has developed in the post-war world, these economies steadily acquired a stronger potential for long-term growth.

Between 1950 and 1980 Australia chose to retain a type of economy which had served the nation well in the past. Meanwhile, however, a new kind of global trading economy emerged, one characterised by an accelerating rate of technological change and growing competition for export markets.[4] Globalisation became a more distinctive phenomenon in the 1980s. Because Australia delayed so long in reacting to these new conditions, the task of restructuring the economy has become more difficult. Australia's early lead has gone. Now it has to build new industries and integrate them with the global economy when the levels of investment and technology required have lifted sharply in the last ten to fifteen years, and where other nations are equally determined to consolidate their own position. Australia has to diversify its economy and catch up with leading competitor nations which have been establishing themselves at the global level for twenty years or more.

Diversifying through restructuring is essential to protect living standards in the future. In relative terms Australia is still a rich country. National comparisons of income per head do not tell the whole story: there is other evidence to suggest that the overall quality of life for most Australians still compares very favourably with that experienced by citizens of countries with higher average income levels.[5] The point is, however, that Australia's relative affluence is the result of a set of circumstances which have now changed markedly. It is conceivable that many people have not grasped the full implications of this point; partly, no doubt, because the full effects of the economic slide which has already occurred have been obscured by extensive borrowing in the 1980s in both public and private sectors. Australian living standards do not appear to have changed too markedly because the nation borrowed extensively to pay for its large imports. But such borrowing cannot continue indefinitely: it has already produced a net foreign debt in excess of $160 billion. The full cost of the borrowing has yet to be felt (this is discussed later in this Chapter).

Those who assume that the recent history of slow decline is not too much of a worry, that it is part of a cyclical downturn which will in due course stabilise and recover, may receive a rude surprise. Similarly, those who suggest that since Australia is still a relatively wealthy country, what is really required are better policies to share out the existing wealth more equitably, are also missing the point. The plain fact is that Australia's economy is not generating sufficient wealth to satisfy its citizens' collective requirements for the good life, where that includes both higher real personal incomes and governments providing a wide range of public goods. If one looks, one can see the signs of creeping national poverty in the extensive cutbacks in government spending, especially at the state level. Or one may ponder where the country will find the huge sums now required to either renew or extend the nation's infrastructure. One recent report estimated that Australia needed to spend an extra $8 billion each year for the next decade to restore crumbling roads and sewers, upgrade the railways, maintain the quality of water supplies and service schools and hospitals.[6] One should recall that real wages fell for large numbers of people during the later 1980s, and remember also the growing numbers of structural unemployed, the 350 000 people who have been unable to find any kind of job for over twelve months.

All these are symptoms not just of economic downturn but

of the fact that Australia has, in important respects, the wrong type of economy to survive in the kind of global economy which now exists. What is more, the structural weaknesses within the economy, especially productivity levels well below those of overseas competitors, create a disturbing potential for a continued and ultimately more serious decline in national wealth and living standards in the 1990s. One should recall the economy now carries a double burden: it has to generate sufficient wealth to stop living standards falling further, and close the current account deficit and halt the rise in foreign debt. Further decline would reduce the sums available for infrastructure spending which would in turn make it more difficult to develop the kind of industries and jobs which Australia now requires to compete at the global level.

Creating a stronger production structure has to be a high priority. Can Australia adapt? One should be hopeful without being overly optimistic. The Australian economy is widely perceived to be one of the more fragile in the OECD. The Swiss-based World Economic Forum in 1991 named Australia as one of five economies 'most vulnerable' to recession. In 1992 the Forum's annual survey of levels of competitiveness and general economic prospects among OECD countries placed Australia sixteenth out of twenty-two.[7] The Forum's indicators are discussed further in Chapter 6. Briefly, however, they showed that by comparison with other countries Australia was not a particularly attractive site for international investment and development opportunities. Australia ranked twenty-first on the internationalisation of the economy; nineteenth on the quality of management; seventeenth on the strength of the domestic economy; and fifteenth on the strength of its science and technology. In fact, on all but one measure, infrastructure, Australia fell in the bottom half of the survey. The Forum also criticised the pace of restructuring as too slow. In 1992 the OECD also produced a gloomy assessment of Australia's economic prospects commenting adversely on high unemployment, low productivity, the slow pace of micro-economic reform and the probable link between wage policies under the Accord and Australia's record of inflation.[8]

It is not just the vulnerability of the economy which is a cause for concern: it is the fact that Australia's problems are cultural as much as economic. The eventual success of restructuring depends not only on the right choice of policies, but on changing the mind-set which has developed over a long period of time under conditions of protection and insularity. A range of factors—early prosperity, geographic isolation, climate and environment—produced a syndrome of somewhat myopic and complacent attitudes, well described by Horne and others and best epitomised by the great national slogan 'she'll be right'. These gave rise to distinctive attitudes towards the relative importance of work versus leisure, enterprise and reward. Now many Australians have to come to terms with the realisation that the attitudes and assumptions with which they grew up—and which are very much part of their identity—are a contributing element in the overall economic problem, a threat to their own economic futures. As Kahn and Pepper recognised in 1981[9], prospects for restructuring depend very much on whether Australians generally are willing and able to alter the attitudes entrenched during the years of affluence. Restructuring now requires, among other things, the national will to persevere with policies which, especially in the labour market, go against ingrained habits.

Restructuring must be seen as part of a larger project—nation-building. Creating a more productive workforce or an export culture depends crucially on getting people generally, and in the workplace particularly, to think and behave differently. That in turn means raising levels of education and awareness. This may seem obvious enough, but one wonders if some free marketeers give as much weight to the importance of social education, and to the cultural dimension of economic change, as they should. Free market policies are a necessary part of restructuring, but there are limits to relying on market forces to coerce people into behaving differently. Creating a more durable market economy will depend very much on persuading the workforce to accept and implement the necessary changes willingly. One returns to the importance of mobilising the consent required to facilitate change, which also entails providing adequate compensation for people hurt by structural change, plus assistance with retraining. Free market theories represent a resource to be used thoughtfully.

The bottom line is that reform has to be implemented through the political process—it cannot just be imposed. The electorate's commitment to long-term objectives cannot be taken for granted, especially when the immediate costs are very real. This calls for significant qualities of political leadership and political education. This is not just a matter of giving orders but rather renegotiating the degree of consent required for reforms to proceed smoothly, even if this does slow down the pace of change a little. The success of structural reform depends very much on providing people with a vision and a strategy which can mobilise both their allegiance and their active cooperation: Dr Hewson's crash-through approach could well have been counterproductive. Whether the requisite political skills exist in this country is unclear. Hitherto there has been too much emphasis on policy selection, on pulling the right levers, and not enough regard for the process of cultural re-education. The electorate also is attitudinally ill-prepared for the long haul. In fact, we have all grown so used to the emphasis placed on economic 'solutions' that it may be hard for Australians to recognise in time that the real test of national resilience and character is going to come in the political rather than the economic sphere.

The major problems in more detail

Between 1950 and 1980 Australia drifted into a position from which recovery is proving difficult. For this one may certainly blame the ruling elites, in all sectors and institutions. However, blaming individuals should not obscure the main point—Australia's economic vulnerability is due to a combination of more deeply-rooted structural and cultural factors whose full effects were relatively slow to appear, and which cannot be remedied overnight. Their adverse impact has been further accentuated by the kind of global economy which has emerged in the last ten to fifteen years. The globalisation of world trade, especially in manufactured goods, has underscored the weaknesses in the Australian economy. There is no easy way to correct this situation because the solution involves breaking with previous patterns of development and putting Australia on a quite different trajectory.

Over-reliance on commodity exports

Australia's prosperity was built on exports of primary commodities, initially foodstuffs (wool, grains, meat, sugar) and later minerals. There is a good deal of truth in the adage that Australia was built on the sheep's back. In 1950, exports of raw wool provided just under half the value of all exports, a figure which had declined to 8 per cent by 1989–90 (Table 3.1). From the outset the rural industries were geared to compete in world markets and this stimulated their efficiency. The same can be said of the mining industry. Australia in fact developed something of a dual economy: efficient export-oriented agricultural and mining sectors, with an inward-looking, protected and, on the whole, inefficient manufacturing sector.

One reason for Australia's failure to industrialise more extensively at an earlier stage was due to the initial strength of the wool industry and to a lesser extent gold mining. The high productivity of the former reduced the incentive to shift resources

Table 3.1 Australia's chief commodity exports

Year	Rural				Minerals			Total covered
	Wool	Grains	Meats	Sugar	Coal	Iron ore	Other ores and concentrates	
1951–52	47%	15%	5%	1%	—	—	7%	75%
1959–60	40%	9%	9%	3%	0.5%	—	4%	65.5%
1964–65	29%	13%	11%	4%	2%	—	5%	65%
1969–70	19%	9%	10%	3%	4%	7%	8%	60%
1974–75	9%	15%	5%	7%	8%	8%	6%	58%
1980–81	10%	10%	8%	6%	10%	6%	12%	62%
1989–90	8%	7%	6%	2%	12%	4%	10%	50%

Note: Some of these categories include some processing.

Source: Developing Australia's national competitiveness Report to the Business Council of Australia, Business Council, Melbourne, 1991, p.48

Table 3.2 Australia's exports: by sectoral groupings

Year	1960–61	1965–66	1970–71	1975–76	1980–81	1981–82	1989–90
Sectoral grouping			(% of total merchandise exports)				
Food	37	38	36	34	33	31	15
Agricultural raw materials	40	34	15	12	12	12	17
Fuels	3	3	6	13	13	16	17
Ores and minerals	9	13	24	23	25	25	32
Manufactures	10	12	19	18	16	15	19

Source: Developing Australia's national competitiveness Report to the Business Council of Australia, Business Council, Melbourne, 1991, p. 48

into manufacturing. It may also have diverted funds for research and development away from the manufacturing sector. Indeed, the early success of the rural industries reduced the incentive to develop a more competitive manufacturing sector and locked economic development into a pattern which has proved difficult to change.[10]

Since 1960 or thereabouts there has been a steady decline in Australia's reliance on agricultural exports. The share of food-stuffs overall (raw and semi-processed) fell from roughly three-quarters of the value of all exports in 1960 to just under a third by 1989–90 (Table 3.2). Their place was taken largely by the export of ores, minerals and fuels. In 1989–90 these accounted for 49 per cent of the value of Australia's exports. In 1988 Australia was the world's largest exporter of coal and the third largest exporter of iron ore. Also important were exports of bauxite and alumina, gold, mineral sands, non-ferrous metals, oil and uranium. Historically, commodities and commodity-based exports have provided between 80 and 90 per cent of all merchandise exports. Although exports of manufactures have recently begun to grow, this pattern has persisted right up to the current time. Australia has retained an export profile which has diverged increasingly from most other OECD countries. In 1985 for example, commodity-based exports made up roughly 80 per cent by value of Australia's total merchandise exports, while the average among advanced market economies was only 24 per cent.[11] Table 3.3 illustrates the degree to which Australia has gone against a major trend in world trade. The table shows how rapidly world trade in primary products has declined, from 45 per cent in 1963 to 28 per cent in 1987 (and to 26 per cent

Table 3.3　Percentage share of world merchandise trade by major categories of goods

Category	1963	1987	Australia's trade in 1988–89 by comparison	
			Exports	**Imports**
Primary products	45	28	48	7
Semi-manufactures	16	18	42[1]	34
Consumer goods and complex manufactures	37	52	10	59
(Balancing item)	2	2	—	—

Note:　[1] This includes a large proportion of commodity-based exports, e.g. semi-processed raw materials

Source:　R. Evans, 'The *Global Challenge* report and the clash of paradigms', in M. Costa and M. Easson (eds), *Australian Industry: what policy?* Sydney, Pluto Press and The Lloyd Ross Forum, 1991, p.20

in 1989). Trade in manufactures has increased correspondingly. By comparison Australia's trade profile has changed little in forty years. Even if one includes a number of semi-processed raw materials within exports of manufactures, the latter only accounts for roughly 30–33 per cent of merchandise exports. In the world's most powerful economies the picture is very different. Manufactures make up 98 per cent of Japanese merchandise exports, 93 per cent of German, 89 per cent of Italian, 84 per cent of British and 82 per cent of American.[12]

There are two related weaknesses in relying so heavily on commodity exports. The first is that primary and mineral export prices fluctuate a good deal in world markets, sometimes dramatically. They are also more sensitive to special factors such as drought and wars. Australia's export earnings are therefore less stable than those of countries which rely predominantly on manufactured exports. The second is that world prices for Australia's chief commodity exports have been declining for some time. This is due mainly to over-supply but that in turn has been caused partly by changes occurring in the nature of modern manufacturing.

Fluctuations in commodity prices

Between 1972 and 1985, global agricultural output rose by one-third to an all-time high. The reasons for this were various. Output has been rising steadily in most developing countries, especially in India and China, in the wake of the Green Revolution. Several former grain importers have become nearly self-sufficient. Western Europe has become a substantial food exporter and is now plagued by a massive food surplus in all kinds of products, from dairy produce to wine and from wheat to beef. Wool has also encountered greater competition from synthetic fibres. Although Australia still dominates the world trade in wool, supplying some 70 per cent of the market, wool now accounts for less than 5 per cent of the total fibre market. The huge stockpile of 4.6 million bales accumulated by the Australian Wool Corporation, and the ensuing collapse of the floor price scheme in 1990, is a graphic illustration of the problems created by over-supply in one of Australia's key export industries.

Over-supply brought about a massive across-the-board collapse of commodity prices in 1985–86. The rapid drop of export earnings from the rural sector was one reason why the current account deficit doubled between the middle of 1984 and the middle of 1986 to reach $14.3 billion (Table 3.7). By the first quarter of 1986, world prices for beef had fallen 24 per cent since 1984, barley prices by 51 per cent since 1982, those for sugar by 51 per cent since 1979, for wheat by 29 per cent since 1981 and for wool by 21 per cent since 1982.[13] Although markets recovered briefly in 1987 and 1988, prices again fell sharply in 1989–90. Between late 1988 and the end of 1991, the index of world commodity prices fell by a third to a level below that recorded during the 1985 collapse. The total value of Australia's rural exports in the early 1990s was back to the level of the mid-1980s.[14]

This situation was aggravated by the worsening trade war between the European Community (EC) and America. In 1990 the EC reportedly spent $US12 billion on subsidies to its farmers while America spent $US1 billion on subsidies under its Export Enhancement Program.[15] By mid-1991 the subsidy war had driven down the world price for wheat to $US125 per tonne, which was below the cost of production for Australian farmers. Although the price recovered to $US175 per tonne by early 1992, it was projected to fall again. Australian wheat farmers faced the prospect of subsidised American wheat invading Australia's traditional markets in the Middle East. In 1991 an American meat import law placed restrictions on imports from Australia, while Australian beef producers also faced the prospect of subsidised European beef being dumped in Australia's Asian markets.[16] With wool prices also falling by between 20 and 30 per cent in 1991, farm incomes fell sharply in 1991 and were projected to fall a further 25 per cent in 1992.

The 1985 collapse also affected minerals. By early 1986 raw material prices were at their lowest levels in recorded history in relation to the prices of manufactured goods and services.[17] Prices for iron ore fell 20 per cent between mid-1982 and mid-1986, aluminium prices by 34 per cent, and coal prices 25 per cent since 1981–82. The main reason was again over-supply. Production of metals, minerals and forest products increased 20–35 per cent between 1975 and 1985. Because coal prices are directly related to the price of oil, which fell steadily throughout the 1980s, the price of coal fell. Australia has also met growing competition from mineral producers in South Africa, Canada and South Korea. Although markets recovered a little after 1985, the prices for three of Australia's main exports, coal, iron ore and alumina, have remained weak.

The problem is not only that Australia's traditional exports have been earning less on world markets. Around 90-95 per cent of Australia's imports are manufactured goods, the prices of which are much more stable. In recent years, Australia has imported a growing volume of manufactured goods, either consumer items (TVs and VCRs, personal computers, fashion clothing, luxury cars) or machine tools and the office and computer equipment required by industry. These goods have become increasingly expensive for Australia to buy as this country's earnings from its traditional exports have either declined or failed to keep pace with the prices of manufactured goods. This disparity between export earnings and import prices was a significant contributory factor to the large current account deficit which opened up in the mid-1980s.

This disparity between declining prices for exports and the rising cost of imports can be summarised by saying that the terms of international trade have been moving steadily against Australia for some while. The terms of trade represent the prices received for Australian exports expressed as a percentage of the prices Australia has to pay for imports, or the ratio of export prices to import prices. In the period after 1945 the ratio was extremely favourable to Australia. In fact, using 1980 as a baseline of 100 to represent parity between export and import prices, the index in the 1950s ranged between 140 and 200 points—meaning, in layman's terms, that the income generated by Australia's commodity exports was high relative to the prices of the goods Australians wished to import. The index then declined before the resources boom of the early 1970s saw it jump sharply but temporarily. Since then, there has been a steady decline. From 120 points in 1975, it fell to between 85 and 90 following the commodity price collapse in 1985. It has since recovered slightly to reach parity in 1989–90. The problem is, however, that it is highly vulnerable to further falls in world commodity prices.

What this means is that, in recent decades, as the terms of trade for Australia have declined, Australia has had to export more in order to pay for what we import. As Gruen explains: 'On average over the last 30 years, it has taken 2 per cent more exports each year to pay for the same volume of imports. Since 1970 . . . it has required on average 3 per cent more exports each year to pay for the same volume of imports.'[18] The same point was made by a recent report on behalf of the Australian Manufacturing Council:

> . . . it takes exports of 300 tonnes of coking coal today to pay for imported word processing, PABX and other equipment for one executive and a secretary. The volumes of such high value-added items that we require are growing quickly . . . In a few years, we may need to export 400 tonnes of coal to equip a comparable office, then 500, and so on.[19]

Clearly, this process cannot continue indefinitely without impacting upon domestic living standards. Because Australia started from such a favourable position in the 1950s, the long-run impact has been delayed. Now, however, Australia is effectively in a position where export income is no longer sufficient to pay for all the imports which Australians collectively wish to consume. If existing living standards are to be maintained, and the *overall* deficit on current account all but eliminated, Australia must find more lucrative forms of export.

The changing character of manufacturing

This brings us to the second problem referred to above: the changes taking place in both manufacturing production and world trading patterns, and their significance. Very simply, commodity prices are declining because world demand for all primary commodities, including raw materials, has been declining for some time. This is not entirely due to over-supply. It is also because there has been an ongoing shift in the nature of manufacturing production which has accentuated the problem of over-supply.

Industrial production worldwide has been moving away from products that are heavily material-intensive and/or labour-intensive. In the last decade especially, world manufacturing has shifted decisively towards both processes of production and products that are not only capital-intensive but which have a much higher knowledge-based (and often high-tech) component than before. We have moved in a number of modern industries from the era of high volume mass production to that of high value production where the emphasis falls increasingly on designing specialised, sophisticated or luxury items for more discriminating consumer markets.[20] (This shift, and the wider phenomenon of globalisation, are discussed in Chapter 7.)

Meanwhile, as Drucker makes clear, this shift forms part of a long-term secular trend in the nature of production. The amount of raw material required for a given unit of economic output has been dropping all century, except in war time. One study by the International Monetary Fund (IMF) calculated the decline at 1.25 per cent per annum, compounded, since 1900. The amount of industrial raw materials needed for one unit of production is now no more than two-fifths of what it was in 1900. And this decline is accelerating. The Japanese experience is striking: in 1984, for every unit of industrial production, Japan consumed only 60 per cent of the raw materials used for the same volume of industrial production in 1973.[21]

This decline reflects the quite phenomenal impact of techno-logical innovations in recent years. Nowadays, 25 to 50 kilograms of fibreglass cable transmit as many telephone messages as did one tonne of copper wire. The rapid drop in the raw material intensity of many manufacturing processes lowers energy use too.

To produce that 50 kilograms of fibreglass cable requires no more than 5 per cent of the energy needed to produce the tonne of wire. Modern plastics, which increasingly replace steel in car bodies, represent a raw material cost, including energy, less than half that of steel. (Concern about the environment is also leading to increases in the efficiency with which raw materials are used; the recycling of materials like aluminium, paper and plastics is growing.) Reich records that, in 1984, 80 per cent of the cost of a computer was in its hardware and 20 per cent in software. By 1990 the proportions were reversed. The raw materials contained in a semi-conductor micro-chip account for between 1 and 3 per cent of its total cost.[22]

This change in the nature of industrial production has two significant implications for Australia. First, economies which rely extensively on exporting commodities and raw materials to other more heavily industrialised economies are likely to be at an increasing disadvantage in the future. They face a probable decline in the prices obtained for their exports as the new manufacturing expands and as knowledge and technology become ever more central in the supply of products demanded by both consumers and other industries. The tendency towards over-supply in world markets for minerals further underlines this vulnerability. Brazil has already overtaken Australia as a major producer of iron ore. Aluminium smelting was Australia's biggest export growth industry in the 1980s but growing competition, especially from Canada, has lowered prices and stalled its growth. With coal and iron ore one never knows where new reserves will be discovered. And in overseas markets, importers in Korea, Taiwan and even Europe may well follow the example of the Japanese who import coking coal through a single buyer, thereby exercising a strong control over price.

Second, in seeking to diversify exports and create more stable and lucrative sources of export income, Australia's general strategy is to produce more value-added goods, i.e. products whose often considerable market value depends on adding inputs of capital, technology or skill to relatively small amounts of raw materials. This is a major goal in trying to secure greater returns from Australia's natural resources (Chapter 6). However, Australia would also be well advised to participate in trade in what are termed elaborately transformed manufactures, or ETMs. The most dynamic and most highly profitable sectors of modern manufacturing are the high-tech complex-factor industries, especially consumer electronics, analytic instruments, information technologies and computers, telecommunications, pharmaceuticals, medical and scientific equipment and more sophisticated cars. Such industries are characterised by rapid rates of techno-

logical innovation and diffusion and by the very rapid growth of
consumer demand. In 1970 the total demand for computers in
OECD countries amounted to $A56.8 billion. In 1985 it was
$A200 billion and growing.[23] These sectors are at the core of a
modern industrial economy; their products are the areas growing
fastest in world trade. They offer one of the best prospects for
economic expansion. It is by no means easy to develop expertise
in such areas, or to penetrate world markets, but there are strong
incentives for doing so. World demand for these products is
growing and will grow further. The more living standards rise
in other countries, notably in Asia, the more people will spend
on cars, TVs, VCRs, fax machines, etc. The more developed or
high-tech other economies become, the more need they will have
for specific ETMs within their own production processes. It
would also be helpful to reduce our import bill for certain types
of ETMs such as computers because, collectively, these are
expensive things to import. Australia's trade deficit in consumer
electronics and computers, cars, telecommunications, aerospace
and pharmaceuticals is of the order of $10 billion a year. In
1988, Australia imported $2.9 *billion* of office equipment and
exported $4.9 *million*.[24] Some improvement here would be
welcome.

The effect of tariffs

The main reason why Australia did not respond more quickly to
shifts in the composition of world trade was the disincentive
effect of tariffs. From Federation in 1901, Australia relied on
tariffs to foster the growth of manufacturing industries whose
principal function, apart from providing employment in the cities,
was to supply the home market (i.e. to replace imports) rather
than exporting overseas. By the 1920s Australia was one of the
highest tariff countries in the world. This profile persisted through
the 1930s, in common with many other countries, but continued
post-war when most other countries were gradually dismantling
their tariffs in response to the policies of economic liberalisation
encouraged by the US in the 1950s and 1960s. By the mid-1970s
Australia and New Zealand had the highest manufacturing tariffs
in the world. The drawbacks of these were attacked increasingly
by professional economists, who demonstrated that they produced
higher prices for consumers, especially for such items as shoes,
clothing and cars. For example, the Industry Commission calculated in 1990 that industry protection added about $4000 to the
cost of a family car. If all the assistance to the motor industry
through tariffs and other means were provided instead by direct

government grants, it would cost taxpayers about $1600 million a year. The overall cost to the economy imposed by tariffs was quantified by the Industry Commission in 1989 at around $7 billion.

The absence of external competition in many sectors of the domestic market also destroyed the incentive for manufacturers to seek out more efficient means of employing labour and capital. High tariffs attracted too many resources into industries which lacked long-term competitive strength, the prime example being the Textiles, Clothing and Footwear industries (TCF). Employment in these still exceeds 100 000 people, despite the fact that for many products Australia cannot match low-wage industries in other countries. Despite the protection the industry receives, Australia is still a net importer of TCF products. The further problem with tariffs is that those whose employment depends on protection, both employers and unions, spend their energies trying to maintain such protection when, from the perspective of the economy overall, it would be better to redeploy the labour and capital employed into sectors with a better growth and export potential. (There is of course room for argument as to how quickly one should force such redeployment, and what compensation should be offered to those affected, especially if the workers displaced cannot readily find alternative sources of employment.)

The chief criticism of tariffs is that over time their political and economic side effects tend to nullify the effective operation of the price mechanism which would otherwise provide signals as to how and where capital and labour might be employed more efficiently. Tariffs tend to lock up resources in established industries which, in so far as they are more or less guaranteed market share, become both inward-looking and progressively less efficient. In Australia, lack of external competition produced a manufacturing sector which, by the early 1980s, was high cost, fairly indifferent to the pace of change in the world economy, and marked by a host of restrictive practices which were the long-term result of employers and unions accommodating each other while enjoying the relative security of life within a closed market.

Tariffs were adopted originally to foster Australia's infant industries and the policy was by no means unsuccessful. The development of BHP between the wars was due partly to the shelter provided by tariffs. By the 1970s, however, the costs of tariffs outweighed the benefits. Despite protection many Australian industries could not match the price or quality of the imported alternative. Australian consumers perceived a growing gulf between the standard of home-produced goods and the features and reliability of imports. The manufacturing sector found itself less and less competitive even in its own home market. After World War II, manufacturing output as a percentage of GDP had grown from around 16 per cent in the early 1950s to 22 per cent in 1964–65, where it remained for several years before declining towards the end of the 1960s. Between 1970 and 1985, partly as a result of the severe recession in 1981–82, manufacturing output as a percentage of GDP declined from 21.3 per cent to 16.7 per cent; the numbers employed in manufacturing also fell from 24.5 per cent of the workforce to 16.7 per cent.[25] (They are currently around 15.7 per cent.)

Some tariff reduction did occur in the 1970s, notably an across-the-board cut of 25 per cent in 1973. In most manufacturing industries the effective rate of protection was down to 14 per cent by 1981–82. However, in response to industry pressure and fears of unemployment, import quotas were extended in the TCF and car industries. These in fact were now more heavily protected than before: their average rate of protection trebled from 45 per cent in 1973–74 to 130 per cent by 1981–82. So although the average effective rate of protection for manufacturing as a whole was roughly 27 per cent between 1973 and 1983, there was a 'phenomenal increase' in quota protection for TCF and cars which offset the fall in protection elsewhere.[26]

By the time Labor came to power in 1983, it was widely agreed that protectionism was no longer appropriate in a world where production had become more globally integrated than ever before. Tariffs were a major barrier to developing stronger export-oriented industries. It is noticeable that countries with high levels of protection export only a small proportion of their total output of manufactured goods, usually between 5 and 10 per cent. In the mid-1980s the figure for Australia was about 7 per cent. Countries with lower protection often export between one-third and one-half of manufacturing output.[27] The Hawke government began cautiously. It announced a series of five and seven-year plans to restructure key industries—heavy engineering, steel, cars and TCF, committing itself initially to a gradual policy of phased tariff reductions as part of the process of making those industries more competitive. It then came under increasing pressure to reduce tariffs more quickly. Mr Keating's Economic Statement of May 1988 announced that tariff levels for most manufacturing would be reduced to either 15 or 10 per cent by 1992. He also announced a quicker withdrawal of protection for the two most highly-protected industries, TCF and cars. A new six-year plan for restructuring the TCF was announced. TCF industries were told their rate of assistance would be reduced to between 40 and 55 per cent by 1995 and all quota restrictions would be removed by March 1995. The car industry was told that tariff reductions would be accelerated: the level of tariffs in 1992 would be reduced to 35 per cent.

Towards the end of the 1980s, the average rate of assistance for manufacturing, excluding cars and TCF, had dropped to less than half that of the mid-1970s. However, pressure for more radical cuts continued from the Industry Commission, and from Treasury which reportedly favoured the abolition of all tariffs within five years.[28] In October 1989 a major report by Professor Ross Garnaut recommended that Australia commit itself to a policy of zero tariffs by the year 2000.[29] On 12 March 1991, Mr Hawke announced that the general level of assistance to industry would be further reduced, in a series of annual steps, to a flat level of 5 per cent by 1996. Tariffs on passenger motor vehicles would be phased down from 35 per cent in 1992 to 15 per cent by the year 2000, in a series of eight annual cuts of 2.5 per cent each. Tariff reductions in the TCF industries would be further accelerated so that the maximum tariff would be down to 25 per cent by the year 2000, while the termination of quota assistance was brought forward two years to March 1993. (A mid-term review of the current six-year plan was scrapped.) General agricultural assistance would also be reduced in line with the pace of tariff reform in manufacturing.

This statement sharpened the debate over tariff reform. Business leaders, unions and industry groups expressed misgivings over how far and how fast it was sensible to lower tariffs. Previously there had been general agreement on the broad strategy: lowering tariffs was intended to pressure those industries which were uncompetitive to restructure. If they could not, then they would wither away, freeing up resources for other industries which offered better growth prospects. Now, however, debate began to polarise between those who saw the virtually complete phasing out of tariffs as the highway towards a more efficient economy and those who saw tariff reductions as one important element of the strategy to boost productivity and exports, but who thought it should be balanced by other policies to reduce overall business costs, such as micro-economic reform, and by other policies to encourage business investment. (This is discussed further in Chapters 5 and 6.)

Protection all round

'Protection' in Australia does not just mean tariffs. The word has a wider cultural and political resonance. It is really synonymous with the belief held implicitly by many Australians in the past that governments existed to provide assistance, and that citizens should be protected from all manner of threats to their security, whether these originated in the economy, the environment or the wider political context. Tariffs persisted so long partly because protectionism has roots in the political culture, in popular expectations of government. As Hancock observed, in describing how Australians viewed the state as a vast public utility: 'protection in Australia has been more than a policy. It has been a faith and a dogma . . . The very word appeals to [Australians], because they believe in their hearts that both their enjoyments and their existence need to be protected against extraordinary dangers.'[30] For a government to seek to eliminate tariffs is to confront attitudes developed in Australia for well over a century, and which are again a product of a distinctively Australian mindset in which the sense of isolation and vulnerability, feelings of insularity and insecurity, have been prevalent, at least in the past.

From this mindset sprang a distinctive style of politics, that of protection-all-round. Australians have long looked on governments as convenient milch-cows, and have favoured government-determined ahead of market-determined outcomes, often at the expense of efficiency. They have tried to equalise, more or less, the share of national income going to the major producer groups in society. In this way, the reliance on tariffs was a central part of protection-all-round. Manufacturers wanted high tariffs because this offered them more secure profits than trying to compete overseas. Organised labour acquiesced because a protected market plus a centralised arbitration system made it easier to secure wage increases, which could often be passed on to the domestic consumer in higher prices. The rural producers acquiesced because they also received a form of institutional protection through government subsidies and price support schemes. Governments acquiesced because commodity exports generated the income which met and underpinned the claims made by the separate producer groups. Protectionism, therefore, was a central part of the set of interlocking policies and institutions which grew up to equalise the flow of resources between the major interests in society. A pattern of development emerged in which each major interest or producer group acquiesced in policies designed to accommodate the others in return for a special *quid pro quo* for itself.[31] The politics of protection-all-round was legitimised expressly by Mr McEwen in the 1960s when he tried to link assistance for rural interests with tariff protection for manufacturers.

Economic protectionism and protection-all-round together created a series of special interest groups concerned to maintain the benefits accruing to themselves. A pattern of rent-seeking behaviour emerged in which these interests concentrated their energies on extracting benefits and concessions (i.e. special 'rents' of one kind or another) from governments, rather than focusing on how to create new sources of wealth. Manufacturers, often tacitly assisted by unions, were more interested in pressuring governments to maintain or extend the height of the tariff walls, or seeking various benefits from those in office, than in raising efficiency.

The point of this is that high levels of protection in a small society like Australia's helped create a pattern of political behaviour which both detracted from the productivity of industry—'because the best human resources will be devoted to seeking rewards from the political system rather than increasing the production of goods and services'[32]—and set up cultural and institutional barriers to change. This underlines the problems and the potential political costs facing any government in Australia which sets out to engineer structural adjustment by reversing the traditional belief in protection. Such a policy challenges the attitudes many Australians have about the role of the state and the preferred relationship between government and industry, and challenges also long-established patterns of rent-seeking behaviour. This helps explain why free marketeers are so fearful of policy measures which threaten a U-turn in the reform process: they fear to encourage those forces and interests in Australian society which would welcome a return to the 'mendicant mentality'.

So while one recognises that protection is no longer a wholly viable policy to pursue in the face of globalisation, it is more than tariff barriers which have to give way. Integrating with the global economy may not be easy for a small and sometimes insecure society which is by no means sure of its own national identity or its place within the region. Switching to a new developmental track, creating a new kind of economy, requires some fairly deep-seated changes in the Australian psyche as well. Once again, the success of economic reform depends on the more elusive (and often subterranean) processes of cultural change.

Failure to share in the growth of international trade

Between 1950 and 1974 (the 'long boom') world trade grew faster than at any previous time. It roughly doubled in the 1950s and more than doubled in the 1960s. Between 1960 and 1987, world trade grew at an average annual rate of 6 per cent in real terms.[33] As trade expanded, the sources of national wealth and prosperity were linked increasingly to a country's participation in international trade. The countries which recovered fastest after 1945, and those which have grown fastest in recent decades, were the ones which took most advantage of the surge in trade, and the burgeoning markets for manufactured goods in particular.

In recent years, therefore, wealth has come from trade and the strongest economies have been export based. Unfortunately, these developments largely passed Australia by. Not only did Australia remain a commodity exporter, but our overall position in world trade has eroded. In 1949, in the wake of World War II, Australia's share of world exports was just under 2.8 per cent, which in fact made her one of the leading trading nations. In 1973, Australia was still the thirteenth largest exporting nation in the world, with 1.6 per cent of world exports. By 1990, we had fallen to twenty-second place with approximately 1.2 per cent.[34] As one study observed, if Australia had only maintained the percentage share maintained in the 1960s (around 1.6 per cent) exports would have been one-third, or about $15 billion, higher than they currently are.[35] In fact, as the Hughes Report commented, Australia was the only industrialised economy which did not increase its proportion of merchandise exports to GDP in the last thirty years. The figure of 13.5 per cent had not changed since 1958 and this was markedly lower than the ratios of other industrial economies of comparable size.[36] (It has since risen to around 20 per cent.) And as Drake and Nieuwenhuysen observe: 'The Achilles heel of the Australian economy today is that, although its structure is geared to international trade, its participation in trade has declined, while that of market-industrialised countries in general has increased.'[37]

Again the point to emphasise is that this decline also reflects (a) the steady decline in the share of world trade of primary commodities as compared with manufactured goods (Table 3.3): Australia is unlikely to improve its position in world trade simply by exporting more primary commodities; and (b) Australia is weakest in the most dynamic area of world trade, trade in value-added goods, especially in complex factor products, or ETMs. Indeed, between 1969 and 1986, manufactured exports declined from 26 to 23.4 per cent of Australia's total merchandise exports.[38] These figures also tend to overstate the proportion of manufactured goods by including various semi-processed goods in that category. Over 70 per cent of what are classified as manufactured exports are actually semi-processed raw materials like alumina, primary metals such as aluminium or gold, or agricultural derivatives like raw sugar or milk powder. The problematic nature of Australia's position is best shown by Table

3.4: in 1987–88, total manufactures amounted to just over one-fifth of merchandise exports. The key category, ETMs, was not only small but the figure of $4.5 billion also included $1.3 billion worth of goods exported to New Zealand and Papua New Guinea, including re-exports. $1.8 billion of the $4.5 billion is also accounted for by just eleven companies, with BHP Steel by far the biggest. The relatively tiny sum—$3.2 billion of ETM exports to the world—reflected Australia's lack of strong tradeable goods firms. Canada has thirty times more exports of non-resource based goods from large export firms (those with exports worth more than US$500 million per annum) in proportion to its GDP than Australia.[39] (See also Chapter 6 for evidence of improvement.)

An uncertain relationship with Asia

Australia may be the world's most isolated continent, but it is on the outer edge of one of the most dynamic regions in the world economy, east Asia, especially north-east Asia. The economic development of east Asia, led by Japan, signals a marked shift in the balance of world economic power. By 1984, the volume of trans-Pacific trade exceeded that of trans-Atlantic trade for the first time. Between 1961 and 1981, east Asia's share of world gross national expenditure rose from 10 to 15 per cent and was projected to reach 18 per cent by 1990.[40] North-east Asia has been the fastest growing region in the world economy over the past decade. The average annual growth rate was 7 per cent during the 1980s compared with the OECD average of 3 per cent. Between 1980 and 1987, the combined GDP of Japan, China, South Korea, Singapore and Hong Kong, plus the rest of ASEAN[41], grew 44 per cent in constant US dollars, while that of Canada and the US grew by 22 per cent, and the twelve EC nations by 14 per cent.[42] The nations of south-east Asia have also achieved remarkably high growth rates in recent years. Malaysia, for example, recorded a growth rate of between 8 and 9 per cent in 1990 and 1991 (Table 3.5).

Also noteworthy is that this growth was based on exports. Japan and 'the four tigers'—South Korea, Taiwan, Hong Kong and Singapore—accounted for 8 per cent of world exports in 1960 and 20 per cent in 1988. Japan maintained a compound growth rate in exports of more than 17 per cent a year, 1960–1980. South Korea increased its merchandise exports by over 35 per cent each year, and Taiwan 25 per cent, between the mid-1960s and the mid-1980s.[43] Manufactured goods account for almost all exports in many cases: 97 per cent in Japan, 94

Table 3.4   Composition of Australia's merchandise exports, 1987–88

	$b	%
Unprocessed primary products	19.7	48.2
Processed minerals and fuel (e.g. gold, alumina, refined petroleum)	5.9	14.4
Processed food (e.g. frozen meat, bulk raw sugar, dairy products)	4.9	12.0
Simply transformed manufactures (e.g. aluminium, chemicals, skins)	4.6	11.3
Elaborately transformed manufactures	4.5	11.1
Balancing item	1.3	3.0
	40.9	100.0

Source: The global challenge: Australian manufacturing in the 1990s, Final Report of the Pappas Carter Evans and Koop/Telesis Study, Australian Manufacturing Council, July 1990, p.6

Table 3.5   Annual average growth of GDP

	1979–80 (%)	1980–89 (%)
OECD Europe	3.0	2.3
United States	2.8	3.0
Japan	4.7	4.2
South Korea	8.2	9.3
Singapore	9.0	6.9
Malaysia	8.0	5.5
Thailand	6.8	6.5
Indonesia	8.0	5.0
Hong Kong	8.2	7.6
Taiwan	9.1	7.9

Source: Developing Australia's national competitiveness, a Report to The Business Council of Australia, Melbourne, 1991, p.19

Table 3.6   Australia's export markets

Area	1962–63 (%)	1975 (%)	1988 (%)
Japan	16	29.2	26.9
Other East Asia	10	13.3	20.2
North America	12	13.1	12.4
Western Europe	35	17.2	16.6
Rest of world	27	27.2	23.9

Source: P. Drysdale et al., The Australia–Japan relationship: towards the year 2000, Australia–Japan Research Centre, Canberra, 1989, Chart 6A. *Australian Exports: performance, obstacles and issues of assistance* (Hughes Report) AGPS 1989, Table 2.4

per cent in South Korea, 95 per cent in Hong Kong and 96 per cent in Taiwan.[44] Malaysia too increased its manufactured exports, from 22 per cent of total exports in 1980 to 60 per cent in 1990, with a target of 75 per cent by 1995.[45] Such figures are in stark contrast to the Australian case.

Australia's trading profile has already changed greatly in response to the rise of the east Asian economies, however. In 1950, half of Australia's exports went to Britain. By 1990, that figure was under 4 per cent. Exports to Western Europe have also decreased markedly (Table 3.6). Meanwhile, exports to Asia rose from under 15 per cent in 1950 to 47 per cent in 1988 and to a possible 55 per cent in 1990–91.[46] Half our imports now come from south and east Asia. Japan alone takes almost 30 per cent of Australia's merchandise exports and supplies one-fifth of our imports. All but two of the economies of north-east Asia are among Australia's top ten markets, South Korea is Australia's third largest overseas market and 27 per cent of tourists and 20 per cent of foreign investment come from north-east Asia. East Asia is also by far the most important market for Australia's growing education exports.

Against this background, the Garnaut Report in 1989 emphasised that integrating the Australian economy more tightly with expanding economies in the Asian region must be a major priority. Professor Garnaut argued that there was a significant complementarity between a number of Asian economies and the Australian economy. This provided great opportunities for Australia to expand its exports to the region, not only foodstuffs and raw materials, but manufactured goods also. There were opportunities for Australia to export expertise in the areas of engineering, construction, transport and communications to assist with the further development and industrialisation of the Asian economies. Australian financial and educational services could also find new, profitable outlets in Asia. The Report stressed that the future of the Australian economy lay in promoting closer cooperation and interdependence with other regional economies. To do this, Australia would need to modernise its own economy at a speed sufficient to keep up with the rapid rate of structural and technological change occurring in Asia. To fail to keep abreast of such changes was both to risk losing market share and to remain permanently on the outer edge as regional economies in first north-east, and then south-east Asia, matured and formed closer links with each other. There was also a real risk of Asian countries either forming their own trading blocs or creating special bilateral trading arrangements among themselves. Australia, therefore, should press for free trade and multi-lateral trade agreements. It should also dismantle its remaining tariffs as quickly as possible, both to promote the further liberalisation of trade and to stimulate the process of structural change within Australia. To this end, Garnaut recommended that Australia embrace a policy of zero tariffs by the year 2000.[47]

Despite the controversial nature of this recommendation, the Garnaut Report both outlined the opportunities open to Australia through sharing in Asia's economic expansion, and underlined the risks of failing to do so. If Australia fails to take advantage of opportunities in Asia, it is very difficult to see how and where else we can improve our participation in world trade, especially as both North America and Europe are each developing their own increasingly exclusive trading zones. If Australia cannot achieve a higher level of integration with east Asia in particular, it runs the real risk of becoming a permanent odd man out in a world parcelled up into three main trading zones—the North American, European and Asian. This would make it extremely difficult for Australian firms and industries to remain abreast of the crucial technological and productivity improvements now occurring more or less continuously throughout the world economy and would tend to confirm Australia's current effective status as a quarry or a farm for the rest of the world, a position which, as we have seen, is untenable in the long run.

To date Australia has made uncertain progress towards integrating with Asia. Exports have grown rapidly in absolute terms: sales to ASEAN expanded by 164 per cent between 1987 and 1991, and those to Hong Kong, South Korea and Taiwan by 78 per cent. Nevertheless, Australia has struggled to maintain market share. In 1980, Australia supplied 4.3 per cent of imports into north-east Asia, but this fell to 3.8 per cent between 1987–90, reflecting the strengthening performance of other economies.[48] World Bank data also showed that whereas Australia supplied 6.2 per cent of all *east* Asian imports in 1980, this had fallen to 3.5 per cent by 1987.[49] More encouragingly, manufactured exports to north-east Asia grew from roughly 10 per cent of all Australian exports to the region in 1984 to nearly 20 per cent by 1990. Exports of ETMs also expanded from $429 million in 1984 to $1.2 billion by 1990. This figure equalled the value of Australia's meat exports to the region, while service exports were twice the value of exports of iron ore.[50]

The government has placed a high priority on strengthening links with Asia. It has fostered the concept of an Asia-Pacific Economic Cooperation (APEC) forum. However, in 1991 Senator Button found it necessary to criticise the 'intellectual laziness' of some Australian company managers for failing to shift their focus away from Australia's older and more familiar markets in Europe and America towards Asia, and for failing to invest in the developmental opportunities offered by the latter. Only 10 per cent of Australian overseas investment ($9 billion out of $84 billion) was in Asia.[51] In 1992, Mr Keating as Prime Minister attempted to talk up the importance of Asia for Australia, arguing emphatically that Australians should, culturally as well as economically, distance themselves further from Britain and take a more positive view towards migration and investment from Asia. Australia should try to involve itself more thoroughly in Asian regional associations and should redefine its national identity and cultural affiliations by seeing itself as a part of Asia rather than a distant outpost of Europe. His efforts received a mixed reception. While Anglophiles opposed his attempts to distance Australia from Britain, opinion polls also suggested a latent unhappiness and resistance in the electorate to the idea that Australia would or should find its future, its sense of national identity and purpose, in closer ties with Asian nations. As one reporter put it: 'Australians sit with palpable unease, and a sense of displacement, on the southern rim of Asia.' Their perspective 'is very much that of outsiders looking in'.[52] Once again, the kind of economic adjustment which Australia really has to make requires a significant process of cultural re-orientation.

Until now, Australians have been able to assume implicitly that theirs was a developed country, by comparison with the newly industrialising countries of Asia. Now that contrast is no longer so clearcut. It is Australia which has failed so far to create the kind of production structure necessary for economic security in the new global economy. If the comparative performance of the last twenty years is repeated over the next ten, Australia will find itself increasingly marginalised from more powerful economies to the north. One forecast suggests that by the year 2000 Hong Kong and Singapore will have passed Australia in per capita incomes.[53] By 2000 it is likely that there will be upwards of 80 million people in our immediate region with average incomes in excess of $10 000.[54] (Australia's average income is currently close to $12 000.) Helen Hughes put the matter neatly in 1985:

> Australia today maintains a relationship vis-a-vis the ASEAN countries by the relative weight of its total national income. Australia with its [16] million people, is small compared to the 265 million or so people of the ASEAN countries, but Australia's total GDP of some US$171 billion [in 1981] remains significant compared to the total ASEAN countries' GDP of US$200 billion . . . However, at 1970–81 rates of growth, in 30 years time the Australian population would be about 23 million, while the ASEAN population would total about 540 million. Australia's total GDP would be about US$453 billion while the ASEAN total GDP would have risen to US$1726

billion. In contrast to, say, Switzerland's or Sweden's role with respect to their major European neighbours, Australia's relationship would be more like that of Ireland, or Portugal.[55]

Although such projections can be deceptive, this again illustrates the real, underlying vulnerability of Australia's position. If the economic slide of recent years continues, Australia might well find itself sinking into a position which will threaten its security and autonomy as a nation state.

Holding the line or a deepening crisis?

Is Australia getting on top of its economic problems? By early 1993 it was not easy to say. Certainly, the policies for structural reform set in train by the Labor government were producing some promising signs of change. The government accepted, however, that the pace of reform must be increased. The whole debate over how best or how fast to restructure the economy was further complicated, first, by another structural problem which had emerged during the 1980s: the expansion of the current account deficit and the related increase in the net foreign debt; and second, by the onset of recession in 1990–91. This section provides a short overview of what has become a particularly complicated situation.[56]

The *current account* provides a summary statement of all the economic transactions, other than flows of capital, between Australia and the rest of the world. (The *capital account* records transactions in the general area of capital investment, i.e. capital moving into or out of Australia. The current and capital accounts together make up the *balance of payments*, which records a country's total economic transactions with the outside world. While Australia is said to have 'a balance of payments problem', it is what is happening with the current account which forms the core of that problem.)

The current account contains two main categories:

1. The trading account or trade balance and the property, income and services account. The trading account records the movement of what are called 'visible' goods or trade in merchandise. It compares, on a monthly and an annual basis, the total value of Australia's merchandise exports (including commodities) with our merchandise imports. Ideally the former should exceed the latter, i.e. the trade balance should record a surplus rather than a deficit.

2. The property, income and services account, or the balance of 'invisible' items. This category includes the cost of all

transactions which are not directly visible in the way traded goods are. It includes, for example, the cost of services involved in merchandise trade, such as transport, freight and insurance; and travel, or the money spent by tourists on goods and services in Australia compared with that spent by Australians overseas. Most important, it records flows of property income, i.e. the money derived by Australians from their ownership of foreign financial assets, as compared with the money which flows out of Australia to people overseas who own assets in this country. This sub-category includes dividends, royalties and interest payments, and it is this area which now constitutes the great bulk of Australia's overall current account deficit.

In the past Australia has quite often run current account deficits, mainly due to shortfalls occurring among invisible items such as services, tourism and property income. The deficits were rarely large enough to create serious economic concern. In the 1980s, however, Australia began to record a series of deficits on the trading account. In the twenty years between 1959–60 and 1979–80, the trading account was only in deficit on four occasions, and even then by relatively insignificant amounts. In the ten years since 1980–81 it has recorded eight deficits, including one of over $4 billion in 1988–89, and another over $5 billion in 1989–90.[57] The causes lie with the matters mentioned previously: weakening terms of trade accentuated by the collapse in commodity prices in the mid-1980s, and growing demand for relatively expensive manufactured imports. The deficits on the trading account were financed largely by borrowing from overseas. This in turn led to a rapid increase in the size of Australia's net foreign debt which, because of the interest payments on that debt, then contributed to a rapidly growing deficit on the 'invisibles' account. This situation was further compounded by the effects of financial deregulation from 1985 onwards which both facilitated the movement of capital in and out of the country, and encouraged many Australian entrepreneurs and financial institutions to borrow heavily from abroad for a variety of purposes. The overall effect has been to greatly increase the amount of money Australians now have to pay to service the loans taken out in the 1980s. While the very large current account deficits recorded in the mid-1980s (Table 3.7) were mainly caused in the first instance by the weakness of exports vis-a-vis imports, more recently the continuing high deficit is due to interest payments on the debt.

In fact, after two particularly adverse results in 1988–89 and 1989–90, the current account deficit has been improving due to strengthening exports. Australia recorded a merchandise trade surplus of $2.6 billion in 1990–91. Between December 1990 and May 1992, the trade balance was continuously in surplus. Whereas in 1981 Australian exports were 11 per cent of GDP, in 1991 that figure had risen to 19 per cent.

This figure provided some evidence that a structural shift in favour of exports was occurring.[58] It was also gratifying that exports of manufactured goods, including ETMs, had increased. In Autumn 1991, Professor Garnaut took some pleasure in pointing out that thus far in the financial year 1990–91, the value of exports of all manufactured goods exceeded the value of rural exports (although that fact also reflected the then severe slump in rural export prices). However, the value of ETMs, excluding metals, in the second half of 1990 was roughly as large as the value of all Australia's food exports.[59] This, too, suggested that structural change was occurring. Still of concern was the fact that import levels had remained surprisingly high during the recession, declining only marginally from their peak in 1989–90. Although in the second half of 1992 it was difficult to identify a clear trend, it did appear that imports had begun to grow more strongly again, while exports were growing more slowly than in 1991. There was some fear, therefore, of the trade gap re-opening.

Despite the undoubted improvement, Australia to the end of 1992 was still running an average monthly deficit of close to $1 billion, now almost entirely due to interest payments on the debt. A further substantial improvement was required to eliminate that deficit, or at least bring it more nearly under control. Among economists, estimates of what represented a sustainable deficit varied between 3 and 4 per cent of GDP. Throughout the 1980s

Table 3.7   Australia, current account deficit, 1980–81 to 1991–92

	Aggregate totals ($B)	% of GDP
1980–81	5.9	4.1
1981–82	9.2	6.0
1982–83	6.7	3.9
1983–84	7.8	3.8
1984–85	10.5	5.2
1985–86	14.3	6.0
1986–87	12.3	4.7
1987–88	11.2	3.8
1988–89	18.5	5.4
1989–90	22.3	6.0
1990–91	16.0	4.2
1991–92	11.8	3.1

Source: Budget Papers

the Australian deficit averaged 4.9 per cent of GDP, the third worst in the OECD.[60] Although the result for 1991–92 seemed to bring the deficit once more within the margin of safety, the disturbing fact remained that to date, financing the deficit (which now means more or less funding the existing level of debt) has consumed all of the increase in export earnings. It has not yet been possible to make any reduction to overall debt levels. So, although Australia may be on the verge of getting on top of the trade deficit which opened up in the 1980s (if recent improvements can be sustained), a much larger trade surplus will be required to stabilise the situation with external debt. It is not immediately obvious how or where that surplus can be generated.

Australia's external debt problem at first sight is intimidating. By the end of 1992 net external debt[61] was still growing steadily and had reached a figure of $168 billion, or around 41 per cent of GDP. (It had grown from around $5 billion or 6 per cent of GDP at the start of the 1980s.) In addition to this, net equity liabilities (overseas holdings and investments in Australian companies and shares) amounted to a further $51 billion, making a total of just under $220 billion or just over 50 per cent of GDP.[62] Concern, however, focuses on the figure for debt liabilities rather than equity, since it is reasonable to assume that the latter substantially represents productive capital investment and involvement by overseas interests in Australian companies. How problematic is the net debt total? Once again, informed opinion is divided. The Australian figure as a percentage of GDP is only a little higher than the OECD average, which was just over 36 per cent in the late 1980s. Australia is also distinct in that the greater share of the debt, around two-thirds, is owed by the private sector (firms and banks) rather than the government. (The massive debt problems which help to create and define 'banana republics' are usually associated with massive and unstainable government borrowing. This is not the case in Australia.) In fact, a good many economists take the view that private sector debt should be seen as the result of economically rational decisions by profit-oriented firms and individuals who borrow, presumably, to develop their enterprises, and who may be relied upon to borrow sensibly and with some plan for repayment. The behaviour of some entrepreneurs and organisations in the 1980s might suggest this is a slightly optimistic assumption: it is not obvious that all private sector borrowing was in the best long-term interests of either the borrower or, indeed, the nation.

The government and its advisers certainly argued (or hoped) that a principal underlying cause of the import boom in the later 1980s and the associated high rate of private sector borrowing was Australian business investing in the plant, machinery and technology required to modernise Australia's industries. Mr Keating, especially, initially saw the deficits and the debt as facilitating a necessary expansion in the nation's productive assets: in time, a revitalised industry would generate the growth and the exports which would close the deficit and repay the debt. This, too, seems to have been a trifle over-optimistic. The growth rate in real manufacturing investment over the period 1984–89 averaged 13 per cent a year[63] but the evidence is ambiguous as to whether any large-scale modernisation occurred. There is little sign of a marked surge in investment in the late 1980s: investment levels in manufacturing seem to have been fairly constant in relation to GDP throughout the 1980s. It also appears that Australian manufacturing investment during the 1980s did not rise above the average in other OECD countries. This is especially worrying given the general recognition that Australia's industrial infrastructure was outdated and an investment spurt was needed simply to catch up with other countries.[64]

It is thus rather doubtful that the borrowing of the 1980s is going to produce the hoped-for extensive revitalisation of Australia's production base. It is quite likely that a fair (if unspecified) proportion of the money borrowed was used to sustain current consumption, and was not invested in developing Australia's long-term economic future, in which case repayment will become a problem if the economy does not grow in the manner envisaged. Again, repayment does not appear to worry those economists who envisage dealing with the problem either through the sale of domestic assets or by persuading overseas lenders to exchange debt for equity holdings in Australian enterprises—in which case one wonders at what point growing foreign ownership of Australian firms or resources constitutes a threat to this nation's economic sovereignty. How far would it be compatible with the goal of restructuring itself, which is to build more Australian firms and industries which can compete in the global economy? Might there not be a certain temptation for overseas interests to take over, in order to close down or move offshore, their potential Australian competitors? Australia is certainly seeking to integrate with the global economy, but there must be a risk that if we were forced through debt repayment pressures to relinquish control of key assets, firms and resources to overseas competitors, we would end up becoming even more of a marginal player vis-a-vis stronger industrial/regional economies—more of a quarry, a farm, a tourist resort, or simply a market—than we already are. This would almost certainly cause a further decline in domestic living standards, because the sectors we would be left with do not in general provide the high value exports which will enable us to pay our import bill. Nor, for that matter, do they generate or sustain a large number of well paid jobs. Although the volume of private sector debt may not constitute quite so much of a problem as one's first acquaintance with the actual total might suggest, nevertheless the bottom line is surely that all debt is ultimately a charge against the whole economy. In the last analysis, all our foreign liabilities need to be serviced and the only way to do that is to create a more productive and competitive economy and to maintain a sustainable level of economic growth. Without the latter, debt repayment will become an increasingly serious problem, no matter who the borrowers are.

Australia's growing levels of external debt increase the vulnerability of the economy—a point recognised by the international agencies who rate the credit worthiness of governments.[65] The size and the continued growth of the debt has to be seen in the context of the known weaknesses in the Australian economy. Currently the current account deficit is running at an annual rate of approximately $12 billion, almost all of it directly due to the cost of servicing the existing debt. The aim of restructuring is to increase exports of both goods and services and reduce imports somewhat, thereby gradually closing the deficit and reducing the continuing need to borrow to finance the latter. This requires a much greater improvement in trade than has so far been achieved. Australia's commodity exports are vulnerable to fluctuating world prices, and the recent rise in manufactured exports has yet to be consolidated. The residual fear is that Australia may not be able to make or sustain the kind of improvement still required. But unless we can do so, borrowing will simply continue and the size of the debt will increase. If this process continues for long enough, the final outcome is Australia falling into a debt trap, or a vicious circle of debt. In this scenario, a country which borrows heavily and/or continuously to finance a persistent deficit on current account first finds that the cost of servicing the debt becomes the more significant element in the deficit itself (Australia's current position); and then finds that because it cannot boost exports sufficiently it has to keep borrowing to meet the interest cost on its initial borrowings. Whatever it earns through trade is immediately swallowed up in interest: it can never get into a position to reduce the size of the principal. This situation causes a steady deterioration in living standards.

This kind of debt trap is usually associated with 'banana republics' but Australia has moved uncomfortably close to this position, underlining the seriousness of the situation. The country has to earn a more substantial and increasing surplus each year to meet the cost of servicing the debt already incurred and eliminate the need for fresh borrowing. One criterion of how serious the situation is becoming is provided by the 'net debt servicing ratio', or the proportion of export income which has to be used to cover the cost of servicing net external debt. Reportedly, the World Bank regards a figure of 20 per cent as the benchmark beyond which it would be increasingly reluctant to advance loans to developing countries.[66] In 1982, 8 per cent of Australia's export income was used to service debt. In the June quarter of 1990 the figure rose to 21 per cent. In the September quarter of 1991 it had fallen to 19.3 per cent, and in the last six months of 1992 it had declined to around 15 per cent, the best result since 1985.[67]

A further complicating factor is the impact of exchange rate fluctuations on both the size of the debt and the cost of repayments. Approximately 60 per cent of Australia's foreign debt is denominated in foreign currencies. A fall in the value of the Australian dollar vis-a-vis such currencies immediately increases the interest bill and the cost of new borrowings. One unpleasant scenario envisages the dollar falling in value—perhaps in the wake of the steady decline in interest rates, or perhaps due to loss of confidence by foreign exchange dealers in Australia's economic prospects—thereby causing a serious and even unsustainable increase in Australia's net interest bill.[68]

Reducing the current account deficit and stabilising the debt situation has itself become a major policy goal. By early 1993 it was widely agreed that Australia needed a growth rate of at least 3 per cent throughout the 1990s to stabilise the external debt. (It needed a much higher growth rate to reduce unemployment substantially.) While this underlined the case for continued restructuring, the question now was whether such growth rates were both achievable and sustainable. Between 1984 and 1989, GDP growth in Australia averaged 4 per cent per annum. That period, however, had ended in a severe balance of payments crisis as strong domestic demand resulted in ever-increasing imports. The government's use of very high interest rates to curtail demand had one main beneficial effect. Inflation, which had been above 7 per cent for most of the 1980s, fell to below 1 per cent by the latter half of 1992. Unfortunately, unemployment rose from just under 6 per cent to a peak of 11.4 per cent in early 1993. The economy (i.e. GDP) contracted by over 1 per cent in 1990–91. It began to grow again very slowly in late 1991 and 1992, reaching an annual growth rate of just over 2 per cent. The recession also caused a sharp drop in business investment.[69]

The problem for the government was to secure the kind of growth rate required to cope with both the debt and the unemployment without setting off either renewed inflationary pressures or another import surge. The latter could lead to a balance of payments crisis of the kind similar to the one which produced the policies which caused the recession. Without substantial growth, Australia's economic prospects were bleak. Too rapid a growth rate, however, could produce an outcome equally grim. After the election, the government announced it would make a dash for growth and set a target figure of 5 per cent. It also foreshadowed increased public sector spending, especially on infrastructure, and a reduction in company tax which had been announced during the campaign (Chapter 4). It envisaged a federal budget deficit close to $16 billion in 1992–93, with the budget not returning to surplus for at least three years. This forecast, coming after the fanfare which greeted the announcement of a massive surplus two years previously, unsettled both the financial markets and the Reserve Bank. Under some pressure from both, the Treasurer, Mr Dawkins, announced the government would give a higher priority to reducing the deficit. Once again the government was caught in the proverbial cleft stick. Without the stimulus of public sector spending it was unlikely that the private sector would grow quickly enough to make much impression on unemployment levels. Such spending, however, and the resulting budget deficit at once exposed the government to the charge of financial irresponsibility. One could say that the government had embarked on a high-risk gamble, but it was a gamble it felt impelled to take. The gamble depended very much on the successful pursuit of structural change. By April 1993 Australia's economic situation left no margin whatsoever for further delays or errors. Quite how many in the community appreciated this is difficult to say.

4

Labor and structural reform

The major aims of structural reform can be stated easily enough: to create a more productive and competitive economy, better integrated with the global economy, with a more diversified export base. These, together with the need to reduce the current account deficit and stabilise external debt, form the core of Mr Keating's 'main game'. The major means of achieving these aims have been tariff policy, reinforced first by deregulation and competition policy, and more recently by a growing emphasis on micro-economic and infrastructure reform. The general reliance on the price mechanism (or market forces) to compel both private and public sector organisations to boost their productivity in order to stay competitive was reinforced by a rigorous commitment to reducing the role of government in the economy and cutting out government assistance which might shield firms or whole industries from the need to respond to competitive pressures. The program for tariff cuts was outlined in Chapter 3. The industry policy debate is discussed in Chapter 6. The other main components of policy are discussed below.[1]

Deregulation and competition policy

Deregulation was a major part of the strategy to internationalise the Australian economy. This policy began with financial deregulation, partly because the internationalisation of the world's capital and financial markets had already proceeded so far that it was more or less impossible for a small country like Australia to resist moving in the same direction. However, the government also hoped that integrating Australia's financial system with international markets would increase the availability of capital and make the flow (and cost) of capital more sensitive to informed foreign assessments as to which Australian industries provided the best prospects for development. It hoped this would facilitate the growth of those sectors which were internationally competitive.

On 9 December 1983, Mr Keating announced that in future the value of the dollar would be determined by a free float in the currency markets, i.e. its value would depend on what dealers were prepared to pay for it and not on what governments decided. In the next three years, the government removed virtually all regulations governing trade in international currencies, as well as those controlling banks' asset structures. In September 1984, over forty non-bank institutions were licensed to participate in foreign exchange transactions. In February 1985, sixteen foreign banks were allowed to enter Australia. Between 1985 and 1987, most controls on foreign investment were either removed or relaxed substantially.

Financial deregulation was followed by a series of policies designed to increase price competition in hitherto regulated industries, notably domestic aviation. The two-airline agreement under which the market was shared exclusively between Ansett and Australian Airlines ended in October 1990. Additional airlines were licensed to compete in the domestic market and price competition was encouraged. In 1992, Qantas gained limited access to domestic routes, in part as a result of its merger with Australian Airlines. Ansett gained access to selected south-east Asian countries and New Zealand. 'Deregulation' became the umbrella term for the government's overall aim of breaking down local monopolies by exposing them to competition. This was pursued with greater vigour after the July 1987 election. The crude oil market was deregulated from 1 January 1988 by ending the obligation of Australian refineries to take prescribed quantities of domestic crude oil, as they had been required to do since 1965. This exposed local producers to overseas competition. Early in 1989 the government decided to deregulate the domestic wheat market mainly because the cost of transporting grain by rail to the ports was thought to be excessive. With some minor exceptions, grain growers had been required since the 1950s to use the railways for transport. Lack of competition had made the railways inefficient: the government thought competition with road freight would reduce transport costs (and hence wheat prices) considerably. In the face of strong opposition from rail unions in Victoria, most of the National party and the Queensland government, it legislated to exempt the Wheat Board and other grain-trading corporations from state regulations that impeded the efficient storage, transport and marketing of grain.

In May 1992 the government foreshadowed a change to the regulations governing company mergers. Before 1977 a merger could be disallowed by the government if it thought it would produce a 'substantial lessening of competition'. In 1977, the Fraser government modified that rule to allow a merger to proceed unless it led to a situation of 'market dominance' (a move Mr Fraser later described as a mistake). Labor now proposed to reinstate the pre-1977 test, to be administered by the Trade Practices Commission. Its aim was to re-affirm its competition policy although in this case the decision was problematic because it could obstruct the development, through merger, of larger 'world-class' Australian firms strong enough to compete in world markets.

Deregulation also meant trying to reduce the plethora of regulations which hampered business operations. These were indeed legion, the long-term result of Australia's fondness for statism, compounded by the effects of federalism. One mining company, seeking approval for a particular project, was said to have dealt with no less than 54 government departments, 34 state and 20 commonwealth.[2] The Confederation of Australian Industry had estimated in 1979 that federal regulatory agencies employed about 12 500 people and spent about $300 million, while the regulatory transaction costs incurred by business amounted to $1.1 billion. The direct costs of state regulation were estimated at more than twice as high again.[3] In 1986 the Business Regulation Review Unit set up in 1985 by the Hawke government reported that approximately 16 400 commonwealth officials were engaged in regulatory activities at a total cost of $700 million, although not all of this was directly business-related. Another report suggested that approximately 20 000 pages of legislation and delegated legislation was enacted in Australia each year, much of it relevant to business.[4] The Hawke government claimed 'to have embarked on a deliberate program of reviewing the broad field of business regulation with the object of rescinding those requirements that have outlived their usefulness'.[5] However, it was not easy to identify substantial results from this process. Business, especially mining companies, protested about the adverse effects of new regulations designed to protect National Heritage areas, Aboriginal land rights, or the environment in general, upon their operations. In September 1992 the Business Council and the Australian Chamber of Commerce called for a thorough review of all existing regulations to ensure that by 1994 no regulations would exist that were more than ten years old.[6] Given the mix of federal and state jurisdictions in these areas, the overall problem seemed to verge on the intractable.

Micro-economic and infrastructure reform

From 1988 onwards, deregulation became part of a broader emphasis on micro-economic reform, aimed at making markets work better by removing 'impediments which discourage or prevent resources being used in the most efficient manner, or which limit the flexibility and responsiveness of workers and enterprises'.[7] A more particular aim is to improve the efficiency of public sector utilities and enterprises, once again by exposing them to some form of price competition or by increasing their sensitivity to price signals. In such organisations micro-economic reform represents a concerted attempt to break down rigid and inefficient work practices, promote better management, raise productivity, secure a better return on capital investment, and expose and question the hidden subsidies to particular groups frequently incorporated in an organisation's pricing policies. By these means micro-economic reforms are intended to reduce overall costs to both consumers and business. The latter views micro-economic reform as crucial: without significant reductions in the cost of key business inputs such as electricity and transport, many businesses fear they will be unable to meet the increasing competition created by lower tariffs.

The growing support for micro-economic reform was due in large degree to the previous work of the Industries Assistance Commission (IAC) which for years campaigned for lower tariffs and a more efficient use of national resources. After the 1987 election, the IAC was first transferred from the Department of Industry to Treasury and then, from the start of 1989, revamped into a new body, the Industry Commission, which also subsumed the Inter-State Commission and the Business Regulation Review Unit. The Industry Commission, strongly supported by Treasury, then spearheaded the move for lower tariffs and substantial micro-economic reform (i.e. 'structural adjustment'). Beginning in 1989, the Commission began releasing a formidable range of reports on particular industries and public enterprises. In the case of micro-economic reform, it argued trenchantly that Australia's government enterprises, state and federal, were performing well below maximum efficiency (some of them abysmally), that much more competition was needed to shake them up, and that change was not proceeding fast enough. Its views are summarised usefully in its annual reports.

In 1989–90 it noted that productivity levels in most public sector utilities supplying electricity, gas and water were less then half those found among leading OECD nations. It suggested that a concerted package of reforms in transport and communications, utilities and electricity supply, together with further reductions in the level of manufacturing and agricultural assistance could, in the longer run, generate a permanent increase in Australia's GDP of around $22 billion, and a net addition of 53 000 jobs.[8] In 1990–91 it noted the problems with Australia's railways, which record losses of around $4 billion each year. The railways' very low productivity levels meant that operating costs were at least 50 per cent higher than they might otherwise be—although in Western Australia Westrail's productivity was around 50 per cent higher than in other large mainland states. Since the railways collectively invest about $1 billion each year and employ about 75 000 people, if overall productivity levels improved to match Westrail or, still better, international best practice, the savings in the capital and labour employed could be considerable. Although railway employment had declined by around 30 per cent since 1981, it was still at least one-third higher than 'best practice' should allow. Similarly with electricity: that sector 'overcharges manufacturing industries by up to 34 per cent'. Low productivity 'has led to capital and labour costs in 1989–90 being 12 per cent and 33 per cent higher respectively than necessary'. The Commission estimated that increasing labour and capital productivity to international best practice levels 'would reduce costs by $1.2 billion and yield a $1.8 billion increase in national output each year.'[9]

Corporatisation and privatisation

The potential savings to consumers and business from micro-economic reform are large. The Commission also emphasised, first, the overall significance of developing first-rate infrastructure facilities in Australia. These can make a major contribution to a firm's competitive advantage in the global economy. They may also help to induce leading international companies to locate some part of their operations here.

Australia's geographic isolation increases the importance of having well-performing infrastructure services. We do not have the option of purchasing electricity or water at lower cost from other countries as we can with goods such as clothing or chemicals. Where Australia's infrastructure services are not provided and priced as efficiently as possible, user industries carry a penalty with them when they compete with foreign suppliers at home or abroad. The large distances between Australian cities, between resource deposits and processing sites, and between many farms and ports or city markets, underscore Australia's need for cost effective and reliable rail, road and shipping facilities.[10]

Second, given the size of the investment tied up in infrastructure, it was imperative to secure an optimum rate of return on it. One estimate put the replacement value of water, sewerage and drainage assets at some $80 billion. The stock of capital used by the railways was valued by the Commission at around $15 billion. In Australia these services, together with electricity, gas and telecommunications, are under public ownership. The Commission emphasised 'that much public infrastructure has performed badly' with the average rate of return on investment being often very low. 'Taxpayers have an obvious stake in ensuring that their investments in public infrastructure are earning an adequate return.'[11]

The Commission, backed by Treasury, urged all governments 'to put government business enterprises (GBEs) on a commercial footing and to open them up to the rigours of competition'. It argued that significant improvements in productivity and ensuing cost savings could only be achieved by exposing them to the kind of market discipline experienced by most private sector organisations. To this end it recommended a strategy of opening up public sector monopolies, wherever possible, to some degree of competition, and corporatising the GBEs. This meant, in general, 'establishing an arm's length relationship between governments and their business enterprises'. It also involved such things as:

- Providing clear and non-conflicting objectives that relate to commercial performance only
- Identifying, costing and directly funding any community services from the budget so as to make subsidies transparent
- Vesting management in a commercial board accountable to Parliament through a minister
- Introducing performance monitoring based on financial and non-financial targets, and establishing a system of rewards and penalties for managers related to performance
- Separating out regulatory functions because an enterprise should not be both an umpire and a player
- Making authorities liable for all taxes and government charges;

requiring dividends at all levels equivalent to similar private companies; removing special regulatory exemptions and privileges and placing GBEs on an operational footing as similar as possible to their private sector counterparts.

The Commission also recommended that privatisation be considered where appropriate:

> Even fully corporatised authorities subject to market competition would not face all of the incentives for efficiency faced by private firms. For example, they would remain immune from takeover and insolvency and the type of performance monitoring implicit in changing share prices. There always remains the possibility that governments will interfere in operating decisions and apply pressure for political ends that damages economic performance. Thus private ownership brings with it a dimension of competitive discipline which cannot be replicated in the public sector.[12]

It recommended, therefore, 'the progressive sale of a range of government assets', e.g. all electricity generation assets and at least some distribution assets; some railway tracks and other railways assets; and some statutory agricultural marketing authorities. It emphasised that privatising public sector enterprises should be accompanied by other measures to increase competition in that area, i.e. privatising was not an answer in itself.

The federal government accepted the case for corporatising federal GBEs, and the states, led by the Greiner government in NSW, followed suit with varying degrees of reluctance, Victoria being the slowest to act. By the early 1990s, however, there was widespread recognition that Australia had no choice but to improve the performance and productivity of its quite substantial GBEs as rapidly as possible. Privatisation caused the Labor party more problems because the public ownership of essential services remained an article of faith to many within the party. The party's Platform also contained a residual commitment to public ownership as a means of dealing with perceived shortcomings in the private sector. For nearly three years, 1987–1990, the party resisted the efforts of Mr Hawke and senior ministers to prod it in the direction of privatisation. Finally, however, at a special one-day national conference called on 24 September 1990, the party endorsed proposals for privatisation in three areas. It approved the sale of 30 per cent of equity in the Commonwealth Bank to allow it to raise money to take over the State Bank of Victoria (which had been severely weakened by the collapse of its subsidiary, Tricontinental Holdings, with debts approaching $3 billion). More significantly, by 58 votes to 43, the Conference voted, first, to merge Telecom with the international carrier, OTC, to create a strong international competitor; and next to sell AUSSAT to a private sector consortium to provide 'a vigorous commercial alternative' to the restructured Telecom. Telecom was also required to relinquish its monopoly over the domestic trunk telephone network. (On 8 November, the government went further by announcing that this duopoly would end in 1997 when unlimited network competition would be allowed.) The Conference also voted, by 60 votes to 39, to sell the whole of Australian Airlines and 49 per cent of Qantas to the private sector. This decision also was subsequently taken further when, on 30 May 1992, Mr Keating announced that the government would merge Qantas and Australian Airlines and privatise 70 per cent of the new organisation. Two days later, cabinet approved a total sell-off of the merged airlines.[13]

By 1992, one could say that attempts to create the underpinnings for a more competitive and productive market economy were well under way. The Industry Commission's annual report for 1990–91 took 27 pages (Appendix 1) to set out reforms in and to the economic infrastructure—energy, roads, rail, waterfront and telecommunications; and another 26 pages (Appendix 2) to list micro-reforms achieved at state and federal levels. Together these suggested considerable progress towards corporatisation and the improved supply of crucial services to user industries. It noted that government response to reform pressures 'had been quite variable', although the effort to bring about substantial reforms in and to the federal system, set in motion by the Special Premiers' Conference held first in October 1990, had encouraged a greater commitment to micro-economic reform from the states, and greater cooperation between them. This had already produced several valuable initiatives (see further below). Nonetheless, much more remained to be done. In judging progress towards reform, one had to keep in mind that in virtually all areas, Australian performance lagged well behind that of competitor nations who were themselves still improving their own productivity. There was a serious question as to whether Australia, striving to catch up, was really moving fast enough. A crucial factor here was the brake on reform imposed by the survival of backward-looking attitudes among both management and unions, and the existence of numerous, cumbersome award agreements institutionalising restrictive practices of various kinds, all of which had to be re-designed, often through long and tortuous negotiations between a whole variety of interested parties. The waterfront was a prime example.

The waterfront

A country like Australia, geographically isolated and seeking to break into world manufacturing markets, must have an efficient transport system including especially efficient ports and docks. A report from the Interstate Commission published in April 1989 suggested that at least $620 million could be saved annually by tackling the inefficiencies known to exist on the waterfront.[14] The Waterside Workers Federation, whose membership had declined from a post-war peak of 80 000 to 8000, exercised a complete monopoly over employment on the waterfront and maintained an impressive list of restrictive work practices: overmanning, restrictions on shiftwork, on who could unload containers, and high penalty rates. Wharfies received around $800 for a notional working week of 35 hours (including idle time); 27.5 per cent leave loading on five weeks annual leave plus very generous sick leave provisions. The report found that productivity in Australian ports was barely half that of levels overseas. It was well known overseas that Australian ports were 'black holes': a ship might disappear into one of them for weeks at a time.[15] As *The Age* editorialised: 'It is a picture of an industry that has lost its way; a service industry in which customers are too often regarded as a nuisance. It . . . often acts as a barrier, not a conduit, to the smooth passage of goods.'[16] In addition, 33 per cent of wharfies were over 50 and 14 per cent had a disability of some kind. The report said the workforce should be cut by one-third. It proposed 3000 of the older wharfies be retired within three years with the aid of generous redundancy payments, and 1000 workers younger than 30 be hired. It recommended a comprehensive review of work practices, and changes to union coverage which would weaken the union's effective veto on productivity improvements.

The report was rejected outright by the Waterside Workers Federation who were supported initially by the ACTU. After two months hard bargaining, the government announced in June 1989 a $290 million redundancy program, financed equally by itself and the employers, to make the recommended changes. However, it did not at the time pursue proposals to reduce union coverage of certain categories of workers, and it did not secure agreement on a number of key proposals to increase productivity, such as lifting the restrictions on just who was allowed to load and unload containers. The union agreed to implement the main features of the package in October 1989 and an In-Principle Agreement on waterfront reform, designed to lift productivity by 30 per cent, was signed. There then followed nearly two years of hard negotiations aimed at reducing the workforce and consolidating the nineteen awards covering waterside workers into one. On several occasions, negotiations aimed at granting wage increases in return for union cooperation in securing productivity increases threatened to break down altogether. Ministerial intervention by Senator Collins and, on one dramatic occasion, by the then Prime Minister, Mr Hawke, kept the parties talking.

Finally, towards the end of 1991 a single skills-based award replacing all previous awards was accepted. Enterprise agreements covering the main ports were signed in October 1991, and by late 1992 a total of 70 such agreements were in force at 37 ports. By then the waterfront workforce had been halved, while 1000 younger workers had been hired. Some progress had been made towards multi-skilling and introducing career paths (albeit rather rudimentary) for employees. The agreements usually gave management greater flexibility to assign employees varying duties during the course of their shifts, while employees were given incentive schemes which could allow them to increase their annual salary by up to $10 000. The Waterfront Industry Reform Authority claimed substantial productivity improvements: labour productivity at container terminals had doubled. Cargo handling rates had increased by between 25 and 50 per cent since 1989. Australian grain ports were now among the most efficient in the world: loading times had halved and costs had been reduced by up to 50 per cent. Following the manning reductions, national stevedoring costs had fallen by about $170 million, and con-tainer-handling costs had dropped by about a quarter.[17] However, these improvements had not yet produced significantly lower freight charges, creating some suspicion that the shipping com-panies had profited most in the short run from the reforms. And although the reforms had certainly produced gains, it appeared that similar reforms in New Zealand had produced larger gains more economically. By early 1992 the provisional conclusion was that the reforms had gone some way towards improving the fairly awful reputation of Australia's ports; the reform process was moving, with the occasional hiccup, in the right direction, but it was still too early to agree with Senator Collins' claim that the reputation for gross unreliability had been permanently reversed. In both port reform and coastal shipping, where the controversial policy of cabotage still existed,[18] it was still essential to maintain the momentum of reform.

Reforming federalism

Micro-economic and infrastructure reforms included many mat-ters which were part of the constitutional responsibilities of the states. Structural reform required their active cooperation. In July 1990 Mr Hawke revived the call for greater cooperation between all Australian governments to improve national economic perfor-mance and the quality of government services. He proposed a series of Special Premiers' Conferences (SPCs) to explore the issues, an idea received enthusiastically by the states. The first Conference was held in October 1990 and the second in July 1991. At these, the states and commonwealth agreed to:

- Establish a National Rail Corporation to provide a single company to run all interstate rail freight operations on strictly commercial lines. An Act to establish such a body was drawn up by the commonwealth in 1992, although progress was delayed by arguments over funding.
- Establish a National Road Transport Commission to develop uniform regulations across all states for heavy transport, especially in regard to licensing, inspection, road charges and pollution. Its aim would be to recover the full cost of highway maintenance and construction from the transport industry by 1 July 1995. Federal legislation to establish this body was passed in 1992.
- Establish a National Electricity Grid which would coordinate the supply of electricity through the eastern and south-eastern states, including Tasmania.
- Establish a National Food Authority to draw up and apply uniform standards throughout the food industry. This body was established in 1992. The states also agreed to implement the principle of 'mutual recognition' of goods, services and occupations across Australia, meaning that where goods or occupational qualifications were accepted or recognised in one jurisdiction they could be recognised in another. They also agreed on the need for common regulations for all financial institutions. In February 1992 all governments approved an Intergovernmental Agreement on the Environment which provided for a National Environment Protection Authority to coordinate environmental policies at all levels of government.

The agreements and the level of goodwill generated by the SPCs were a very welcome departure from the normal squabbles of federal–state relations. Unfortunately the momentum was halted in October 1991 when Mr Keating, speaking as a Labor centralist, and in the course of staking his own claims to the Prime Ministership, persuaded the Labor caucus not to support Mr Hawke's apparent willingness to entertain state proposals for the commonwealth to return to them a fixed (and known) proportion of income tax revenues. The states, arguing that any permanent improvement in the quality of Australian federalism depended on their having sufficient revenue to fund their responsibilities adequately, refused to attend the next SPC in Perth. That meeting had been due to discuss a major proposal from the states to establish a standing Council of the Australian Federation, a new decision-making body made up of heads of government, which would meet once or twice a year to focus on 'strategic cross-jurisdictional and cross-portfolio structural issues'. It would also discuss all 'issues relating to the creation and maintenance of economic union' within Australia. The states were also due to present for approval four principles intended to give a greater degree of coherence to the vexed question of how to allocate roles and responsibilities between the levels of government, at least three of which affected structural reform directly.[19] These receded into the background during 1992. The entire episode demonstrated once again just how hard it is in Australia to generate the political will and momentum required to drive through desirable reforms. In so many ways the political system— or the way politics is played in this country—acts as a barrier to reform.

Some momentum was restored in 1992. Commonwealth and states agreed on the need for extensive spending on infrastructure and the Better Cities program. *One Nation* committed $2 billion for a common gauge rail link between Brisbane and Perth, and for highway construction. Mr Keating reconvened a Heads of Government meeting in May (but not the SPC) to discuss how to implement the earlier decisions. Nevertheless, at a fairly crucial moment in the reform process, a valuable opportunity to mobilise greater efforts for structural reform had been lost.

Labour market reform

Australia's system of industrial relations had given it a reputation as an unreliable country in which, or with which, to do business. Industrial disputes were frequent and unpredictable. It was known for its practice of referring disputes to a complicated system of industrial courts and tribunals, which operated at both the state and federal level, rather than dealing with them at the workplace. It also relied on a central Arbitration Commission (as it then was) to determine the overall structure of wage levels throughout the economy. The system of conciliation and arbitration had proved quite successful as a method of containing and resolving conflict within the highly adversarial culture of industrial relations. The Arbitration Commission had also safeguarded the interests of lower paid workers and secured a measure of comparative wage justice. However, during the 1980s the overall system received increasing criticism for being excessively rigid and cumbersome. There were growing demands from employers' associations, and from the political right, to replace it with a more decentralised system in which wages, terms and conditions could be settled by direct negotiations between employers and employees at each individual workplace.[20] Such a system, it was thought, would allow firms and employers greater flexibility in responding to increasing competition.

By the 1980s, as the global struggle for competitive advantage became more acute, large parts of Australian industry were saddled with problems whose roots were once again entrenched in the national culture. The unions and, indeed, many Australians had become accustomed to regular wage increases delivered either through the national wage decisions of the Arbitration Commission or through the flow-on effects which invariably followed a new wage award in a major industry, notably the metal trades. The labour movement looked to outcomes in the arbitration system as a primary defence of their members' standard of living, even ahead of the welfare system. The general populace regarded regular wage increases as their just entitlement. The whole system of industrial relations, an arcane mystery to most people, operated increasingly as a state within a state. The real cost was that over time, its internal rules and calculations—and the kind of materialistic self-interest which drove it—was increasingly divorced from the new economic realities confronting Australia. In particular, the nexus between pay and productivity was quite obscured. So too was the residual problem of how to create the wealth to be parcelled out through the wage awards. By the 1980s employers and others were arguing with a growing sense of desperation that many industries could no longer afford the national across-the-board increases handed down by the Arbitration Commission. Wage increases had to be related directly to an industry's competitive position, to its capacity to pay. They also complained that national wage increases, plus the mandatory requirement to employ labour at national award rates, in the absence of productivity improvements, added continually to their costs. Because employers were forced to raise prices in proportion, this gave rise to significant inflationary pressures.

It was also evident that one major reason why productivity in Australia lagged behind the OECD average was the number of restrictive work practices which had built up in the average Australian workplace; under the existing system of industrial relations, neither management nor unions had sufficient incentive to tackle reform. The problem was due partly to the number of unions in Australia, partly to the effects of the award system, and overall to the kind of industrial culture which had developed over the years.

In 1984 there were 329 unions left in Australia, most of them small and craft-based, relics of a previous industrial era. There were often five or more unions represented at medium-sized workplaces, while there might be ten or more at workplaces with more than 2000 employees. The unions competed fiercely for members. Over time they had established rigid groundrules defining what work their respective members might and might not do which gave rise to frequent demarcation disputes. Furthermore, the number of state and federal awards governing wages and conditions at medium-sized and larger workplaces varied between four and seven. The awards were often long and complicated, recording the concessions and privileges won from employers over the years. They were institutionalised through both the state and federal arbitration systems, and their provisions were jealously and zealously protected by union officials. The unions were especially concerned to see that any unusual departure from normal working practice (tightly defined) was compensated by penalty rates and/or over-award payments. By and large, unions had been less interested in securing efficient production than in consolidating the gains won by their members. Having won the 38-hour (and in some cases 35-hour) week, 4 weeks annual leave, sick leave, and the 17.5 per cent leave loading, unions frequently placed restrictions on the length and amount of shift work, enforced rigid manning requirements, and imposed a variety of restrictions on who could do what work, with whom, under what conditions and for how long.[21]

While the most obvious abuses could be blamed on the unions, management (especially middle management) also left something to be desired.[22] Again, for many managers, negotiating their way through the labyrinthine award and arbitration system took more time and will than many felt able to spare. There is little doubt that managers and unions too often defined their roles in opposition to one another. Many employers and managers came to view their workforces as akin to recalcitrant children whose cooperation had to be gained by a combination of coercion, cunning and bribery. Many unionists were only too willing to play this game. While protection remained, managers had no overriding incentive to confront the legacy of restrictive practices which accumulated over the years. Similarly, unions and workers had no incentive either to think about the problems of wealth-creation—or the long-term security of their own jobs—so long as they could rely on regular wage increases and institutionalised protection under the Arbitration system. The culture of mistrust and opposition set up a major inertial barrier to reform: because of the complexities of 'the system', no one person would think of going against it given the plethora of rules, sanctions and bodies he or she would have to confront. The result was a prolonged disregard for issues of productivity and competitiveness. Workplace reform is just as important as low-ering tariffs, but far more complicated. It is the area which most requires a cultural revolution in behaviour and attitudes, on both sides of the industrial fence.

First attempts at reform

The government was initially a strong supporter of centralised wage-fixing and the role of the Arbitration Commission (in March 1989 this became the Industrial Relations Commission or IRC). It first opposed the idea of deregulating the labour market, or creating 'a free market in labour'. Then, gradually, it swung round in the later 1980s to support a more decentralised form of wage fixing. It also came to support, as did the ACTU, the core idea of 'enterprise bargaining'. By mid-1992, with some important differences, it appeared to be going in the direction urged by the Opposition, towards a more highly deregulated labour market, with a minimal role for the IRC.

Throughout the 1980s the cornerstone of the government's wages and labour policies was the Accord, which institutionalised Labor's special relationship with the trade union movement. The Accord began life as an agreement negotiated between the industrial and political wings of the labour movement prior to the election in March 1983.[23] Its main feature initially was an agreement to index wage increases in line with increases in the consumer price index (CPI). By this means, the government hoped to prevent the kind of wages breakout which had occurred in 1982. Both the government and the ACTU were agreed that economic recovery and reducing unemployment required both wage stability and some degree of wage restraint. In the event, as Australia's economic vulnerability became more evident, and the full complexity of structural change appeared, the unions were required to accept a greater degree of wage restraint than first anticipated. In 1983 and 1984, wages were adjusted sub-stantially in line with increases in the CPI. Thereafter, following the sharp deterioration in the current account in 1984–85, the fall in the value of the dollar and renewed inflationary pressures, the IRC, with the government's agreement, began the practice of discounting wage increases to reduce inflationary flow-on effects. In the later 1980s, the Accord became, implicitly, a convenient means of bringing about a fall in real wages for the majority of wage-earners in the greater interest of improving business profitability. By 1988, real unit labour costs had fallen back to the level of the late 1960s, and the share of national income going to labour (59 per cent) had also returned to the level of 1970. Overall, between 1983 and 1991 average weekly (ordinary time) earnings fell at least 2 per cent in real terms. Those at the lower end of the labour market suffered a larger fall in real incomes.[24] This contributed to a significant increase in corporate profitability, prior to 1989, but not all of the increase flowed into productive investment. The Accord also brought one of the longest periods of industrial peace in more than twenty years. Since 1982, the number of days lost in industrial disputes declined steadily, except for a small increase in 1988; on an annual basis, the number of days lost since 1982 has been the lowest since 1967.[25]

After 1987 the terms of the Accord—and the central principles underlying the national wage-fixing process—were overhauled continuously as the government accepted the urgency of workplace reform. By late 1986, it was willing to tackle the problem of restrictive work practices. In the national wage case decision in March 1987, the IRC, following a line of argument proposed by the government and the ACTU, more or less abandoned the system of wage indexation in favour of a two-tier approach. Under this, the first tier provided a uniform minimum wage increase for all industries, taking account of the CPI and general economic conditions. The second tier allowed for an additional wage increase, based on a demonstrated improvement in productivity, to be negotiated between a firm and a union, or between employers' associations and peak labour associations. This was a significant development for two reasons. First, it was a step away from centralism towards decentralisation. Second, it marked an historic shift in the position of the union movement. Hitherto the ACTU had demanded wage increases directly in response to increases in the cost of living. Now it was accepting that future wage increases should take account of productivity and efficiency factors. It did this partly in response to growing union dissatisfaction with the Accord and wage indexation: the unions wanted another principle on which to justify additional wage demands. However, this opened the way for a more flexible wages system to emerge.

Succeeding national wage cases went further in this direction. In August 1988 and March 1989 the IRC accepted the ACTU's recommendation that it deal with award restructuring; i.e. in the course of making decisions based on individual awards (and the Business Council estimated there were at least 2000 such awards throughout Australia) it should encourage the parties to eliminate those provisions which created demarcation disputes or which stood in the way of efficiency gains. Instead, it should progressively build into awards new provisions to encourage skill formation, training and the acceptance of greater responsibility for workplace efficiency among the occupational groups involved.

The IRC has since been concerned to establish a wages system which reflects the principle of structural efficiency. It has tried to restructure awards to reduce detail and anomalies, trying to create fewer, more broadly-defined job classifications (broadbanding) linked by skill levels which provide a career path along which, ideally, workers may progress throughout their working life by acquiring additional skills and competence. The emphasis is on encouraging workers to acquire a variety of skills (multiskilling), to think of themselves as members of a team, and to be able to carry out a greater range of jobs at the workplace rather than being confined, like cogs in a machine, to narrowly defined and usually dead-end jobs. In determining individual wage rates, therefore, the IRC has been moving steadily away from the previously central nexus between the CPI and wage rates. It has focused more on setting new minimum rates of pay across industry sectors, taking greater account of the levels of skill or responsibility entailed.

The shift towards enterprise bargaining

In early 1990 the government and the ACTU went one stage further by agreeing that unions and employers should be free to negotiate productivity bargains at the level of the enterprise or company rather than the whole industry (although employers pointed out this would not work properly while the number of unions represented at each enterprise remained so high: see also below). This marked a further step towards a more flexible and decentralised labour market. In particular, the government and the ACTU were more willing to acknowledge that wage levels in particular industries might vary according to their economic circumstances. By early 1990 there was growing recognition that in future the function of the national wage case would be to provide, if the conditions warranted, a relatively small across-the-board increase to all workers, most likely in the shape of a flat dollar amount rather than a percentage increase, while more substantial wage increases might be negotiated on a specific industry or company basis, and would have to be justified by productivity increases. The latter would be monitored by the IRC and would only be ratified if the IRC was satisfied by their bona fides. A notable example of this approach was the agreement negotiated in the Metal Trades Industry in March 1990. To obtain the second 3 per cent (productivity-related) pay rise granted by the previous national wage case, the metal unions agreed to scrap nearly 360 job classifications in favour of fourteen new categories. The agreement established more flexible working conditions on the shop floor, permitted longer shifts, provided training facilities for multi-skilling and an orderly career path for employees. The agreement was welcomed by all parties as leading to 'a quantum leap' in productivity, and a benchmark for other industries to follow.[26]

To this point the government and the ACTU had worked together with the IRC to promote workplace reform. However, for reasons which lie outside this book, relations between the ACTU and the IRC began to deteriorate during 1990. The rift came to a head when the IRC, in deciding the national wage case in April 1991, refused to provide further endorsement for enterprise bargaining as requested by the government and the ACTU. In effect, the IRC accused the unions of treating enterprise bargaining more as a means of securing additional wage increases than as a device for raising productivity. It implied that the ACTU saw productivity deals as akin to the kind of over-award payments which had existed hitherto. Enterprise bargaining could not succeed without a fundamental change occurring in attitudes to work and pay, but 'the parties to industrial relations have still to develop the maturity necessary for the further shift of emphasis now proposed'.[27] Until the parties involved clarified their ideas and objectives, which were currently vague and conflicting, the IRC refused to endorse any new form of enterprise bargaining.

These remarks brought a bitter response from both the ACTU and the government. The Secretary of the ACTU Mr Kelty, remarked: 'The Commission spent six months incubating a decision and produced a rotten egg. We are not about to eat it.'[28] Mr Keating suggested that the IRC had completely mistaken its role in the decentralised system now emerging, and should be abolished.[29] (He later qualified this remark.) Both the government and the ACTU were incensed that the IRC had also refused to endorse the provisions of the Accord (Mark VI) previously agreed to by them. The IRC rejected the claim for a flat $12 weekly increase and granted instead a structural efficiency adjustment of 2.5 per cent in paid rates and minimum awards, in exchange for demonstrated productivity gains. It also adjourned the ACTU claim for a phased 3 per cent increase in superannuation entitlements.[30]

The ACTU, backed by the government, rejected the decision outright and attempted (without much success) to fight for the Accord through workplace bargaining in specific industries. This produced a series of damaging encounters between the government and the IRC over who had the final authority to set wage levels. One of these almost wrecked the delicate process of waterfront reform when the IRC refused to ratify a productivity deal negotiated under the auspices of the Prime Minister, Mr

Hawke, because it exceeded the wage guidelines laid down in April. The IRC did, however, accept that wage rises beyond the 2.5 per cent were possible for genuine productivity agreements which could be treated as special cases. Finally, in the October national wage case the IRC gave considerable ground by accepting that a further move towards enterprise bargaining was necessary and desirable. It acknowledged that employers and unions might now strike productivity bargains through direct workplace negotiations. The IRC would not place a ceiling on possible wage outcomes. Unions would not have to give a no-extra-claims commitment to get an agreement ratified by the IRC. Moreover, the IRC said, henceforth it would restrict its own role to that of conciliator if required: it would not arbitrate on disputes over agreements. If employers and employees were agreed, they could press ahead and implement their own bargain. The IRC repeated its earlier warnings that unless there were clearer criteria for defining and measuring efficiency gains, enterprise bargaining would turn out to be a rhetorical term of convenience, and not a genuine avenue for addressing structural efficiency at the workplace. However, its decision placed the responsibility for developing enterprise bargaining very much on employers and employees.

The breakdown of consensus

The 1991 dispute was a major hiccup in the process of workplace reform: much of the year was taken up with jurisdictional disputes between the reforming bodies themselves. It also contributed to a permanent souring of relations between the IRC on the one hand, and the government and the ACTU on the other. A major ancillary cause of this was a long-running dispute over the structure of the IRC and the pay and judicial status of its members. By early 1992 the government was widely perceived to be conducting a campaign to reduce the independence of the IRC, and to make it more subservient to its own policy wishes— and by implication those of the ACTU as well.[31] The government now wished to speed up the process of enterprise bargaining, but the way in which it proceeded created doubts, especially among employers and presumably in the IRC, as to the genuineness of the productivity 'deals' it was advocating. The employers evidently feared that the government's reform agenda was being driven too much by its political ties and obligations to the ACTU in this the run-up to the 1993 election.

In March 1992 the government foreshadowed changing the relevant sections of the Industrial Relations Act to require the IRC to approve enterprise agreements so long as they met only certain, rather general, criteria. The government legislated in June and the legislation came into force in July. Hitherto the IRC had emphasised that the primary criterion for its approving productivity bargains was the demonstrable presence of 'efficiency measures designed to effect real gains in productivity'. The new legislation removed that criterion, meaning that the IRC could no longer demand that wage increases contained in enterprise deals be linked to improvements in productivity. Instead, the government substituted more general criteria for approval: that deals maintain community standards on pay and conditions; the terms of an agreement must not disadvantage employees; there must be adequate procedures to settle disputes; and there must be single bargaining units of the relevant unions. The legislation also removed the requirement that the IRC consider the public interest in deciding whether to approve a deal. The minister, Senator Cook, announced that he would hold this power in reserve for 18 months but it would only be used 'in the most extreme circumstances'.[32] This debarred the IRC from disallowing a deal because, for example, it was concerned about the precedent set, and/or the likely flow-on effects.

This legislation was not well received by employers. Indeed, it may well have been the point at which many key employers decided they would be better off with the more radical version of enterprise bargaining proposed by the Opposition (see also Chapter 5). Previously the employer groups had disagreed among themselves in their support for the IRC and the desirable balance to be achieved between centralism and decentralisation. Several had favoured moving carefully towards enterprise bargaining under the scrutiny of the IRC. They valued the IRC's support in upholding the principle of structural efficiency. Now they felt that the new rules, by giving little or no explicit emphasis to measurable productivity increases or to the public interest, had tilted the balance of their particular playing field too much towards the unions. In particular they were concerned that there would no longer be any attempt to place a ceiling on wage increases won at the level of the workplace: whatever could be extracted was permissible. They were especially concerned at the likely flow-on effects: a large wage increase won at one site would inevitably place pressure on employers elsewhere. They did not think they had sufficient protection from the illegitimate use of union power, partly because they did not think a Labor government would be willing to invoke the penalty sections of the Industrial Relations Act against recalcitrant trade unions. And, given the new open-endedness of enterprise bargaining, they opposed the continued existence of national wage case hearings. Overall, employers feared that the IRC's earlier concerns were increasingly well-founded: in the absence of a more responsible workplace culture, which had still to be developed, the new system gave too little emphasis to productivity, and too much scope to the unions to pressure for wage increases.

It was particularly significant that the Metal Trades Industry Association, hitherto sympathetic to Labor's model of managed decentralisation within the auspices of the IRC, called the new legislation 'reckless, ill-advised and ill-thought-out'.[33] The Confederation of Australian Industry (CAI), the largest employer group and a traditional supporter of compulsory arbitration, had already reversed its position as a result of the 1991 dispute. It called then for an end to the exclusive right of unions to represent employees, an end to national wage case hearings, and for fundamental rationalisation of the complex array of state and federal arbitration bodies as a means of reducing the number of awards which applied to enterprises. It also thought awards must be confined to particular industries and be subject to only two minimum standards, an hourly wage rate and an annual leave allowance. It preferred to retain a monitoring role for the IRC, but by June 1992 it was frankly sceptical of the unions' good faith vis-a-vis productivity bargaining.[34] Its position was now much closer to that of the Business Council of Australia which had always favoured single bargaining units and direct workplace negotiations over wages and conditions. Ideally it wanted one award per workplace with employees allowed to bargain for themselves, without the presence of a union. It strongly opposed negotiations involving more than one employer or one union. Previously it had seen a role for the IRC in ratifying agreements and checking the unions' single-minded focus on pay.[35] If the IRC could not provide that check, there was little point keeping it.

The ACTU's position

In response, one should certainly note that by 1992 the ACTU (if not all of its members) supported the principle of enterprise bargaining. This indicated the magnitude of the attitudinal shift which had occurred since 1983, a shift which vindicated the early critics of centralism, but it could not have happened without the support provided by the leadership of the ACTU, especially the Secretary, Mr Kelty, the previous President, Mr Crean, and his successor, Mr Ferguson. They shared Mr Keating's strong belief that the future of many wage and salary earners was bleak without restructuring to secure the longer-term viability of the sectors in which many of them worked. The leadership played a crucial role in explaining to unionists what had to change and why. The single most important factor was to persuade the union movement to adjust wages for reasons other than the cost of living, i.e. to shift from wage indexation to productivity bargaining and award restructuring. As Mr Crean put it, 'What the union movement came to realise in the eighties is that the easy road to wage fixing is closed. Unless wealth creation is promoted, distribution is limited.'[36] The leadership at least recognised that productivity deals afforded virtually the only prospects for real wage increases in the 1990s.

The union movement, slowly and grudgingly in some cases (especially in the public sector), was coming to recognise that it had to adapt to new social conditions. This recognition was reinforced by declining union membership, which by 1988 had fallen to just over 40 per cent of the workforce, a figure buttressed by much higher rates of unionisation in public sector enterprises. Mr Kelty emphasised the imperative need to reduce the number of unions, a reduction essential to eliminate demarcation disputes and facilitate enterprise bargaining. He set a target of just 20 large industry unions by 1996. However, movement towards amalgamation was slow. There were still 275 unions in June 1991.[37] ACTU leaders acknowledged that the tribal character of the union movement, plus personal and ideological disputes among union leaders, posed severe impediments. Within each of the 21 broad industry groups identified by the ACTU, there were often between 8 and 17 unions still to be amalgamated. Seventy-six per cent of the 275 unions had fewer than 10 000 members each in June 1991.[38] The ACTU remained optimistic, claiming amalgamation was gaining significant momentum. Bill Kelty wrote that by mid-1993, '98 per cent of union members . . . [would] be covered by just 21 unions organised on industry lines'.[39] The ACTU also fully supported breaking down rigid job demarcations, encouraging training, multi-skilling and teamwork. It agreed with the government's policy of extending superannuation to as many workers as possible, both to boost national savings and to forestall the rising cost of the old age pension caused by an ageing population.

The unions had two major reservations about enterprise bargaining. First, they resisted the idea that wages could go down as well as up. They suspected some employers would be over-keen to force down wages and conditions as a cost-cutting measure. Hence the unions wished both to protect and to build on from the existing structure of award rates. (Employers were nervous that this would escalate labour costs and, without wage ceilings, produce exactly the same effects as the previous system of over-award payments.) The unions initially saw the IRC being responsible for safeguarding award rates. As the IRC pursued the principle of structural efficiency, it proved less willing to treat the existing structure of award rates as establishing a firm floor to the market.

Second, the unions wished to preserve their monopoly right to represent all employees in all wage negotiations. The problem with the proliferation of single bargaining units was that in effect it resulted in the balkanization of the whole industrial relations system. And, since perhaps half the workplaces in Australia (especially the smaller ones) had no trade unionists among employees, the unions suspected that a decentralised bargaining structure would tend to favour employers. In particular the unions feared that unless a union was present to defend the collective interests of individual workers, many of those rights, notably the length of the working day, sick leave, four weeks annual holidays and especially the 17.5 per cent leave loading, would be whittled away in the course of enterprise bargaining.

The government's eroding position

The government agreed that employees were best represented by unions. It favoured the creation of industry unions, one of which ideally might represent employees at a particular workplace. It supported agreements reached at 'greenfield sites' (i.e. industrial developments starting from scratch) for one union to represent all workers at that site.[40] It welcomed the progressive reduction in the number of awards applying to particular enterprises. It appeared to accept that national wage case decisions would diminish in importance and would provide more of a defence for lower-paid workers. This became clearer in August 1992 when it proposed that in 1993–94 the only centrally-determined pay rise would be a flat increase for low-paid workers receiving minimum rates of pay under certain awards. All other increases should occur through productivity bargains at the workplace. In effect this abolished the traditional national wage case. The ACTU wanted to expand the category of low-paid workers, but otherwise seemed disposed to agree.

Between 1990 and 1992 the government had clearly changed its mind on one central point: it no longer believed in centralism, and although it seemed to think the IRC should assist with the process of award restructuring, it no longer favoured the IRC supervising, still less directing, the shift to enterprise bargaining. The IRC's responsibilities for implementing the structural efficiency principle were unclear. This left a major question mark over the government's whole strategy of managed decentralisation. The IRC was evidently going to occupy a more marginal role in the future system, concerned primarily with protecting minimum rates and, perhaps, with comparative wage justice for female and/or lower-paid workers. Ostensibly at least, the government was now in favour of wages being determined mainly by productivity bargaining in the labour market. This meant that, on the one hand, it had once again pinched a substantial portion of the Opposition's policies; but on the other, it had gone some way itself to bypassing and even undermining the centralised system. In that respect it had laid the groundwork for a more fully deregulated labour market of the kind preferred by its political opponents.

By mid-1992 it was hard to resist the conclusion that although the whole tortuous and arthritic system of industrial relations was beginning to move, slowly but perceptibly, towards greater flexibility and decentralisation, the system itself was unstable for three main reasons:

- The series of compromises and accommodations which had allowed the system to emerge from within the chrysalis of centralism could not be sustained any further. In particular, what had to be decided was whether the new system was one based on a genuine pursuit of productivity and structural efficiency, or whether it was just another means of achieving a further round of wage increases. On this the government was equivocal, the ACTU committed in principle but fuzzy in practice, and the employers increasingly sceptical. After five years of evolution and experiment, the latter felt that the system was delicately poised at the point where it could either slide back into old habits and practices or develop into a genuine system of productivity bargaining. Many employers felt that the government and the ACTU were unable, for a variety of historical and political debts and ties, to make a decisive break with centralism and commit themselves fully to a new kind of system. The government had hoped that the new would simply grow out of the old; many employers, well aware of the complexities involved, had been willing to go along with this approach. But many of them felt it was now or never: either Australia committed itself unequivocally to basing wages on productivity, or the competitive position of many industries would be gone for ever. What had happened to the IRC, and what was not happening at the workplace, left employers less inclined to support the government's agenda of gradual, managed reform.
- The IRC had been the crucial facilitator of managed decentralisation. It had now lost the powers it needed to back up its views. Its relations with the government and the ACTU were poor and, according to press reports, its morale was

extremely low. Employers felt that the IRC had been emasculated. If, therefore, they had to fend for themselves in the market place, why not adopt the Opposition's agenda which would remove national wage case hearings and very likely give employers stronger powers to deal with 'illegitimate' union actions?

• It was difficult to say how well enterprise bargaining was going, but press reports suggested that progress was slow and painful. By March 1992, some 50 deals (half of them in the metal trades) had been approved in the industrial courts, touching only 100 000 workers out of a workforce of 7 million.[41] However, these did include some noteworthy precedents and substantial reforms.[42] The rate of progress may have improved in the next few months: a figure of 130 deals was mentioned in June while Bill Kelty claimed in July that more than 700 enterprise agreements, with terms varying from six months to two years, had already been negotiated at (mostly) single bargaining units across Australia.[43] The concurrent process of award restructuring was moving more rapidly, with substantial progress reported towards broadbanding, multi-skilling and provision of training opportunities. Problems arose frequently, however, with penalty rates, shift work, leave provisions and changes to the span of daily hours.[44] Employers found the issues confronting them bewildering, especially in designing productivity measurements; in trying to produce flatter, less hierarchical styles of management; in devolving responsibility for efficiency and quality control downwards to the workplace; encouraging teamwork and trying to develop a greater sense of collective responsibility for the enterprise and its products. For employees, enterprise bargaining demanded from them a complete change in attitude towards work and pay. Many found this hard. Although the overall system was moving in the right direction, the 'new workplace culture' required for productivity bargaining to succeed was only just emerging. As one observer put it:

Almost certainly, left to its own devices, the system in its present state will revert to its old and destructive ways of conflict first, conflict last. There will of course be the moderating influence of the recession and an ACTU leadership in general support of government policies and objectives. Yet these will not in themselves be enough to contain the crudest elements of the system. The enlightenment of employers and union officials has not yet advanced to the stage where the system can operate without checks and balances, especially given the industrial legal framework. The early signs of a maturing of the Australian workplace are there, but it remains a long way from full-blown.[45]

After the election Mr Keating, in an important speech to the Institute of Company Directors, announced that the government would move more decisively to encourage a more fully decentralised system of enterprise bargaining.[46] He signalled that the future wages system would be based predominantly on workplace agreements between employers and employees. Although the arbitration tribunals, state and federal, would still provide minimum safety nets for low-paid workers, the great majority of workers should expect wage increases only on the basis of genuine productivity bargains. Moreover, Mr Keating accepted the criticism that hitherto unions had been too inclined to use enterprise bargaining as a way of adding on to existing awards. He indicated that the government would need to find a way of extending the coverage of workplace agreements so that these, rather than the awards, became the primary means of defining an individual's terms and conditions of work. He foreshadowed legislation 'to renovate the legal and institutional structure of . . . industrial relations' and make it fully compatible with the concept of enterprise bargaining. He also accepted that a more credible means of enforcing workplace agreements would be required, with 'clear, substantial and easily enforceable penalties for breaches'.

This speech heralded a further reduction in the role and functions of the IRC. Symbolically, it appeared to mark the point at which the Labor government made the decisive shift away from the tradition of centralised wage fixation towards a much more flexible and decentralised system. Indeed, as Mr Keating emphasised the priority of workplace agreements, it was difficult to see what separated his version of enterprise bargaining from the Opposition's. For the unions, the speech left a number of issues to be resolved. Did Mr Keating really intend that enterprise agreements should replace awards for many workers? How many workers would be covered by the safety net, and would this still set a floor to the entire wage structure? And, of most importance, if the government was committed to establishing full enterprise bargaining, what would happen to the 70 per cent of workers in the private sector who did not belong to unions? Who would represent them? It seemed very likely that the consequence of shifting to a system of local-level agreements would bring an end to the monopoly right of trade unions to represent all workers in negotiations leading to registered agreements on wages and conditions. Whether the union movement would accept this—or accept even that sub-branches of national unions could bargain

as autonomous units with their immediate employers—remained
to be seen.

Education and training

Until very recently Australia was a relatively under-educated
society. Lack of education reinforced complacency and hindered
the process of cultural adaptation: too many Australians remained
both ignorant of, and indifferent towards, the need for reform.
Lack of suitable skills has hindered the pursuit of productivity.
This has now begun to change, but the benefits cannot be realised
overnight.

The 1981 Census showed that just on half the adult population had left school between the ages of 13 and 15. In 1981,
71 per cent of adults had no formal post-school qualifications:
10 per cent had some kind of tertiary qualification; another 19
per cent had a trade certificate of some kind.[47] (By 1991, the
percentage with no formal post-school qualifications had fallen
to 59 per cent.) Australia began the 1980s with approximately
1 in 3 students proceeding to Year 12. By 1992 the national
retention rate was 70 per cent, and in Victoria 86 per cent. The
numbers proceeding to university increased from 348 000 in
1983 to an estimated 530 000 in 1992.[48] Following the abolition
of the binary division between universities and the college system,
the number of universities increased from 20 in 1988 to 36 by
mid-1992. The government saw these changes producing a clever
rather than a lucky country. Mr Dawkins argued that higher
education especially, once organised in a unified national system,
should make more of a contribution to Australia's economic
problems by increasing the supply of more highly-skilled and
clear-thinking people.[49] The government also tried to encourage
study and research in a number of priority areas (see Chapter
6).

Although the government deserved credit for catalysing the
expansion of higher education, and for linking its further development to the overriding national imperative of structural reform,
it must be said that in the short run the benefits and the costs
of the 'Dawkins reforms' were evenly balanced. With hindsight
perhaps not all of the forced amalgamations were sensible;
reforms supposed to make the universities more enterprising only
appeared to increase central control and regulation of the system
by DEET (the Department of Employment, Education and
Training). And, although the government increased total expenditure on education, funding per student fell by at least 10 per
cent (some said more). Although the government tried hard to

increase funds for research, there was simply too little money to support the research aspirations of all universities. OECD figures showed that Australian government spending on education in 1989 was 4.72 per cent of GDP, which placed Australia seventeenth out of 24 countries.[50] The OECD average was just over 5 per cent. The government, or perhaps DEET, could be accused of failing to appreciate quite how far education, especially higher education, is labour intensive. Tutorials often ranging in size from 18 to 30 made a mockery of small group discussion as a primary mode of learning. One wondered how many of the graduates emerging from the much larger institutions were really going to make a substantial contribution to creating the clever country.

There were also doubts as to how many generalist degrees the economy could absorb, especially with the current squeeze on middle management positions. It was recognised that the universities were producing too few engineers, scientists and mathematicians. Neither were they producing sufficient skilled personnel to meet the requirements of industry. The federal government first tried to make business itself responsible for training by requiring all firms with annual payrolls over $212 000 to contribute a minimum of 1 per cent of their payroll to training expenditure. By 1990, however, a better answer to the problem was seen to lie in modernising education's Cinderella, TAFE, or Technical and Further Education. The TAFE system, established in 1974, comprised some 220 colleges, mainly old technical schools and adult education colleges. Well over one million Australians were enrolled in courses each year, although at least a third of these were hobby courses. The problem with TAFE was it was stereotyped by its trade school beginnings and by its focus on craft apprenticeships, which were of declining significance in modern industry (one-third of TAFE students were industry apprentices). Modern industrialists did not value the kind of training TAFE provided. School-leavers too often saw TAFE as a last option. From 1983 the number of 15–24-year-olds with degrees rose by 43 per cent, while the number with trade qualifications fell by 11 per cent.[51] By the late 1980s three factors had combined to bring about a radical reassessment of the potential contribution of TAFE to the economy.

First, manufacturing industry required more people to operate the increasingly high-tech equipment appearing on the shopfloor, especially automated and computer-operated design and processing equipment. Jobs demanded a different combination of theoretical instruction, technical training and skill—a higher all-round level of industrial and workplace competency—than before. If such people were not coming from the universities, then TAFE would have to provide a more sophisticated brand of technological instruction, along with some business training. Second, in the wake of award restructuring and multi-skilling, the ACTU also realised that formal industrial training was essential to create a more flexible workforce. Employees had to be given better opportunities to upgrade their skills and qualifications. This should also occur on a continuous basis, given the scale and rapidity of technological change. Both sides of industry were agreed, therefore, that 'doctors and lawyers were not going to save the nation but the expansion of value-added jobs in industry might'.[52]

The third and increasingly ominous factor was the changing nature of the youth labour market. The number of jobs suitable for young unskilled workers had been falling continuously, from around 600 000 in 1966 to perhaps 240 000 in 1992. In the mid-1960s nearly six in every ten 15–19-year-olds had a full-time job. In 1992 the figure was two in ten. This change was mainly due to the effect of technological change upon the structure of the economy. Previously, teenagers found work as clerical workers and typists, book-keepers and cashiers, telephone operators and postal workers. Many of these jobs were now handled by computers or advanced communications technology. In many other occupations, rising qualification levels, usually related to technological change, meant these jobs were no longer open to early school leavers. The casualisation of the workforce also seems to have proceeded faster in Australia, perhaps an employer response to the structure of award rates. The net result is that for those who do not stay in school, finding a fulltime job is more difficult. In 1992, 857 000 15–19-year-olds were still in fulltime education. Of the remaining 364 000, 124 000 or roughly a third, were unemployed. The conclusion: teenage years should be seen very much as a period of vocational preparation; teenagers required much higher levels of education, job training, preparation and information than before; and, increasingly, the kind of jobs available in the future technological society would require higher educational and/or skill levels, plus a greater degree of flexibility and maturity in the workforce.[53]

Two federal reports (and at least one state report[54]) argued strongly for restructuring both schools and TAFE to break down divisions between work and learning, and to establish better access routes to vocational education and training for much larger numbers of young Australians. In August 1991 the Finn Review of post-compulsory education[55] recommended that schools become more concerned with issues of employability and vocational education; that TAFE provide the skills and competencies required by a technological society; and that industry play a greater role in integrating training with employment. It noted that 400 000 teenagers did not stay in the education system after Year 10 and that their numbers swelled the unemployed and the homeless. The Review urged the need for firm targets: by 1995 (nearly) all 18-year-olds to have completed either Year 12 or a Level 1 traineeship. By 2001 all to have gained a Level 2 traineeship or be progressing towards a higher level vocational or academic qualification. Altogether, 95 per cent of 19-year-olds to have completed Year 12 or the equivalent, or be in training by 2001. It proposed that governments agree to introduce a post-compulsory Education and Training Guarantee whereby all young people would be guaranteed a place in school or TAFE after Year 10 for two years of full-time education or training, or its equivalent part-time for up to three years. Staying at school until the close of Year 10 should be compulsory throughout Australia. It stressed that all young people develop certain key competencies to help prepare them for employment: language and communication; maths, scientific and technological understanding; cultural understanding, problem solving and interpersonal communications. It suggested ways of developing minimum standards in these areas within a national curriculum. It also recommended improving cross-accreditation between TAFE and universities, and ways to develop training programs. Altogether there were more than 200 specific recommendations. The snag was the cost: an extra $1 billion a year for the next ten years, mainly from governments.

In March 1992 the Carmichael Report on the Australian Vocational Certificate Training System[56] broadly endorsed the call for nearly all 19-year-olds to complete Year 12 or a post-school qualification. Its key recommendation was to merge all existing forms of traineeships and apprenticeships within a new national Vocational Certificate Training System, to 'provide a flexible range of fully articulated, substantially work-based, vocational certificate training pathways'. The Certificate would be gained through a combination of work experience and study. This Report was more critical of the conventional academic content of many Year 11 and 12 subjects, calling for the development of more vocational options in Years 11 and 12, and for the creation nationwide of 'public and private Senior Colleges' to promote the study of practical work-related subjects. It also called for more systematic integration between schools, TAFE and employers so that young people could get a better sense of career paths and how best to pursue them. In particular, there should be greater opportunities for students completing Year 12 to undertake on-the-job training. Ideally all school leavers should have access to a structured training system when they started work. It recommended that the commonwealth provide a new training allowance to top-up the incomes of trainees under 20 who were doing part-time study plus part-time work programs to match the minimum 18-year-old rate of the Job Search Allowance. The new Certificate was intended especially for trainees in semi-skilled, trade and technical occupations. The Report envisaged replacing the standard time-based four-year apprenticeship with a vocational traineeship which could be completed in 27 months, in which a person would be required to demonstrate competency in a number of designated areas. Youth wage rates could then be based on skills-testing rather than age.

The core idea behind both reports was to provide a more flexible system of training to develop the skills (both technical and personal) required by the rapidly changing nature of work and the workplace;[57] and by so doing, to eliminate the current waste of Australia's human resources and improve levels of skill and competitiveness in industry. The commonwealth, already concerned at the variation in course standards and criteria for course accreditation between the states, was receptive to these ideas. The commonwealth currently provided about 15 per cent of the $2.4 billion cost of TAFE. In October 1991 it offered to take over TAFE and fund it itself. There followed the usual depressing saga of commonwealth–state wrangling over the implications of the offer. Mr Keating re-stated it in *One Nation* in February 1992 and later threatened to set up a parallel system to TAFE if the states could not agree. Eventually, in July 1992, following a creative suggestion from Mrs Kirner, Mr Keating announced the formation of the Australian National Training Authority, to run both TAFE and the training and labour market schemes administered by the commonwealth. The new body would enforce national training standards from the start of 1994. It would be funded through existing state funding for TAFE plus $720 million from Canberra spread over three years.

The Authority offered a way through the impasse over TAFE, although making it work looked to be an administrator's nightmare. By July, however, the unemployment crisis made further action on training imperative. Following a Job Summit on 22 July, Mr Keating announced four training initiatives as part of his response to teenage unemployment:

- The 35 000 teenagers who had been out of work for more than one year would be offered a 6 month vocational training course at TAFE or a private institution, and would be paid a formal training allowance while studying. On completion they would receive a Job Start card to show potential employ-

ers they were eligible for a wage subsidy of between $70 and
$230 per week, depending on their circumstances and length
of unemployment.

- The government allocated $32 million for a new Career Start
  Traineeship Program, aimed at young people who did not
  complete 12 years of schooling. This program would pay early
  leavers at least $125 a week for a combination of work and
  training.
- The government would spend $55 million over two years to
  trial the introduction of the Carmichael Australian Vocational
  Certificate, through employer subsidies and topping-up the
  wages of trainees placed in dozens of large companies.
- It increased the subsidies payable to employers who hired
  (after 30 June 1992) trainees under the Australian Traineeship
  System to $3000.[58]

There were now four training schemes in operation: apprenticeships, the Australian Traineeship System, Career Start Traineeships and the Australian Vocational Certificate. The ACTU
had also agreed that the unions would change industrial awards
to allow employers to pay training wages to young workers who
studied during work time.[59] There seemed a real prospect that
the fundamental changes urged by the Finn and Carmichael
reports would occur if the new National Training Authority
proved effective. The snag, as with other key structural reforms,
was the timespan and the huge amounts of money required for
their successful implementation—not to mention a greater degree
of inter-governmental cooperation. For Australia to become internationally competitive, these reforms were essential, but their
feasibility depended on the economy both coming good and
holding good in the immediate future. It was all very much a
race against time.

5

The Liberal alternative

In the run up to the election the government claimed, with some justice, that it had placed Australia on a different trajectory of development. In most organisations, public as well as private, there was evidence of reform under way. However, there was a question as to whether the reform process was working quickly enough: did Labor have the policies and the energy to take structural reform through the next critical phase? The Opposition thought not but, while many in the community were beginning to feel that some change of policy was required, the Opposition favoured a stronger dose of free market policies. It promised a more determined assault on 'big government' and welfarism, a greater emphasis on the virtues of individual self-reliance, a firmer commitment to zero tariffs and competition policy, and a 'crash through' rather than a consensual approach to structural reform. The Opposition's support for both a Goods and Services Tax (GST) and a fully deregulated labour market placed many voters who were disenchanted with Labor between a rock and a hard place. The Coalition was undoubtedly correct to emphasise the gravity of the economic situation and to say that the momentum for reform had to be increased. Whether its policies could achieve this was more doubtful.

Fightback!

The radical intent of Opposition policies was clear from *Fightback!*, a 335-page policy document (plus another volume of supplementary papers) launched on 21 November 1991. In this remarkably explicit statement of intentions, delivered well in advance of the election, the Opposition proposed 'to bring about an historic redefinition of the role of government in Australia', and to make Australia a more attractive base for international capital and technology.[1] *Fightback!* rested fairly explicitly on the value system most associated with classical liberalism in its heyday between 1760 and 1860. It thus represented, depending on one's political values, either a positive return to the fundamental tenets of liberalism, or a negative reaction to twentieth century welfare liberalism.[2] Three principles were central: a distrust of government or the state; faith in the individual; and reliance on the market.

A central belief of many liberals in the 1980s, especially on the right of the party, was that public revenues had been increasingly and relentlessly exploited by private and sectional interests for their own benefit. The selfish claims of 'special interests' had overshadowed the public interest. This trend had been encouraged by the pork-barrel style of politics in modern democracies: the electoral power of special interest groups was seen, increasingly, as a growing threat to the efficiency of the production system. It was also a notorious feature of protection all round, reinforcing the populist view of the state as a milch-cow and strengthening the handout mentality. For the Liberals a primary aim of structural reform was to restructure the state itself, to redraw relations between state and society and eradicate servile dependency relationships.

The Liberals believed with increasing conviction that the steady growth of a welfare state, a state which assisted people or groups who could not, apparently, help themselves, which siphoned off the wealth of society from the real producers and subsidised an ever-growing category of dependent interests, was a major obstacle to both economic growth and social (and individual) vitality. Their aim was to reverse this trend, to stop the state carrying out the numerous redistributive functions it had accumulated, to free up and reward the energies and talents of the more productive members of society; also, by radically reducing the size and expenditure of the state (or the public sector) to make it crystal clear to everyone that henceforth self-reliance would be the norm. The main thrust of this strategy was to shrink the state, returning as many functions as possible to the private sector, and apply the discipline of the price mechanism (or market forces) to all aspects of resource allocation. This, it was hoped, would ensure that the nation's resources were utilised more clearly in the public interest.

The kind of state the Liberals envisaged was a framework (or 'nightwatchman') state—one which upheld a framework of clear, general laws which applied equally to all people. Government was there to provide an orderly and predictable environment within which individuals could realise their own interests. Or, the purpose of government was to provide the minimum and necessary conditions for free markets to work efficiently. Once the government had established the right framework, the rest was up to individuals, whose responsibility (or duty) to work, to stand on their own feet, was emphasised. *Fightback!* referred frequently to the importance of incentives, rewards and the need 'to help average Australians help themselves':

> The whole purpose of this great reform package is to give individual Australians the chance to fight back for a better life. This reform package will put Government in its place and put Australians back in control of their own lives . . . The whole thrust of our policy is to strengthen the individual against the state—in particular, to strengthen the forgotten people, the low and middle income earners, against the forces which control and limit their lives.

Liberals emphasised the rationality of markets in preference to the political calculations of governments; and the impersonal efficiency of the market in preference to the deals negotiated between bureaucrats and special interests. Free markets maximised individuals' freedom of choice. The logic inherent in the operation of the price mechanism, or the 'invisible hand' of the market, could reconcile the pursuit of private interest with the public good more efficiently than government regulations. In the 1980s these ideas gained strength as command-style systems collapsed in eastern Europe. However, this emphatic argument for the superior rationality of market decisions derived almost entirely from the thinking and the principles embodied in the neo-classical model of perfect competition: i.e. the case for implementing much more radical free market policies rested almost entirely on a revival of the nineteenth century liberal faith in laissez-faire and the minimal state—at root, there were no new arguments adduced. The Liberals appeared to take no account of the practical experience with markets—or the intellectual reaction to laissez-faire—since about the middle of the nineteenth century. In particular they seemed indifferent to the many criticisms and warnings, made by persons of all political and intellectual persuasions, concerning the adverse—and sometimes disastrous—impact of completely free markets upon the fabric of society. *Fightback!* rested on very narrow intellectual foundations and its supporting rhetoric reflected a limited historical and comparative perspective. This was disturbing given that it was presented as the answer to Australia's problems. The Liberal leadership did not seem to appreciate the utopian quality of their own program, or the degree to which they were proposing a course of action which had been tried and found wanting before.

As with the argument for economic liberalisation, one could accept there were good reasons to correct the inefficiencies of Australian statism and reform the rent-seeking culture by relying more on markets. However, given that Australia's economic problems left no margin for error, *Fightback!* seemed a very high-risk proposal in the circumstances. It was not just that *Fightback!* embodied an ideologically-inspired program to remake Australian society in a different image: there was, after all, a good case to be made for strengthening civil society against the state, for empowering the individual against bureaucracy, and asserting the paramount value of individual freedom, and of markets as a means to realising that value. What was disturbing was that those in charge of *Fightback!* seemed to have a rather limited grasp of both the social ramifications of the ideology they were promoting, and the intense ideological battles they were proposing to refight. Notwithstanding the scale of the document and its good intentions, one sensed a formidable ignorance too about the internal complexities of liberal democratic societies and the actual balance of forces within Australian society. One might agree at several points with *Fightback!*—in the problems it identified and the solutions it proposed—but how far could one support a program whose progenitors seemed so unaware of the passage of social and intellectual history since about 1860—including, especially, the history of liberalism itself? It was really a program for true believers. It was as if one hundred years or more after the close of the religious wars in Europe a new party had emerged in a particular country which proposed to re-order society according to the principle of *cujus regio, ejus religio.*[3] This did not seem the ideal way to mobilise collective support for structural reform.

One must acknowledge that some at least of those who helped draft *Fightback!* were not unaware of these problems. There was an undercurrent of tension between the prevailing rhetoric of 'rugged individualism' and faith in markets, and a recognition that the tenets of economic individualism could be pushed too far: they had to be reconciled with another crucial idea in liberal (and Christian) thought: society should also be understood as, in principle, a moral community made up of consenting adults who, through their in-principle status as morally autonomous beings, enjoyed certain rights in common with one another as citizens. *Fightback!* acknowledged that 'a decent society must be based on a strong sense of fair and ethical dealing and a commitment to the interests of the community beyond the market place'—'Freer markets can achieve a great deal but they cannot achieve everything'. The reform program was 'not based on a blind faith in markets. Markets are simply one of the means available to society to achieve a better life'. The most important relations between people were not necessarily commercial ones. Ideally, full provision for economic freedom and a proper regard for society as a moral community should complement one another. 'Properly functioning markets are a by-product of ethical community.'

The problem was how to reconcile the market view of society as a competitive struggle for private advantage between self-interested individuals, whose social relations were organised primarily by contract rather than fellow-feeling, with a concept of society which stressed the greater importance of moral obligation, recognition of collective responsibility and non-contractual forms of human association. Market or economic liberalism generally took a strongly individualistic approach to society: society was no more than the sum of its individual parts or atoms, whose own individual good or self-interest was paramount. The idea of society as a moral association took a more communitarian approach to social life and organisation: society was a collective enterprise with a legitimate interest in its own viability or wellbeing which was qualitatively different from, and arguably superior to, any one individual's private good. The state was the instrument for defining and pursuing the collective interest which a society had in its own cohesion, development and future.

The previous argument in the Liberal party between the Dries and the Wets was very much over which aspect of liberal thought to emphasise, the individualistic or the communitarian.[4] The victory of the Dries, and the emergence of a committed free marketeer, Dr Hewson, as leader tipped the balance in favour of the former. Although *Fightback!* did contain references to moral community which were reminiscent of the Wets, the tenor of the document as a whole favoured individualism. It did recognise that the good society required both free and open markets and a strong sense of 'ethical community': each helped to support the other. Overall, however, it took the view that 'because markets are based on voluntary cooperation and decentralised decision-making, they also create the only conditions in which a moral community can emerge and be sustained'. The document's dominant appeal, therefore, was to individual self-interest modified, hopefully, by individuals' awareness that there were meant to be moral as well as legal limitations on their pursuit of private advantage.

Fightback! said enough about the social and moral limitations to free markets to suggest there was a more balanced way to pursue the central values Liberals had in mind—greater individual freedom, pride in Australian citizenship, a more productive culture, and a smaller but more effective state. One suspects, too, that many Liberals would have preferred a greater emphasis upon communitarian values, and a greater regard for the normative framework of structural reform. In practice, however, the main policy emphasis fell on markets and competition, economic efficiency, a negative approach to the state, and on creating new opportunities for individuals to acquire wealth. In the public debate there seemed little difference between the central thrust of *Fightback!* and the position of economic rationalists. When Liberals tried to rebut the Labor charge that they were a party of accountants with little or no regard for non-quantifiable social values, their speeches too often seemed like afterthoughts intended to put a more attractive gloss on a fairly hard-nosed package of economic reforms.[5]

The economistic approach to structural reform which emerged from *Fightback!* cast a rather different light on the vision which it claimed to offer, and detracted from it. The Liberals were intent, rightly, on creating a more productive and a more responsible society. But the essence of their strategy was to benefit the community by making individuals (and especially those who gained most from the income tax cuts) better off. Their strategy rested very much on an appeal to individual betterment—or self-interest—not community values or the public good. The Liberals hoped that by creating a society of achievers, self-reliant rugged individuals, Australia would be better off—in time. But this approach always reflected the limitations and, indeed, the narrowness of the neo-classical view of human nature which informed it. The opinion polls regularly showed that a good many in the electorate were unhappy with the combined emphasis on economic individualism and materialism: the kind of vision they wanted had more to do with a clearer emphasis on community values, or the national interest.

The more one looked at *Fightback!*, or the way it was presented, the more one was struck by the ultimate narrowness and deficiencies of its approach to structural reform. Its central thrust was to create a society geared to wealth creation, in which it would be much easier for individuals to acquire and to keep wealth. This thrust had two main prongs: to move further and faster than the government to create a completely open and competitive economy responsive to, and regulated by, the discipline of the market—or market forces. This, it was thought, would maximise the opportunities, for both firms and individuals, for wealth creation. Next, to encourage individuals to work harder by offering them tax incentives, and by making it very plain that individuals who could not take advantage of the increased range of opportunities in the market place would only receive limited or temporary assistance from the state. The latter would act as a kind of comfort station to provide a short breathing space for individuals who were then expected to return, suitably revitalised, to the competitive fray.

This approach was open to many criticisms from the political left, shared by some on the conservative right. For example, it took the emphasis on self-interest and material acquisition too far, reviving the discredited value system of 'possessive individualism'; it showed too little regard for mounting social inequalities; it made too little provision for those worst affected by structural change, notably the long-term unemployed.[6] With regard to structural reform itself the broad strategy envisaged by *Fightback!* appeared to have two serious deficiencies. First, it paid little direct attention to the relationship between economic reform and cultural change. The Liberals hoped that the combination of the carrot (tax incentives) and the stick (coercion by market forces) would produce a more disciplined and more highly motivated workforce. But the liberal timetable left little or no room to engage in consultative negotiations with disaffected groups. If people did not respond as 'rationally' as neo-classical theory predicted they should, there was little sense of alternative processes or mechanisms to maintain the momentum of structural reform, which was crucial.

Second, *Fightback!* left the success of structural reform almost wholly to the rationality of market forces, in effect placing its faith in the profit motive. It eschewed any steering role for the state. It also made little attempt to set out a systematic and coordinated timetable for reform, apart from its commitment to zero tariffs by 2000. Judging both from the behaviour of many 'entrepreneurs' in the 1980s, and how other market societies were currently reacting to the impact of globalisation, the Liberals' near-total reliance on the market and market forces was either very optimistic or naive. If the market did not work, what else was left? Overall, one gained the strong sense that in Liberal hands the turn to the market was in danger of becoming a panacea, a single too-simple solution for a range of complex problems.

Public attention focused on the initial proposals for tax reform. The Liberals proposed cutting revenue from personal income tax by 30 per cent (or by $13 billion) over two years; the tax threshold would be raised and marginal tax rates would be reduced substantially so that, by 1 January 1996, 95 per cent of taxpayers would pay a marginal rate of 30 cents in the dollar or less. The highest rate of tax would fall to 42 per cent on incomes over $75 000. A further range of taxes would be abolished, including the wholesale sales tax, payroll tax, petroleum duties, the coal export duty, the training guarantee levy and, by 2000, all customs duties. Replacing them would be a tax of 15 per cent to be levied at first on the sale of all goods and services, with twelve exempt areas, for example, health and health goods, education, churches, local government rates, rent and mortgage payments, exports and the sale of businesses as going concerns. Low income groups would be compensated for the inflationary effect of this tax (estimated at 4.4 per cent): most pensions would be increased by 8 per cent and family allowances increased substantially. *Fightback!* also promised a massive reduction in, and redirection of, federal government spending over the Opposition's first three years in office. This was calculated to reduce government spending by a net $4 billion. Overall spending on education, social security and family allowances would in fact increase while health would decrease. Medibank Private would be sold and higher income earners pressured to take out private health insurance.

The Opposition indicated that it would accelerate the program of micro-economic reform, taking special account of the recommendations of the Industry Commission. It endorsed the government's proposals for increased spending on infrastructure, TAFE and training. It presented a much wider program for privatisation: it too would sell off Qantas and Australian Airlines completely, and the restructured Telecom, all of the Commonwealth Bank, the Federal Airports Corporation, the Commonwealth Serum Laboratories, the Pipeline Authority, the Snowy Mountains Engineering Corporation, and the remaining shares in both the Australian Industry Development Corporation and the Australian National Line. It would privatise the docks, end the system of cabotage and the monopoly of the Waterside Workers Federation on the waterfront. All proceeds from the sale of public sector assets (an estimated $13 billion) would go to reducing government debt. *Fightback!* also contained proposals for a new national savings strategy,[7] for reinforcing competition policy and boosting growth. The Coalition hoped to halve the unemployment rate and create two million new jobs by 2000.

One could sympathise with aspects of the tax reforms. The income tax system certainly needed a radical overhaul. It was ludicrous that the top marginal tax rate of 46 cents in the dollar cut in at $36 001 p.a. when the average wage was rapidly approaching $30 000 p.a. There was a very strong case for abolishing the payroll tax (a tax on employment), wholesale and petrol taxes: all would be of great benefit to business.[8] One could even agree that there was a case for trying to broaden Australia's small revenue base by introducing a consumption tax, of a kind which already existed in 21 out of 24 OECD countries. Such a tax might or might not tap the black economy, but it might raise a considerable amount of money from tourists to Australia. And in a society of rampant consumers, it made sense to try and leave more money in people's pockets, increase the incentive to save, and tax the individual's choice to spend. In the final analysis, however, none of these points outweighed the fact that the GST meant a tax of 15 per cent on food and clothing. Perhaps if the Liberals had exempted these two from the tax from the outset, the ensuing debate would have followed different lines. As it was, the GST was firmly identified in the public's mind with a substantial rise in the CPI. Dr Hewson's revisions to *Fightback!* in December 1992 (see further below) were not sufficient to deflect or neutralise a relentless Labor assault targeted on one key point: a vote for the Coalition meant a price rise of 15 per cent on many staple items in the household budget.

There were three areas in which the Liberals, once again, could be accused of carrying ideology too far. First, one motive behind their tax reforms was the belief that Australians were over-taxed. Comparative data indicated this was not true. Australian tax revenue as a percentage of GDP was just over 30 per cent, placing it twenty-second in a list of 24 OECD countries. The percentage was lower only in the US, marginally, and in Turkey.[9] The rhetoric of reducing taxes 'to get big government off the people's backs' was misleading. The Liberals argued that substantial cuts in direct taxes would motivate people to work harder, but this reform was only likely to benefit those who had some direct control over the relationship between hours worked and income or fees, such as high-status professionals, small business and the self-employed. The Liberals did not appear unduly worried that, in reducing the revenue from direct taxes and relying more on a substantial GST, they were moving from a broadly progressive to a more regressive form of taxation. One could argue for a GST to help provide additional revenue for necessary public goods such as social infrastructure or to help fund the social wage. For the Liberals, however, the primary justification for the GST was private benefit (plus, perhaps, efficiency in raising revenue). They intended it to fund personal tax reductions which benefited higher income earners a good deal more than lower. Indeed, the GST was really being used to subsidise direct tax reductions which, combined with a projected decrease in spending on the social wage, represented an overall reallocation of resources away from poorer people towards those better off.[10]

Second, the Liberals proposed even larger cuts to federal spending. Labor had already cut commonwealth outlays from 30 to 23.5 per cent of GDP between 1985 and 1991. Despite Liberal attacks upon waste and fraud in the welfare sector, once again the comparative data showed that Australian spending on welfare and social security placed it in the bottom quarter of all OECD countries. The Labor government had also tightened up what was in any case a fairly lean welfare system by targeting services very directly at those in need.[11] In the circumstances the Liberal animus towards 'big government' seemed excessive. The Coalition proposed *gross* cutbacks of around $10 billion. Even allowing for new spending in central policy areas such as Social Security, Family Assistance, and Education, it was clear that many existing commonwealth programs and agencies would be eliminated altogether rather than just pruned back. Half of the $4 billion of *net* savings would also come from reducing funding to the states—although the states would also take over several responsibilities from the commonwealth, such as Aboriginal Affairs. Commonwealth grants to the states to build public housing, for urban public transport and the Better Cities program would be abolished altogether. Funding for a range of miscellaneous welfare, community and cultural bodies, notably the ABC, would be radically reduced.

Given that Australia had a public sector that was smaller than the OECD average, a much smaller welfare sector and a relatively efficient public service and, given that by 1992 it no longer appeared that there was any clear-cut connection between a country's economic performance and the size of its government, one had to wonder quite why the Liberals were proposing such sweeping cuts. There appeared to be no clear economic justification for them at all, only an increasingly dogmatic desire to expand the scope of the market whatever the social costs. It was at this point that conservatives joined the political left in arguing that the fascination with economic rationality, and the attack on all kinds of public institutions, had gone too far. Market solutions such as privatisation and contracting out were being used too indiscriminately. For example, in October 1991 Senator Alston, shadow minister for social security, announced that 10 per cent of the $850 million (federal) welfare administration budget would be privatised when the Liberals won office. He foreshadowed abolishing the posts of all 485 of the Department of Social Security's social workers, saving $13.9 million in wages. The Department's central computer facilities, public advisory services, publishing, valuation and research sectors would all be privatised. Its advertising budget of $30 million a year would be scrapped.[12]

Third, *Fightback!* (until December 1992) foreshadowed a more hard-nosed approach to paying unemployment benefits. It stressed that 'only people who are serious about seeking work have a right to a benefit'. So, during their initial three months on the dole (i.e. in receipt of the Job Search Allowance, JSA), unemployed persons would be asked to provide the names of at least two prospective employers approached in the previous two weeks. Between three and nine months, the unemployed would again have to demonstrate, by evidence from employers, that they were actively seeking work. A tighter work test would apply after six months while automatic entitlement to the JSA or dole ceased after nine months. Thereupon, a Special Benefit would be paid only to 'persons found to be in hardship situations who have been actively looking for work'. *Fightback!* did propose to introduce AUSTRAIN, a special program to allow the unemployed to be employed at training wages, the level of which would reflect the length of their unemployment. The Liberals endorsed the whole idea of retraining the unemployed, and of extending facilities for vocational education. In July 1992, to match Labor's new policies, the Liberals promised to increase spending in this area from the $450 million allocated by *Fightback!* to $945 million. Half of the cost would go on the scheme for training vouchers. The Liberals hoped that savings in unemployment benefits would pay for this funding.

The point of controversy was that the Liberals appeared to see the current, necessary emphasis on education and retraining more as a matter of individuals' responsibility to make something of themselves than as the community's responsibility to deal with the changing nature of the labour market and the effects of structural employment upon the young. To Dr Hewson it seemed to be up to the young to make the sacrifices required for the sake of their own future employment. He suggested in July that it was up to the young unemployed to accept a training wage of $3 an hour or become 'couch potatoes'. His critics suggested that the youth unemployed were already in an invidious position, mostly through little fault of their own. It was not very realistic to motivate those already on the margins of society by asking them to lift themselves up by their own bootstraps while paying them a wage many found derisory.

In unemployment and social security, Liberal policy again reflected a nineteenth century regard for the virtues of self-help. It showed too little recognition that unemployment and poverty had become—in particular age groups and social locations—a chronic problem which required a greater level of community support and a greater range of community services than Dr Hewson, for one, seemed to appreciate. When he spoke of the need to 'quite ruthlessly cut our [welfare] expenditure which is going to those not genuinely in need, who are not pulling their weight'[13], both his implicit social model and his grasp of contemporary social realities appeared deficient. His personal viewpoint was that success in life was very much a function of native talent, hard work and a competitive desire to succeed. He genuinely looked forward to creating a society in which many others could (and should) emulate his own example. He emphasised, therefore, equal opportunities, incentives, freedom of action and security of contract. In Australian society, however, not everyone had quite the same regard for the work ethic, or the same rather circumscribed view of human nature and 'success'. In particular, the neo-classical regard for the individual's self-interest, and the related view of life as a competitive struggle for rewards and recognition, was more problematic than Dr Hewson, perhaps, acknowledged. Geoffrey Barker put it well:

> Tawney's point . . . is that a complex, modern economy cannot be built solely, or even predominantly on exceptional talent, although such talent is absolutely necessary and deserves its reward and advantage. A modern society also depends. . .on 'cohesion and solidarity'. There is a need not only for individuals to ascend to Ferrari ownership if they want it, but also for a high level of general culture and a sense of common interest in which all accept that they have a real and permanent stake . . .
>
> What John Hewson seems not to understand is that individual happiness and social well-being is not secured solely by ensuring that the best and brightest are free to rise economically. It is also necessary that individuals should be able to lead lives of some dignity and decency whether or not they are able to rise on the strength of their individual talent and industry.
>
> That second sufficiency condition is the ultimate justification for the ameliorative and redistributive policies which Dr Hewson appears to find threatening to the potential Ferrari-owner class. He is wrong. It is precisely what ensures the social stability and freedom in which the best and the brightest can aspire to a Ferrari (or, as in Paul Keating's case, a collection of antique clocks).[14]

In some ways, *Fightback!* was an impressive document which

contained more nuances than public debate allowed. For Liberals like Dr Hewson, however, the language of competitive individualism always overshadowed *Fightback!*'s communitarian undertones. In his hands the Liberals always seemed too close to going over the top in pursuit of a free market utopia. Much of what he and others said was right, however. Australians did need to work harder, save more, become more productive and enterprising, stand more on their own feet, and so on. But these virtues were in danger of over-emphasis.[15] The dichotomies drawn between state and market, individual and society, were too sharp, too polarised. The social and political dimensions of structural reform were in danger of eclipse.

Towards the end of 1992 the electorate had clearly begun to have second thoughts about *Fightback!* By November, all four opinion polls showed Labor leading the Coalition for virtually the first time since the last election. Dr Hewson came under increasing pressure from both the parliamentary and the organisational wings of his party to modify his position. On December 18, after some weeks of leaks and speculation, he announced *Fightback Mark 2*, the central element of which was a pledge not to apply the GST to basic foodstuffs such as meat, bread, milk and tinned food. However, it would still apply to restaurant food, snacks and takeaways. Childcare services were also exempted from the tax. Dr Hewson announced that the Liberals would not now withdraw the dole after nine months from genuine job seekers. Tax cuts for those earning over $40 000 p.a. were postponed for three years, while tax cuts for low and middle-income earners would be implemented earlier, from July 1993. *Mark 2* also promised larger rises in Family Allowances and pensions; a $3 billion Rebuild Australia Fund to provide money for infrastructure projects; a new accelerated depreciation allowance for business, and some assistance for particular industries, such as sugar (where the rate of tariff reduction would be reduced) and tourism.

Dr Hewson described the policy switch as 'fairly minor refinements to the *Fightback* package', and justified it as a necessary response to the severity of the recession. While the press and the government interpreted the switch as 'a breathtaking grab for power', 'a shameless somersault' and 'a wholly cynical exercise', it did spark a Liberal recovery in the polls in the New Year. Nevertheless, it left Dr Hewson and the Liberals vulnerable to two major criticisms. Conceivably these may have contributed to their defeat as the implications became more apparent to more people.

First, having argued previously that *Fightback!* had to be accepted (and implemented) as a coherent whole, Dr Hewson had now shown himself willing to make the kind of piecemeal concessions to political pressures and special interests which he had declared he would never make. Of course, he could not have done much else given that, without office, *Fightback!* was of little or no use. However, the change of policy undermined the Opposition's claim that *Fightback!* was a qualitatively superior document which contained a comprehensive solution to Australia's problems. Modifying it in response to electoral pressures dented its status and called in question the credibility of its own internal sums and calculations. *Fightback Mark 2* was just another party manifesto, not a document embodying a special expertise and insight as the original *Fightback!* was claimed to be.

Second, in regard to the GST on food, Dr Hewson had performed the kind of U-turn he had previously resisted at all costs. He was seen to be acting politically having previously scorned to do so. It did not matter that he acted pragmatically, trying to keep the Liberals in the electoral race. In his case, *Mark 2* looked too much like a somersault carried out for obvious electoral ends. Dr Hewson had previously linked his case for office with the claim that he was not just another log-rolling politician. He argued that he could do a better job than Mr Keating because he had a perspective, values and expertise which lifted him, implicitly, above the political process. Now he seemed to be reneging on the very values on which his claim to be a special kind of 'non-political politician' rested. The shift to *Mark 2* compromised his authority and credibility in the eyes of both the press and the electorate. It also marked another loss in the battle for psychological supremacy with Mr Keating.

The labour market again

During 1992 reform of the labour market rivalled tax reform as the central political issue. Here the Liberals saw the course of events trending very much in their favour. John Howard pointed out with some relish that the government had undermined the strongest argument in favour of retaining a centralised wage-fixing system by first rejecting the IRC's decision in April 1991 and then legislating to restrict the powers of the IRC. This meant it could no longer argue credibly for the IRC as a substantial, impartial umpire, there to uphold the public interest and prevent wage outcomes turning into an undisciplined free-for-all in which the strongest would do best. The government's own legislation left the way open for genuine workplace bargaining to emerge. Mr Howard's confidence was supported by opinion polls which showed rising numbers of people in favour of settling wages by direct employer-employee negotiations, bypassing unions.[16]

Mr Howard had been one of the earliest and strongest champions of workplace bargaining. Although there were many liberals who agreed with the H.R. Nicholls Society that the entire system of arbitration, with its special industrial courts and tribunals and its self-contained (and often baffling) body of law should be swept away, labour market reform had been a major point of dispute between the Dries and the Wets. Mr Howard painstakingly persuaded the party to support gradual labour reforms, leading ultimately to a deregulated labour market. By 1990 the Liberal wages alternative envisaged workers falling into one of three categories:

- those who opted to remain within the wage-fixing system presided over by the IRC
- those, probably in larger companies, who would participate in enterprise bargaining, where agreements would still be monitored by the IRC
- a new system of voluntary agreements which would allow employers and employees to conclude deals outside the centralised system. The numbers in the second and third categories were meant to grow as unions and workers realised the benefits to be won via productivity bargaining. The Liberals also favoured the creation of smaller workplace or enterprise unions: in March 1990 the Liberals announced they would allow 5 per cent of workers at any workplace to apply to the IRC to create a new union or branch. This was opposed to the ACTU strategy of creating giant industry-wide unions. The Liberals intended their system to be backed by tougher enforcement measures to deal with those who failed to comply with IRC decisions or who breached the no-strike provisions of voluntary agreements. They also proposed to legislate to outlaw the 'closed shop' and preferential employment for union members; and to establish compulsory secret ballots among union members to approve strike action.

During 1991–92, as it appeared that enterprise bargaining would emerge more rapidly, the Liberals tried to distinguish their model from Labor's. They emphasised that Labor's form of enterprise bargaining was a corporatist model which suited larger employers with big and heavily-unionised workforces. (Companies like BHP, Ford and Du Pont were, in fact, nervous that the Opposition's policy would create too many bargaining units within large, multi-site companies.) The Liberals wanted direct workplace bargaining between single employers and their own employees. To achieve this, they envisaged ending the monopoly right of trade unions to represent employees in wage negotiations, and encouraging voluntary unionism. They foresaw the emergence of many separate agreements outside the framework of industry awards. These, they thought, would reflect genuine productivity deals whereas the kind of bargains the ACTU wanted, and of which the IRC was properly sceptical, were really 'productivity top-ups', a means of extracting more wages from employers. Again, larger employers did not entirely agree: Mr Howard's ideas seemed more in keeping with the situation of small business than the complexities of big business, which preferred a more unified approach to enterprise bargaining.

From the start of 1992 Dr Hewson, using fairly muscular language, signalled a more hard-line approach to unions and labour market reform, one that was less gradualist and favoured instead 'a big bang approach to policy'.[17] He reiterated the Liberals' belief that national wage cases should be abolished and henceforth all wage increases be based on productivity gains. Penalty rates and the holiday leave loading should also go. Under the Liberals, unions would be held legally responsible under the common law to pay damages to employers for losses caused by strikes. Secondary picketing would be prohibited.[18] He also foreshadowed the complete disappearance of centralised wage fixing, i.e. the kind of choices envisaged in Mr Howard's earlier policy would go. At this point Mr Howard disagreed.[19] In May 1992, however, the Liberals did make a significant change in policy. Previously, those who wished were allowed to opt out of the centralised system. Now Mr Howard proposed to reverse the onus of choice by enforcing the expiry date on federal awards: when existing awards and agreements expired, employers and workers would be considered out of the centralised award system unless they chose, by mutual agreement, to opt in. The Opposition also foreshadowed legislation to prevent any automatic fall-back to state awards when federal awards expired.[20] Although Mr Howard envisaged the survival of the IRC and some form of centralised wage fixation, Liberal policy now favoured moving as rapidly as possible to a system of localised workplace bargaining. Mr Howard accepted that 'a de facto abolition of compulsory arbitration is what we are proposing'.[21] Although he personally acknowledged the need for some guarantee of minimum wages, if only 'because it's part of the Australian ethos', Liberal policy now envisaged the progressive dismantling of the award system, with all existing entitlements (or privileges) absorbed into a total wage package to be determined by direct negotiation at the workplace.

In October 1992 Mr Howard announced the Opposition's

overall policies for labour market reform. He confirmed that once federal awards expired on their next anniversaries, employers and employees faced three options:

- They could agree to return to the award system and work within the terms of the existing award. Pay rises would still need to be approved by the IRC but there would be no more national wage cases. Also, unions would lose their monopoly right to represent employees.
- They could strike a new workplace deal redefining the terms and conditions of employment. However, there would still be minimum national conditions on holiday leave and adult workers could not be paid less than the minimum specified under the old award. Youth workers aged 15–17 would be paid at $3 per hour; those 18–20 at $3.50. Individuals as well as groups of workers could strike their own deals with employers.
- If employers and employees disagreed, then previous award conditions would apply, but any change or pay rise would require a new deal. Employers might also hire new staff under a new agreement. Under the second and third options all previous entitlements except holiday leave could be renegotiated. Employees who felt they had been treated unfairly could appeal to a new 'Office of the Employee Advocate'. The Coalition foreshadowed legislation to restrict strikes and prevent secondary picketing, but also specified that an individual who breached an agreement could be fined a maximum of $5000 rather than an unlimited sum as at present.

The major intent behind the reform was to bring about an end to the award system which still covered altogether nearly 80 per cent of Australia's workers, and to break the unions' monopoly over wage negotiations. It also signalled the end of the centralised wage-fixing system. Most, but not all, employers' groups endorsed the proposals. The unions, led by the ACTU, saw the proposals as a coming assault on the powers and the legitimacy of trade unions in Australian society. They also feared for the future of workplace reform, and the gains which were emerging through award restructuring. The latter was aimed especially at creating a more highly skilled, flexible and responsible workforce: the rationale behind it was to create an economy based on both high productivity and high wages, where the competitive advantage of firms would depend increasingly on the all-round quality and performance of their workforce. There was a risk that the Liberals' industrial relations system would send the wrong signals to employers, encouraging them to compete by forcing down wages rather than by lifting productivity and quality. The further risk was that this would encourage the survival of low-wage and relatively low-skilled occupations when Australia really needed to encourage the development of knowl-edge-intensive, high value-added industries, in which higher wages were possible because a firm's competitive advantage rested much more on the quality and reputation of its products. Would the Liberals' system maintain the emphasis on improving struc-tural efficiency? Would it maintain the momentum towards developing more sophisticated ideas of organisation, training and management, or would it encourage employers to focus too narrowly on containing labour costs?[22]

The unions had a point. Management also had failed to pursue productivity in the past, and the Liberals seemed much happier espousing the benefits of a fully deregulated labour market than talking about *how* precisely Australian firms would secure a competitive advantage in the global economy. Beyond invoking 'the market' and 'competition', there was a certain lack of detail. This fostered the impression that some liberals, includ-ing Dr Hewson, viewed the unions as scapegoats for the country's problems, or as 'structural rigidities' to be removed, rather than as necessary partners whose cooperation, for workplace reform to succeed, was essential.

Questioning consensus

By mid-1992 the political issue was as much one of how to pursue structural reform than a direct choice between *Fightback!* and *One Nation*, although the issue of how was bound up with the broader question of what kind of society one wished to see emerge. That issue came down very much to a choice between the government's consensual approach to reform and Dr Hewson's 'big bang' approach, which conceivably carried with it the prospect of more confrontation.

The government's approach could be described as the prag-matic pursuit of radical change. Labor was well aware of the need to mobilise consent for structural reform, of having to coax the electorate and the workforce into abandoning bad habits. In the 1980s Mr Hawke made a virtue out of consensus politics, linking reconstruction with the politics of reconciliation, and tailoring change to suit electoral realities. Although reform went more slowly than one might have liked, it did progress with a minimum of serious conflict. The government also tried, with some success before the recession, to compensate those worst affected by structural change through modest increases in the social wage.

The Opposition under Dr Hewson made it very clear that Australia could not afford to proceed at the pace set by the most reluctant reformer. Dr Hewson especially rejected Labor's emphasis upon consultation and negotiation: to him that amounted to 'one step forward, two steps back'. He favoured a more dramatic approach which might include, for example, enacting essential services legislation to counter the threat of industrial action in key industries, or using troops if necessary to by-pass resistance on the waterfront.[23] Labor had mortgaged its capacity to act by its over-willingness to conciliate (i.e. give in to) special interest groups, notably the ACTU, the welfare lobby and environmental groups. Dr Hewson believed in stronger government on the Thatcher model: once the government had declared its will in legislation, that was it: dissent or opposition became obstruction. The issue was, could such an approach really work? Or, given the controversial nature of the reforms envisaged, would it only serve as a red rag to those truculent old bulls in the Labor Movement who were only too ready to trot out the admittedly old-fashioned rhetoric of the class war? But the Movement and labour values were still a reality, and what was self-evident to Dr Hewson was much less so to many community groups who believed in their values as intensely as he held to his.

The reform process was poised at a delicate stage; it did need to proceed faster, but which was the better route: to carry on negotiating, coaxing, explaining; or to 'press on regardless' in urgent pursuit of a more thorough-going market society? Would the latter undermine the still flimsy degree of trust and cooperation just beginning to emerge? While it was true that the economic situation brooked no further delays, neither could Australia afford delays caused by confrontation. The crucial point, again, was that the success of structural reform depended on achieving real and durable change at the cultural level, by changing attitudes. Was the Opposition fully attuned to the complexities of workplace or micro-economic reform? Was it inherently attracted to a rather old-fashioned view of the rights of management which was already giving way, in a number of larger firms, to more decentralised and cooperative styles of work? The style of the Kennet government in Victoria showed the potential for key structural reforms to be set back by poor strategies for implementing them.

Labor had taken a distinctly political and corporatist approach to structural reform, which drew criticism. The danger with Dr Hewson was the reverse: an apparent lack of political sensitivity, or a strong sense that the truth as he saw it must prevail. Dr

Hewson's lack of flexibility, plus the hint of tunnel-vision, was frequently noted in the press.[24] It did seem that reform for him would not be a matter of reaching pragmatic accommodations where the optimum was impossible. Dr Hewson epitomised the classical liberal faith in the rational solution, where reason and economic rationality possessed a self-evident meaning and authority which only a fool would dispute. Negotiation (and structural reform) seemed to him to be more a matter of convincing the unenlightened of the essential correctness of his own views. For example:

> I believe this government has been particularly characterised by the fact that special interests have had special privileges and gained special access. I've set out, as I said all along, to run a government on the basis of no deals and no special interests. What I'm saying to all of these groups is put your case, I'll hear it. You've got to win on the force of your argument. I feel very strongly about that. We've also said that we will review the amount of money that goes into these groups from Government. Some of them have become more or less fronts for the Labor Party.[25]

Dr Hewson had the welfare and environmental lobbies especially in mind,[26] although from time to time he was highly critical of business leaders for failing to stand on their own feet and for relying on governments for assistance. He was notably impatient with those business groups who suggested that some form of strategic trade policy would suit Australia better than a policy of laissez-faire and zero tariffs. He dismissed warnings from nearly all car industry leaders that their industry could not survive under zero tariffs. The Liberals still found it hard to understand why manufacturers were often cautious in their support for them. Early in 1992 Dr Hewson and other Liberals were critical (to put it mildly) of business groups, mainly in Victoria, for failing to endorse Opposition policies on industry and industrial relations. Responses from employers, while diplomatic, implied they found the Liberals' attitude politically naive, and their policies of uncertain benefit economically.[27] Dr Hewson reiterated his position that there would be no fine-tuning to *Fightback!*. While he would 'listen to what people had to say', whether business or welfare, there would be no change to the Opposition's policies. To Dr Hewson, structural reform was 'a task that had to be done', a personal mission which he seemed to conceive in messianic rather than political terms, and certainly one brooking little opposition from any persons classified as 'special interest'. His impatience with the delays imposed by groups seeking to maximise benefits for themselves was no doubt understandable, but the latent question was how far Dr Hewson's faith in the 'obvious' rationality of free market solutions obscured the importance of bargaining and compromise in a pluralist democracy. In reality, not all people agreed with his view of reform: were their views, in his eyes, legitimate? How much room did Dr Hewson's neo-classical beliefs (or ideology) leave for politics as a necessary and creative activity for reconciling opposing points of view in an open but heterogeneous society?

6

The industry policy debate

B_y 1991–92, the debate over industry policy was at the core of the whole debate over the market and economic rationalism. Here the government was caught in an awkward three-cornered contest. It was under pressure from its principal economic advisers in Treasury and the Industry Commission (IC), as well as the Liberals, to eliminate tariffs and create a thoroughly competitive market economy. The business sector, meanwhile, thought the emphasis on low or zero tariffs misguided without attendant strategies to reduce business costs. Business leaders wanted the government to provide 'a wholly coordinated national vision' on Australia's future directions.[1] Manufacturers from non-resource processing industries wanted, more specifically, an industry policy to address the particular weaknesses of Australian manufacturing, identify growth strategies for particular sectors, and assist firms to get established in highly competitive world markets.[2] Their arguments were fiercely resisted by Treasury, the mining industry and the free market lobby generally. Meanwhile too, there were growing calls in the community to arrest the rate of tariff reform and safeguard employment. During 1992 under Mr Keating the government began to retreat from 'narrow' economic rationalism and to search for a policy-mix which might provide a more viable basis on which to pursue structural reform and sustainable growth.[3] However, if there was a clear conceptually-based alternative to the full free market route, it had yet to be articulated in a form which the government could embrace.

The neo-classical perspective

In the past, 'industry policy' meant protection and assistance. The very term, therefore, had negative connotations for free market reformers, who were on their guard against policies which could return protectionism through the back door. The IC, in particular, was determined that firms should stand on their own feet: 'if a firm is a winner it doesn't need assistance'.[4] Governments could not make firms efficient: they had to become so by themselves and the acid test was survival in the market place. The IC's basic advice to the government was that 'the economy has to cut its losses': resources should not go into 'sectors that are not competitive on a world basis'.[5] Much manufacturing was 'extremely artificial' because of past protection: it was an open question as to how much would survive. The government must be prepared to bear the short-term electoral pain for the greater long-term good. The guiding principles of the policy recommended by Treasury and the IC were as follows:[6]

- To create a fully competitive economic environment by removing all impediments to the free play of market forces, relying on the price mechanism as the most efficient method of allocating resources between sectors.
- To keep all forms of government intervention or assistance to a minimum. Intervention was seen as expensive—it imposed costs elsewhere in the economy—relatively inefficient, and undesirable in principle because it prevented the price mechanism from working as it should. The government should intervene only to address very specific problems of market failure or structural adjustment.
- The government should focus on achieving 'correct' macroeconomic policy settings, especially low inflation, and ensure that markets for capital and labour worked as efficiently as possible. In the eyes of Treasury, once the latter were organised on a properly competitive basis, there would be no need for a distinct industry policy. (Indeed, there might be no need for a separate Department of Industry at all.[7]) Government's job was, through competition policy and micro-

economic reforms, to create an environment in which productive resources would gravitate naturally to those industries which were resourceful, productive—and competitive.

- This approach reflected a strong faith in free trade and free markets as the best way to increase a society's overall wealth and welfare. The cornerstone of this faith was the classical theory of comparative advantage. This advised nations to exploit whatever cost advantages they might have or acquire over competitor nations, due to their possessing favourable or abundant supplies of one or more of the key factors of production: land or natural resources, supplies of capital or relatively cheap labour. A given nation should specialise in producing those items which, because of favourable 'factor endowments', it could produce more cheaply than others. If all nations aimed to export goods in which they had a natural cost advantage, and imported those where, generally, they did not, all should be better off; i.e. free trade between open markets offers potentially greater benefits to all participating nations than any other developmental strategy.

This doctrine further implied that a nation's production structure should be developed in line with its natural resource and factor endowments. It also assumed that factor endowments were mostly given or 'natural'. Free marketeers who accepted the standard version of this theory therefore supported the development of rural, mining and resource-based industries, and services, ahead of manufacturing. Or, they were inclined to think that manufacturers should not be allowed too much latitude to pre-empt resources which could be used to better effect in developing industries where Australia had a clearer comparative or cost advantage. These points were disputed by manufacturers (see further below).

The government did not come to power with such an explicit commitment to market principles. The original Accord envisaged using moderate interventionist policies, and a degree of planning, to revitalise a then-depressed manufacturing sector. This approach took shape in the five-year plans drawn up in 1984–85 to restructure problem industries like steel, heavy engineering, cars and the TCF. These embodied, initially, a fairly moderate rate of tariff reform with some financial assistance from the government to aid restructuring.[8] The thinking behind this approach was gradually submerged after 1987 when the government became more enthused with the Treasury program for economic liberalisation. By 1990 the dominant trend in industry policy was 'unambiguously towards a greater reliance on market forces as the dominant allocator of resources'.[9] The government increasingly adopted a minimalist, non-interventionist policy towards industry. However, before turning to the rising opposition to this policy and the government's change of emphasis in 1992, one should note that in the 1980s the government did experiment with a variety of policies to assist industry. Most of these were justified as necessary responses to market failures or imperfections. However, these responses showed that on occasion 'imperfections' could have a fairly elastic interpretation, and the Department of Industry could take a wider interpretation than Treasury.[10] The five main examples were as follows:

- Incentives for Research. It was widely recognised that Australia's spending on Research and Development (R and D), especially by the private sector, was well below the OECD average, and R and D was crucial to competitive success in most modern industries (see further below). The government introduced a 150 per cent tax concession for R and D in 1985: firms could deduct from company tax one and a half times the cost of eligible R and D. It also introduced in 1986 a Grants for Industrial Research and Development (GIRD) scheme to provide support for collaborative R and D projects involving industry and publicly funded research bodies. This scheme contained several separate programs.[11] In 1990 the government announced a new program for 50 cooperative research centres to bring together scientists from the universities, CSIRO and industry consortia in a range of national priority, especially high-tech, areas. Thirty-five such centres had been announced by December 1991 with funding shared between government and business.[12]
- Providing venture capital and encouraging investment. The lack of patient equity capital in Australia, coupled with an endemic short-term outlook among Australian entrepreneurs (see also below) was a serious hindrance to getting new high-tech ventures off the ground, because the initial start-up costs were high and returns uncertain. In 1984 the government introduced the Management and Investment Companies (MIC) Programme, under which an immediate tax deduction of 100 per cent was available for investors in MICs which invested in innovative, export-oriented and potentially high growth ventures.[13] The government also experimented with an Investment Promotion Program to encourage foreign-owned firms to invest in Australia, especially in resource processing industries. It also provided some assistance to help small companies commercialise new products.
- The National Industry Extension Service (NIES) was introduced in 1987 to improve the efficiency and international

competitiveness of Australian industry by providing better coordination of federal and state resources and advice to industry. This Service also assisted small firms with strategic planning and management and tried to speed up the rate of diffusion of new technology among smaller firms, and to raise their innovative capacity.

- The civil offsets program. This was an attempt to use the government's purchasing power to induce international firms to cooperate with local industry. It was hoped this would assist the transfer of technology to local firms and provide the latter with opportunities to break into overseas markets by supplying the foreign majors. Overseas suppliers of equipment to the government (or its instrumentalities, such as the airlines) were required to offset the cost of the imported item by commissioning some of its production within Australia. The offset could be up to 30 per cent of the value of the imported content. However, this scheme benefited mainly 'a narrow group of firms in the aerospace, telecommunications and computer industries'.[14] Telecom, for example, induced Philips and L.M. Ericsson to manufacture certain products in Australia for world markets. In 1987 the government introduced a 'partnerships for development' program aimed especially at stimulating the growth of the information industries. This scheme encouraged partnership agreements between any Australian government and a transnational corporation (TNC). The latter agreed, in return for the discharge of its offsets obligations and help with infrastructure, to achieve within seven years both expenditure on R and D in Australia equal to 5 per cent of its local turnover annually, and annual exports of goods and services equal to 50 per cent of the TNC's imports into Australia. By 1990 twenty TNCs had signed partnership agreements, including almost all the major firms in the global information industry. A similar scheme was introduced for the pharmaceutical industry in 1988. This was designed to encourage the local development of internationally competitive products. The government undertook to pay higher prices for products listed on the Pharmaceutical Benefits Scheme to firms meeting agreed levels of exports and R and D spending.

- Export assistance. Recognising that Australian industry lacked an 'export culture', and that individual firms faced significant costs and obstacles in trying to penetrate overseas markets, the government continued and expanded the Export Market Development Grant Scheme, first set up in the 1970s. It also established four more specialised schemes to assist High

Technology Exporters, Innovative Agricultural Marketing, International Business Development, and the Export Facilitation Scheme for motor vehicles. It also conducted a major overhaul of the Australian Trade Commission, AUSTRADE, and expanded both its mission and its budget.[15]

These schemes for the most part cost the government relatively little money. They were targeted at whole industries or sectors and not specific firms, and their general aim was to redress acknowledged deficiencies in the market. Nevertheless, free market purists did not altogether approve of them. The IC, for example, was hostile to the offsets and partnerships program. It criticised any attempt to identify and assist industries with special promise as 'picking winners'.[16] The manufacturers strongly favoured building on from what had become, by the time of *One Nation* (see further below) a *de facto* industry policy. They wanted for example, to expand the partnerships program, to make greater use of the government's procurement powers, greater provision for attracting venture capital, tax incentives for business investment and overall a more systematic attempt by government to promote industry development. They were supported by those within the Labor movement who felt it was time to revive some of the ideas with which Labor had come to power, notably policies for sectoral planning and selective intervention. These calls were resisted by free marketeers as special pleading by special interests. After 1990, public clashes between the IC and manufacturers were common[17], and as the government wrestled with the problem of how to restore economic growth, it faced a real and very bitter split between the purists who favoured leaving outcomes to market forces, and those who feared such a strategy was a recipe for disaster.

The manufacturers' perspective

The manufacturers—still less business generally—did not disagree with the general emphasis on competition and lower tariffs, although responses were mixed.[18] They accepted the reasons for integrating more fully with global markets. Their basic point was that pure free market policies were not sufficient to achieve the outcomes desired. Given the nature of globalisation, they could even be counterproductive. They saw themselves arguing not for protectionism but for a more sophisticated approach to free market theory. They believed that some kind of managed industry policy was essential to bring about the kind of structural changes everyone agreed were desirable: these would not arrive just by themselves. What was required was a national strategy to promote long-term industrial development, and a more coordinated or planned approach to the many separate facets of reform. They also believed that competitive advantage in the global economy had to be built over time, by systematic cooperation between firms and government. Their opposition to the pure neo-classical perspective may be condensed into four core points:

- Manufacturing was of much greater importance to Australia's economic survival than most free market economists acknowledged.
- The weaknesses and disadvantages of Australian manufacturing were so pronounced as to require strategic treatment by government as well as firms.
- The market approach rested on flawed assumptions, both in regard to the behaviour of entrepreneurs in Australia, and the real sources of competitive advantage in the global economy.
- The approach to structural reform and economic management in Canberra was marked by a curious optimism that the market approach would work, if given enough time and if the right people learned enough from previous mistakes. Despite improvements, however, the real economic situation was far more serious than most of the government's advisers acknowledged, and Australia simply did not have sufficient time to persist with the current experiment.

The case for manufacturing[19]

The manufacturers disagreed that in seeking to diversify exports Australia should rely primarily on those industries where it had a comparative advantage, notably rural, mining and related resource-processing industries. While these were obviously important, it was also the case that no first world society could survive as such without a strong and competitive manufacturing sector. The only secure foundation for a post-industrial and service-oriented economy was a modernised industrial base. The goal of policy should be to strengthen this base, which already employed 14 per cent of the workforce and contributed between 17–18 per cent of total production—the largest single sector. The apparent willingness of Treasury and the IC to countenance an extensive reduction in manufacturing (de-industrialisation) was extraordinarily shortsighted. The manufacturers made three supporting points.

First, although exports of primary commodities would remain important for Australia, world trade in such commodities had diminished from 45 per cent in 1963 to 26 per cent in 1989. The terms of trade were moving against commodity-dependent countries. Economies which relied extensively on commodity exports to other more heavily-industrialised economies would be at an increasing disadvantage in the future. Certainly Australia should develop natural resource processing industries based on its raw materials. Instead of exporting woodchips, for example, worth relatively little, Australia might invest in pulp mills to reduce its $1.2 billion bill for imported paper. Or again, if all the raw bauxite and semi-processed alumina produced here were smelted to aluminium metal before export, this could add approximately $10 billion to Australian exports.[20] The benefits available from refining Australia's abundant minerals instead of exporting them in raw form were also substantial.[21] Yet developing pulp mills or smelters was capital and technology intensive, and would not happen without suitable encouragement and facilitation from governments.

Second, the largest component of world trade (about 60 per cent) is tradeable manufactured goods. This is the area in which Australia most needs to develop products for sale in world markets. This includes adding value to raw materials. In 1990–91 about 71 per cent of Australia's wool exports went out as raw (or greasy) tops, and only 2 per cent as yarn or fabric. Processing all wool to produce yarn or fabric would theoretically add $8 billion to exports. To go one stage further: the raw wool required to make a fashion jumper costs two or three dollars. The jumper is usually made overseas. The wholesale price when it returns is around ten times the cost of the raw wool.[22] Similarly with Australia's foodstuffs: processing them for sale in specialised Asian markets is a much more lucrative proposition than simply exporting raw commodities.[23]

However, the most dynamic and highly profitable areas of modern manufacturing are the high-tech elaborately-transformed manufactured goods (ETMs) such as cars or consumer electronics. This is where Australia, despite recent improvements, is still very weak. *The Global Challenge* emphasised that the further Australian 'industry moves along the value chains towards high value-added products' the greater the returns: 'the prize for extending successfully into differentiated products is likely to be far larger than that for upgrading raw materials to higher value-added commodities'.[24] For example, iron ore and coking coal produced basic hot-rolled steel: as one advanced through the value chain which led to cold rolled steel, to coated steel, to coated and painted steels custom-made for particular industries, the economic rewards grew significantly.[25] If the overall aim of restructuring is to create a more diversified and more secure export trade, then Australia had to develop a stronger profile in value-added manufactures. Trade in primary and semi-processed commodities would remain important, but only manufactured exports in general, and ETMs in particular, possessed the kind of potential required to overcome the remaining deficit on the current account (i.e. about $12 billion). While manufacturers accepted that productivity improvements in specific rural industries could yield sizeable export gains, Australia could not afford to rely on the latter as a secure or rising source of income.

Third, the neo-classical approach emphasised the potential of service exports. Manufacturers emphasised that the viability of the most lucrative services—financial and business, and education to some extent—depended on the level of development achieved in the business sector as a whole. It was true that the number of tourists to Australia had doubled since 1983 to over 2.1 million persons a year, who in 1990–91 earned Australia $7.3 billion in foreign exchange. The export of education services (including total spending by overseas students in Australia) had also grown from very little in 1983 to over $1 billion by 1990.[26] Services had increased from 17.2 per cent of total exports in 1983–84 to 20.4 per cent in 1990–91 (but even so they ran at a net deficit of $3.4 billion[27]). The small surplus generated in travel-related services in recent years had been offset by much larger and growing deficits in shipping, financial and business services. Although Australia was looking forward to a tourist bonanza,[28] *The Global Challenge* pointed out that 'tourism is highly price-sensitive and will only grow in Australia as long as the wages of many of the people involved are fairly low'.[29] One should not look to tourism to generate a large number of well-paid jobs in the future. Overall, 'the rate of growth of services trade is (slightly) slower than manufacturing trade' and, a key point, 'services trade in areas with high GDP per person depends on Australia having a strong industrial base'.[30] Australia was unlikely to retain a flourishing service sector in the absence of a strong manufacturing sector, and the business requirements that generated.

Manufacturing matters

Strong support for this last point and for the manufacturers' position in general could be derived from an American study which criticised both the abstract view of economic life held by neo-classical economists and their framework assumptions about the nature of economic development.[31] Modern economics lacked concreteness: it was preoccupied with examining particular industries with the aid of theories which stressed the link between competition and efficiency, but took too little account of the economic facts of life with which those industries had to deal. Economists conceptualised economic intercourse as relatively straightforward market relations between buyers and sellers. These relations for them comprised 'the real world'. Their aim was then to identify rational–logical strategies for improving the 'efficiency' of these relations, according to quite specific economic criteria. Each set of relations was usually considered in isolation, and examined from the quantifiable point of view of how to maximise returns, by increasing output and/or lowering cost. All factors—geographic, political or labour—which conflicted with the smooth and efficient operation of buyer–seller relations in the various product markets were regarded in negative terms as 'structural rigidities'.

In fact, modern industrial economies contain a very large number of real-world concrete linkages between industries—tight, medium and weak. Interdependence, though often concealed, is the true reality. The economy 'is not simply a system of slide-in-slide-out linkages' of the kind modelled in conventional economic analysis. A more accurate picture of the economy would portray it as made up of interdependent chains of linkages—almost an ecological metaphor—each helping to sustain the other by the requirements it generates. In a modern complex economy, viability depends on strengthening and extending the chains, not breaking them apart or reducing their number (which is the practical effect of pure neo-classical policy).

If one analysed the economy in terms of its various linkages, one would get a very different idea of how the whole actually worked, and of the relative importance of the different sectors, especially for employment. For example, to say that agriculture now employed a mere 3 per cent of American workers gave no real clue to its actual importance in the US economy, or the linkages which existed between it and other industries, not readily apparent from economic statistics. By tracing the chains that extended back through the economy from the original point of production, and taking account of secondary processing indus-tries, component suppliers, and the links to transport and distribution networks, the authors suggested that the total number of jobs directly related to farm production lay between 6 and 8 million, rather than 3 million, the conventional figure.[32]

Similarly with manufacturing, which formally accounts for one-fifth of the US workforce, but through linkages might well generate between half and two-thirds of total employment; many workers conventionally counted as service workers could well be classified as manufacturing.

Modern economists like to portray the shift out of manufacturing into service industries as akin to the earlier shift of labour out of agriculture into industry—another 'natural' step in the move towards a post-industrial society. The argument is itself fallacious, but the key point here is that the high value-added service roles—the ones so attractive to those who stress the potential of service exports—are directly related to the expansion of high-tech manufacturing. They would quickly be lost if manufacturing moved offshore. Downstream from the point of production, many service jobs would certainly remain in retailing, distribution and advertising. But the key ones which help sustain the productive enterprise itself are upstream. These include design and engineering, payroll and accounting, finance and insurance, plant repair and maintenance, training and recruitment, testing services and laboratories, trucking and transporting, and many other specialised services—waste disposal, pollution, security, warehousing, etc. These form an elaborate cocoon around the manufacturing enterprise itself. The Report to the President on the Trade Agreements Program noted that '25 per cent of US GNP originates in services used as inputs by goods-producing industries—more than the value added to GNP by the manufacturing sector'.[33] Or, manufacturing output plus services sold to manufacturing firms makes up nearly half America's output. So 'talk of shifting out of [manufacturing] is not something that should be complacently contemplated'.

There are other arguments to be made on behalf of maintaining a strong manufacturing sector—its significance for defence, or the degree to which competitive interaction between different high-tech industries can create new products and even new industries, but the general point is plain: the contribution of manufacturing to all-round economic development, and to employment, is much greater than a conventional measurement of its size implies. This point has a good deal of relevance to Australia.[34] High-tech manufacturing and high-value service industries enjoy a symbiotic relationship. To lose both would be to undermine our overall technological and innovative capacity significantly. The conclusion in the American case is worth quoting since it too is directed at neo-classical economists whose models not only induce a certain bias against manufacturing activities, but who have failed for the most part to come up with adequate strategies to counter the competitive success of manufacturing-based economies in Asia and, to a lesser extent, Europe:

> . . . we should be converting low-productivity, low-wage, low-skill production processes into high-technology, high-skill, high-wage activities—whether they are in manufacturing . . . or counted largely as service . . . [The] one needs the other. The process of development is not one of sectoral succession but . . . one of increased

sectoral interdependence driven by an ever more extended and complex division of labor.[35]

A further note on tariffs

Tariff reductions, if unaccompanied by systematic strategies to reduce business costs, raise productivity or improve the competitive position of Australian firms in world markets, threatened to overwhelm the latter or drive them offshore. The latter was, in any case, an attractive option to any firm whose export program utilised economies of scale. The Australian market was usually too small to provide these, creating pressure to relocate in or closer to a larger market. And once a company urged to export gained a foothold overseas, it might be induced to relocate there through incentives offered by that government. By the early 1990s many firms evidently were moving offshore.[36] Again, this did not appear to bother free marketeers: cheaper production meant lower prices and that was all there was to it. The manufacturers argued, in line with the above, that what was happening not only threatened employment, but represented a steady weakening of the linkages which supported all manufacturing industry and Australia's technological base. They wanted the government to take action, either to attack business costs, or match incentives being offered overseas or modify the rate of tariff reform.

Reducing tariffs should not be seen as a self-evident end in itself but a means to the goal of creating more efficient outward-looking industries. The rate of reduction should be related to the competitive circumstances of particular industries, and it should take account of more factors than just the final price to the consumer. The IC's approach to tariff reform made lower prices the decisive, even the sole, criterion of how to increase economic welfare. It had previously stressed that high tariffs in the past represented a total cost to the Australian consumer of up to $4000 per car (i.e. higher prices plus the concealed cost of subsidies). By 1992 the Opposition claimed *Fightback!* and zero tariffs would reduce the cost of the average car by between $500 and $800. The IC thought that unless car makers could match the prices and production standards of overseas competitors, it made economic sense to run down the domestic industry and expand imports. Under the Button car plan the number of car manufacturers had fallen to four, the total workforce had fallen by one-quarter and productivity (and exports) had risen. Car industry leaders warned that raising Australian productivity standards to a level approaching international best practice would take time. Given also the limitations of Australia's small domestic market, some degree of tariff protection was crucial to preserving the industry's competitive position while it modernised further. Zero tariffs meant zero investment and the probable end of the car industry.[37]

The car industry and its supporters agreed that the industry must pursue higher productivity but argued that the price of the final product was by no means the only criterion of the industry's value to Australia. *The Global Challenge* pointed out, first, that one effect of losing the industry would be to increase Australia's trade deficit in motor vehicles from around $5 billion in 1988–89 to nearer $10 billion. Australia would also lose $1 billion of car exports. Which new industries would make up the deficit? Industry leaders pointed out, second, that the loss of the industry and its suppliers would cost up to 60 000 jobs: where were the replacement industries? Third, the car industry was virtually the only 'original equipment maker' (OEM) Australia possessed. The car industry kept not only the main firms but their many component suppliers in touch with engineering and technological change worldwide, and with advances in organisational management and design. The car industry was, in many respects, 'the industry of industries': it linked together makers of steel, plastics, machine tools, glass, paints and, increasingly, consumer electronics, and served as 'a major force in driving quality improvements throughout the manufacturing sector'.[38] Its loss, given the lack of comparable OEMs, would be a major blow to the linkages in the economy.

Instead of pursuing zero tariffs at all costs, Australia should take account of the all-round strategic significance of particular industries for the economy, including their export potential. Policy makers should ask what would happen if an industry were not there: what would be the consequences for imports and for unemployment benefits? In the case of TCF, there was a strong case for a substantial reduction in the size of the industry: the gap between production costs in Australia and those overseas was for the most part too wide to be bridged. Here there was an argument for releasing capital and labour for other uses. But the car industry was a different proposition because of its location within Australia's industrial structure. If continued tariff reductions could assist the drive to raise productivity, and if Australia finally ended up with just one or two firms, then well and good. However, if zero tariffs meant the end of the industry altogether, Australians might still be better off instead, as a community, by paying slightly higher prices for domestic cars. It should be possible to deal with this issue empirically rather than ideologically.

Australian manufacturing: problems and weaknesses

The neo-classical approach assumed that capable firms would respond positively to the opportunities available in free markets. Others might disappear. The manufacturers thought it was not so simple. Australian firms lacked experience of global competition, their productivity levels were low and many practices had to change. All this required time: managers and workers had to lift their game substantially. Leading countries, meanwhile, were still improving their own standards. The manufacturers thought that what the IC had in store for them was not unlike the medieval practice of immersing suspected witches in water (read 'competition') to determine their guilt or innocence. History records the rate of survival among suspected witches was not high. Many manufacturers did not fancy their chances either, and thought there had to be a better way of establishing their bona fides in the stirring times the IC had conjured up. It was all very well to say that Australian firms should 'integrate with the world economy' but Australia was geographically remote from world markets, including Asian markets: Melbourne and Sydney were no closer to Japan than California. Australia's domestic market was usually too small to provide the scale economies required to sustain powerful manufacturing firms. The size of the continent and the scattered population made excellent communications essential, but Australia's railways and ports still left a lot to be desired. These situational weaknesses have been compounded by the effects of protectionism which have left a number of structural weaknesses at the level of the firm. The more important are as follows.

Low productivity

Average productivity levels in Australian manufacturing are 20–25 per cent below 'international best practice' and up to 10 per cent or more below the best-performing Australian companies.[39] Labour productivity growth in the 1980s was less than half the average in the OECD and has lagged consistently behind the latter over the last twenty years. Although there have been some marked improvements in a number of organisations in the last two or three years, productivity growth in much of Australian manufacturing is occurring more slowly than in other leading industrial countries, and a good deal more slowly than in many newly-industrialising Asian countries.[40] This is disturbing because standards of efficiency in these same countries are already ahead of Australia's. Productivity in many public sector utilities was also thought to be half to three-quarters of the levels routinely achieved overseas, thereby raising the cost of essential business inputs. Because the average manufacturing firm directly controls only one-third, approximately, of its total costs, there is a strong implication that unless organisations in all sectors of the Australian economy raise their productivity substantially by adopting as their benchmark 'international best practice', it is unlikely that many exporters of manufactures will be able to build up or sustain a competitive advantage in world markets.[41] 'Best practice' includes all aspects of on-the-job working and greater attention to product design, quality and reliability. The modern consumer expects more than many Australian companies have been used to providing.

Becoming competitive depends crucially on raising productivity, which is the major goal of workplace reform. But in 'the land of the long weekend' it is attitudes that must change first. When one's economy and economic future is as vulnerable as Australia's, it is less than realistic to 'remain locked into the concept of a normal Monday to Friday working week when the rest of the world accepts that some industries must operate 365 days a year, 24 hours a day to meet the realities of business and the demands of the customer'.[42] It is also uneconomic to enforce rigid distinctions between 'normal' work and work that must be paid at, literally, penalty rates. There are many facets of national life which either are, or will become, unaffordable unless productivity improves dramatically—such as closing down in effect for the month of January. Australia also has a major problem with absenteeism: the 'sickie' is part of the national culture. One major study found that in any week 4.5 per cent of employees were absent without approval, compared with 0.23 per cent on strike. This added up to a loss of about 64 million working days a year, almost 19 times greater than the loss from strikes. The study found the rate of absenteeism rose with the size of the workplace and the problem was greater in the public sector (6.6 per cent) than the private (4.2 per cent).[43] In Victoria, documents obtained from the Public Transport Corporation showed that tram and bus employees took 300 000 hours of sick leave in the financial year 1990–91, the equivalent of 200 staff not working for 12 months.[44] Another document showed that about 1000 Public Transport workers were absent on sick leave at any given time.[45]

Productivity problems have been greater in more highly protected industries and in public utilities. In the car industry the labour turnover rate in 1987 was 35 per cent; the figure for other countries was between 4 and 7 per cent. The high turnover levels added almost $900 to the cost of a locally made car. The turnover rate among process workers in the TCF division of a large Australian company averaged 27 per cent.[46] The workforce in these areas often has severe problems with literacy: quite often, a third or more of those employed can be defined as functionally illiterate in English. Such factors, combined with such things as an adversarial culture of industrial relations, too many unions, lack of training, have undermined all aspects of productivity. The car industry provides a graphic illustration of the problems. One international survey (1989) found that, in the number of defects per 100 vehicles, the best performance achieved by an Australian plant was below the average levels in most other countries, and was about the same as the worst Japanese performer. On automation, overall management and use of human resources, Australia ranked last or near last on virtually all measures.[47] (The story in the white goods industries was only marginally better.) While Australia maintains a 1-shift, 5-day week, a 2-shift, 6-day week is normal throughout the rest of the world.[48]

The World Economic Forum and the International Institute for Management Development publish an annual World Competitiveness Report which synthesises data on 22 developed countries to provide an overall ranking of their relative strength and competitive prospects. Altogether, there are around 300 individual measures grouped into ten categories. Overall Australia ranked tenth in 1989, thirteenth in 1990 and sixteenth in 1991, suggesting that the internationalisation of the economy was not proceeding fast enough: the nation's economic environment remained unattractive to companies competing in global markets. On infrastructure, Australia's ranking had fallen from fourth in 1989 to eleventh. On all other categories Australia fell in the bottom half, usually in the bottom third. Of special concern were the criticisms of both management and the workforce: Australia's managers rated bottom in terms of long-term orientation, international experience and employee relations. Australian companies were near bottom for product innovation and productivity. The attitudes of the workforce, despite relatively good levels of education and health, were the worst in the OECD—lacking in competitive values and motivation, over-fond of alcohol and unwilling to retrain. Apart from Greece, Australia was still the most inward-looking country in the OECD. Either both countries restructured their attitudes, practices and institutions urgently, or they would drift into economic oblivion.[49]

Lack of world class firms

Australia has over 700 000 enterprises, the vast majority of which are small businesses employing twenty or fewer persons.[50] Australia has only fifteen firms listed in the world's top 1000 companies, which account for only 0.9 per cent of the top 1000's sales. Only two of the fifteen are pre-eminently manufacturing companies. BHP Steel is the only case of a 'strategic exporter' (a company for whom exports are a primary focus, as compared with those who export from time to time, or opportunistically) outside the resources sector that is clearly of world class. In 1989–90 its export sales exceeded $1 billion. (Ford Australia recorded sales of $502 million in 1991–92.) Otherwise, in 1989–90 there were only eight other complex factor firms in Australia exporting more than $100 million a year and several of these were part of the networks of foreign multinationals.[51]

Outside the resources sector, very few Australian firms compete in export markets. The Bureau of Industry Economics reported in 1990 that the proportion of firms which regularly export 10 per cent or more of their turnover was probably around 10 per cent. Thirty-seven per cent of Australian firms did not export and 42 per cent had exports of less than 10 per cent of sales. 'Australian companies have only modest international goals and few appear intent on building major international competitive organisations.'[52] There was an evident lack of outward-looking, entrepreneurial ambition among many medium-sized firms, also a legacy of protection. Yet, as the Hughes Report found: 'Many exporters told the Committee how exporting forced them to improve design, lower production costs and improve the timeliness of deliveries. It is, therefore, not surprising that there is a high correlation between the growth of trade, productivity and income.'[53]

Australia does not possess many leading edge industries noted for their technological lead or qualities. There are few international brand names linked to Australian firms. Australia does not have significant clusters of firms in related industries which can stimulate or cross-fertilise one another in the way consumer electronics, cars and machine tools sparked one another's development in Japan. There are not many examples of strong rivalry between domestic firms competing in the same industry. Such factors have all been adduced as contributing to the growth of a country's industrial strength and competitive advantage (see also Chapter 7).

Failure to invest in R and D

In the 1980s it became clear that the strength and growth of manufacturing industries everywhere depended on their capacity for technological innovation, which in turn was a function of their willingness to invest in R and D. Innovation, the capacity to invent and market new products and update them, is a major

Table 6.1 Five highest output growth industries

	Australia	Canada	France	Germany	Japan	UK	USA
1	Real estate	Computers	Computers	Computers	Computers	Computers	Computers
2	Communication	Motor vehicles	Communication	Aerospace	Pharmaceuticals	Real estate	Electronics
3	Utilities	Electronics	Electronics	Communication	Electronics	Electronics	Communication
4	Non-ferrous	Real estate	Pharmaceuticals	Real estate	Motor vehicles	Finance	Instruments
5	Instruments	Pharmaceuticals	Aerospace	Finance	Communication	Mining	Social services

Source: Epac Discussion Paper 91/08, 'Science, technology and industrial development', p.26 (citing an OECD study)

source of growth in high-tech economies.[54] In the past Australia has spent too little on R and D. In the early 1980s total spending on R and D was around 1 per cent of GDP, of which private sector expenditure was only 0.24 per cent, or about one-quarter of the average for comparable OECD countries. The Hawke government introduced the 150 per cent tax concession for company expenditure on R and D, which helped to increase business spending on research to 0.45 per cent of GDP by 1990. This figure placed Australia sixteenth out of nineteen ranked countries in the OECD[55], which still compared poorly with business spending on research in the leading countries: Switzerland (2.27 per cent), Sweden and Germany (1.82 per cent), Japan (1.96 per cent), and the USA (1.23 per cent). Including government and the universities, Australia's total spending on R and D rose to about 1.2 per cent of GDP in 1988 (or $2.8 billion) which left Australia eleventh in the OECD league table, a little better, but a long way behind the leading countries which spend altogether, as a proportion of GDP, over twice as much as Australia.

There are signs that Australian firms are becoming more outward-looking—Australian patent applications in foreign countries rose from 5000 in 1983 to 144 000 in 1988—and more technologically innovative: the high-tech output of the manufacturing sector increased by one-quarter between 1984 and 1989, compared with an increase in output of 15 per cent in total manufacturing. Nevertheless, Australian manufacturing is dominated by low and medium technology industries. In 1987 Australia accounted for just 0.2 per cent of total high-tech exports to the OECD area, placing it twenty-second out of 23 ranked countries (Argentina was twenty-third with 0.1 per cent). The list was headed by Japan with 18.2 per cent and the US with 17.3 per cent. Table 6.1 lists the five industries that achieved highest output growth in Australia compared with six OECD countries in a 15-year time period to the mid-1980s. The list almost speaks for itself.[56] If Australia is to participate in the lucrative trade in ETMs, there is still much ground to make up.

Why has Australian business spent so little on research? Partly, perhaps, because the multinationals who own large sections of Australian manufacturing have preferred to import their technologies rather than develop them here—but so too have many Australian firms. One of the standard criticisms of Australian business, highlighted by several prominent examples in recent years[57], is of their unwillingness to spend time and money developing promising inventions made by Australian scientists in the universities or the CSIRO. Here too there is a major cultural barrier to be overcome if Australia is to develop a modern high-tech manufacturing sector. The business culture in Australia has too often been geared to exploiting easy options, usually in the home market, in search of quick returns. The notion of product or market development, of building up productive capacity in the long term, of supporting good people and investigating good ideas regardless of short-term financial risk, has been absent except in a handful of world-class firms. But more and more, success in modern high-tech manufacturing depends on R and D, innovation, product development and taking the long haul. The centrality of researching ideas is better understood overseas. The head of the French company Limagraine, the world's third largest seed company (the world seed market is valued at $20 billion), when asked whether he would back anything with some promise, replied:

> . . . In research, we always take a risk and at such a level of research, we think that probably 20 per cent of the projects would succeed and therefore 20 per cent of the money will be profitable.

> —What are the benefits for companies of backing research like that?

> —The benefit for a company is to survive. It's very simple. If you have no good product [to market] you won't survive.[58]

The head of the US Biotech Corporation held a similar view: with technology generally, and biotechnology especially, no company could afford to focus on short-term profitability. Thinking of the potential of Ribozyme science, which may lead to a new generation of pharmaceuticals whose benefits may exceed those of antibiotics, he said:

> If we work on good ideas and developing them there will be benefits to us as a company and hopefully to society in general. I think there's always a financial risk if you measure the risk in terms of economic reward only. If you measure the reward also in terms of the ultimate benefit and improvement in learning or in benefits for the community in general, the risk is much less though longer term.

The Australian experience and outlook, on the other hand, has usually been the opposite.

As Barry Jones, reflecting on the sale of the gene shears technology to Limagraine, observed:

> Why would industry be interested in something that involves ideas? The great bulk of Australian industry has either relied on know-how that's been imported or, in the case of the major Australian-owned companies, they've been concerned with process-manufacturing, that is, manufacturing things like beer or paper where you've got the same product that goes on approximately for ever; or they're in secondary processing, i.e. manufacturing where you convert iron ore into ingots of steel or . . . bauxite into aluminium. That's the kind of manufacturing for export that we're used to . . . The whole idea

that we can, as a clever country, develop goods and services that are sophisticated, that are very high in value and very small in volume, and that don't cost very much to export; that is a new idea which is as dramatic as Copernicus' idea that the earth moves round the sun or that the earth isn't flat. To a lot of Australian business people, they look out the window and they say that it's apparent to me that the earth is flat and why should I act in any other way?[59]

A lack of savings

Australian entrepreneurs have a reputation for 'short-termism'.[60] In addition, manufacturers have frequently complained of a shortage of venture capital and a lack of patient equity capital to assist the development of high-tech industry. Business generally has complained that banks have been too willing to finance conglomerate expansions and property investment and have not given sufficient weight to funding investment in productive assets. The final, related problem is that, for various reasons, Australians have been saving less and spending more; via the attractions of negative gearing, two out of every three dollars saved goes into property. The household savings ratio declined from a peak of around 14 per cent of household income in the mid-1970s to under 6 per cent in 1991.[61]

Confronting this set of problems is crucial to Australia's economic future. Unless Australians save substantially more, and unless this money can be channelled into long-term productive investment, it is difficult to see where the extra industrial capacity will come from to generate the exports required to eliminate the current account deficit and arrest the growth of the foreign debt. This problem is both cultural and institutional. On the one hand, it means trying to turn a nation of consumers and, it seems, compulsive gamblers (while household savings fell, Australians still spent $27 billion annually on gambling) into a more thrifty society collectively concerned with the problem of wealth creation. On the other, it means trying to build the institutions and the mechanisms to both encourage savings, i.e. domestic capital formation, and channel funds into building up Australia's real productive capacity.

So far the government has not come to terms with the scale of the problem or it has opted, via the compulsory superannuation levy, for a forced rather than a voluntary national savings scheme.[62] The problem with this is that it adds considerably to business costs at a very inopportune time, and it does not directly address the problem of where the money saved will be invested. If, as seems likely, the national superannuation scheme is going to represent virtually the only substantial source of domestic savings, there is a strong case for providing either some limitations, or some direction, on how and where the funds may be invested. Superannuation funds had already reached $140 billion in mid-1992, and were projected to reach $600 billion by 2000. So far there seems to have been no systematic attempt to ensure that fund managers take direct account of Australia's national economic priorities in deciding where to invest, although pension offices do invest in infrastructure developments by investing in semi-government bonds (and may invest more in privatised facilities); at least four of the larger Life Offices have set up voluntarily their own venture capital units.[63] However, given the shortage of 'patient capital', there is a case for earmarking some proportion of the potential funds for certain categories of industrial development, as has been suggested.[64]

Given the seriousness of the situation, the government should also take a more creative approach to encouraging individual savings, perhaps by providing tax incentives to individual savers (as *Fightback!* did: Chapter 5, note 7). Or it might appeal to Australians' gambling instincts and establish Development or Infrastructure Bonds modelled on the UK Premium Bonds scheme, where bond holders are eligible to receive substantial monthly prizes. It should consider abolishing negative gearing and address shortfalls in the rental market via higher-density public housing. It should look, in particular, at the kind of savings schemes and institutions in operation overseas, notably Japan's Postal Banks or Singapore's Compulsory Provident Fund. It should also look at the linkages between banks and industry in Germany or Japan, with a view to developing an industrial banking capacity, which does not really exist in this country, and it should consider building on the experience of the Australian Industries Development Corporation (rather than abolishing it, as *Fightback!* proposed).

Flaws in the market approach

The neo-classical approach assumed that if one created an economy more highly responsive to market signals, then resources, especially fresh capital investment, would flow into more profitable sectors and industries. But could one be sure of this? Would Australian investors favour quick returns or long-term investments? The answer was not clearcut. New ventures in modern manufacturing involved high start-up costs, the result of expensive plant and equipment, expenditure on product development, research and development (R and D) and marketing. Investors and entrepreneurs would not proceed unless they were reasonably sure their product would command both market share and a competitive advantage in the markets targeted. Their decision depended on such things as the availability of suitable infrastructure, tax depreciation allowances, the effect of tax on profits and the quality of the labour force, which were all factors governments could influence. In other words, whether or not the capital and other resources theoretically released by the closure of uncompetitive industries would actually flow 'naturally' into more productive uses depended on a variety of contingencies, linkages and the right structure of incentives. These had to be established by conscious policy. They could not just be assumed.

This point led manufacturers to question the main implication of classical comparative advantage theory—that a nation's economy should be developed in line with its given factor endowments. Manufacturing, or the tradeable goods sector, was the largest single component of international trade. Trade in ETMs was a major source of wealth. Clearly other countries, notably Japan which lacked any advantage in raw materials, had chosen first to develop manufacturing industries, and then to shift resources into specific high-tech industries. This was done despite the apparent implications of comparative advantage theory. The decisive factors required for success in manufacturing still included capital and suitable land. They also included, increasingly, the presence of world-class infrastructure, especially all forms of communications, access to theoretical and technical knowledge and highly-skilled labour and high-grade R and D facilities available through clusters of firms and research institutes. None of the latter were God-given but all could be created by clever policies. The character of modern manufacturing, the growing centrality of high-tech industry, meant there were reasons and opportunities for governments to intervene in the economy to help create the particular factor conditions required by such industry. To fail to do so was to be bypassed in the race to access these new sources of wealth. The manufacturers did not deny the applicability of comparative advantage theory to primary and resource-based industries. In their case, however, the sources of competitive advantage in the global economy required some modification to the theory of comparative advantage. In particular, they required a more pro-active and strategic role from government (see also Chapter 7).

This argument was resisted by the IC, although it began to give ground grudgingly by 1990.[65] The IC believed that the future of manufacturing should be left almost entirely to market forces. The manufacturers believed that a more open and competitive economy would not necessarily bring with it the incentives or, indeed, the opportunities that would induce firms to act in the way free market theory said they should. Such incentives had to be, at least partly, created. As *The Global Challenge* argued, there was no automatic escalator leading from the disappearance of one set of inefficient industries to the appearance of another—not given the levels of competition which now existed globally.

How far are existing policies working?

The IC and Treasury resisted calls for a policy change partly because of their unyielding commitment to neo-classical principles, partly because they feared where change might lead, and partly because they believed existing policy was working. Treasury pointed out that between 1982–83 and 1990–91, although the manufacturing share of GDP fell from 18.5 to 16.7 per cent as a result of strong growth in other sectors, manufacturing output itself grew by more than 20 per cent. In this period labour productivity in manufacturing grew at an annual rate of 2.4 per cent compared with 1.1 per cent for the economy as a whole. Real investment had grown by 45 per cent prior to the recession. Manufacturing was not, therefore, 'in a state of terminal decline'.[66]

Between 1986–87 and 1990–91, Australian exports had grown by over 9 per cent a year, but the fastest rates of growth had been in total manufactures (16.9 per cent a year) and ETMs (18.6 per cent a year). Between 1981–82 and 1991–92, total manufactures had risen from 19.6 per cent to 27.3 per cent of total exports, almost the same as total rural exports, 28.8 per cent. Services had also risen to nearly 20 per cent.[67] For Treasury, therefore:

> . . . the reforms of the 1980s are paying dividends, and . . . manufacturing is becoming more internationally competitive. Further micro-economic reform will bring substantial gains to all industries . . . The gloom which has been expressed about the future of manufacturing is misplaced. There is every reason for confidence that a revitalised manufacturing sector will grow stronger and more competitive in the 1990s.[68]

There were indeed grounds, with some reservations, for arguing that the improvement in Australia's trade balance since the mid-1980s had been led by manufacturing.[69] There were welcome signs of a number of small and medium-sized high-tech firms emerging, producing high value-added goods, often for international firms and overseas niche markets. In the previous decade computer exports had grown from $71 million to $831 million (although Australia still imported around $4.5 billion worth of computer equipment); medicines and pharmaceuticals from $90 million to $453 million; exports of analytic instruments, scientific and medical equipment to $600 million with a projected target of $1.7 billion by 2001 (here too Australia currently imported about $2 billion worth of equipment). Wine exports had risen to $234 million with a target of $1 billion by 2001; quality TCF products provided exports worth $183 million (against imports of $1.5 billion). In computers, electronics, instruments, cars and engineering products, steel and biotechnology, one could see the emergence of a high-tech industrial base and the beginnings of an export culture. One study, undertaken by McKinsey and Company in 1992 for the AMC, identified 700 firms—many of them small and medium-sized—responsible for exports of $8.3 billion in a wide range of high value-added products. Their success confirmed that a promising trend had emerged in Australian manufacturing.[70]

Treasury thought the manufacturers were too ready to cry wolf. The latter thought Treasury projections too optimistic: that Treasury took the survival of some industries under lower tariffs, notably cars, too much for granted. It took too little account of pressures on other firms to shift offshore, and discounted fears that fledgling high-tech firms could be taken over and expropriated by predatory overseas companies. The critical questions were: Was the current rate of improvement sufficient to resolve Australia's economic problems? and Could that rate be sustained? The manufacturers' responses were equivocal, although they accepted that export prospects were better than might have been expected even two years ago, and could improve still more with micro-economic reform. However, they felt the rate of improvement was not sufficient, given the size of the deficit and the debt. The Australian Manufacturing Council noted that to stabilise the debt ratio in the 1990s meant that the value of exports had to exceed imports by 4 per cent a year—the equivalent of adding the combined export earnings of BHP Minerals and Alcoa every twelve months.[71] Although exports had improved, they were only just keeping pace with imports, while commodity exports were scarcely secure, given the volatility of world markets. To consolidate the gains made in manufacturing, Australia had to investigate strategies for turning the small and medium-sized firms into stronger and larger firms. It needed to identify areas with high export potential and look at ways to consolidate the growth of strategic exporters. While it was up to firms themselves to raise their productivity and seek out markets, it was up to the government also to assist business to eliminate obstacles to, and provide developmental assistance for, achieving competitive advantage for Australian firms.[72]

A 'middle way'?

The business sector had other complaints: the effect of state and federal taxes on business, the number of regulations, the high level of on-costs, and having to cope with a currency whose value went up and down like a yo-yo because it was linked to price movements in commodity markets. The basic argument, however, coming from large sections of business, was that Australia's economic survival depended on building a stronger industrial base, creating many more value-added goods for export and participating more in the rapidly growing trade in ETMs. Given the weaknesses facing business, these goals required a more systematic, coordinated, strategic approach from government. In several respects business did not want the federal government to do a great deal more than it was already doing by 1992, but it wanted some things done either better or more quickly. Business leaders agreed with the main components of structural reform. They accepted that business itself had to make more of an effort to raise productivity, and to take advantage of opportunities in Asia.[73] However, they stressed that all these matters required a long-term vision or strategy. The existing approach to structural reform was too much like muddling through. Only the government could create a more integrated approach, could engender 'a collective effort to develop firms, products, and markets'.[74] It followed that relying on the market alone was not sufficient. The government had to do more than simply create the 'correct' environment for entrepreneurs to succeed. How much more was open to dispute, but most agreed that the government could not afford to be merely a spectator: it needed to become more of a player-coach.

From 1989 onwards the manufacturers, with varying support from business, were feeling their way towards an alternative policy mix. This was a tricky exercise as any retreat from free market axioms was invariably attacked as a return to protectionism. The manufacturers and some academics wished to argue that a middle way was possible between, on the one hand, an over-idealised view of markets, and on the other, an old-fashioned and inward-looking protectionism.[75] The middle way was not a concealed argument for protection, as some suggested. It endorsed the emphasis on competition in open markets as the crucial spur to productivity and innovation, but thought that since the nature of trade and competition in global markets had changed, some at least of the prescriptions of neo-classical theory should change too. Its advocates sought to adapt the framework of existing theory to fit new economic realities, not to change it altogether.

They were for the most part concerned not to let protection in by the back door, but they thought Australia had something to learn from Porter's theory of competitive advantage, the growing interest in strategic trade theory in the US, and the responses of other countries to intra-industry trade (see Chapter 7).

The middle way was an attempt to break out of the kind of binary oppositions—state v. market, public v. private sector—which imposed a rigid and unhelpful framework on current policy debates, industry policy especially. It was an argument for a more balanced approach, for the importance of shades of grey, and for a more flexible and imaginative approach to the problems facing industry. It was an argument for bringing the state back in to some degree, and for a more cooperative relationship between government and business.[76] It involved implicitly an attempt to re-evaluate the lessons of the 1980s. There were government failures but they were not so one-sided or so clearcut as to warrant a near-total rejection of government's role in economic development. Indeed the private sector, especially the banks and certain self-styled 'entrepreneurs', were heavily implicated in the scandals in Western Australia and Victoria, and to some extent in South Australia. These were not just failures of government. To condemn all attempts to predict the emergence of potential high-growth firms or sectors as 'picking winners' was as crass as making 'economic rationalism' a wholly pejorative term.

In saying this, advocates for a middle way also thought Australia could learn by studying the approaches of other Asian and European countries to economic development (see also Chapter 7). The latter did allocate a more positive role to the state in 'planning for the market', despite the IC's attempts to argue that they did not. Australia could learn from the developmental strategies followed by several Asian states. It might take note of particular strategies, including tax incentives, tax holidays and infrastructural assistance, used to attract overseas firms and to build up export-competitive firms. There were more options available than pure free marketeers allowed.

Overall the middle way was an attempt to challenge the ruling neo-classical paradigm, to re-order the relations between state and market from a different conceptual perspective. By 1991 there were growing fears that, despite widespread agreement that free markets were desirable, the type of mindset held by pure marketeers had become something of a structural rigidity itself, and as such was blocking the further development of policy. The fear was that those who believed in the market, the whole market and nothing but the market, were sending Australia in a direction which was diverging increasingly from the kind of policies other countries were adopting to deal with globalisation, and relied too much on a rather narrow range of policy instruments predicated on an equally narrow regard for the central value of economic efficiency. There were, in fact, plenty of ideas available: the problem was to get them onto the agenda for discussion. The over-rigid adherence to the ruling paradigm precluded genuine debate. As Colin Carter put it:

> The economists who dominate financial journalism as well as policy-making in Canberra never do us the dignity of discussing why [countries like Singapore] do these things. It's not even considered worthy of comment. So, if you put up a proposition in Australia that there should be an articulated sense of vision or that we should use the tax system to provide differential tax incentives—which Germany does in bucketloads and which each one of the Asian countries does—you are regarded as a neanderthal. The tragedy for the country is, the debate isn't even entered here.[77]

The tragedy was also that the gap between many free market reformers and those who favoured a middle way was not large: a relatively small conceptual shift could well yield disproportionate benefits in policy flexibility. There was general agreement on the continued importance of micro-economic and workplace reforms, and on the need to create an environment more conducive to industry development. There was a growing recognition that the federal government would have to spend heavily on infrastructure works, and on education and training. Nearly everyone agreed in principle on the need for state intervention to promote industrial R and D in particular, and science and innovation in general. This involved the state at a series of points. However, as Barry Jones' experience testified, the government's treatment of science and the CSIRO raised the question of whether it fully grasped the ramifications of 'wealth through innovation'. The government espoused the clever country and high-tech industry, but it not infrequently did things which were quite at odds with its rhetoric.[78]

Nevertheless, in government circles, there was a slowly growing appreciation of the potential importance of the ETM industries, and a recognition that these might need some form of targeted assistance. Or, as the Department of Industry delicately phrased it, 'a major challenge to policymakers will be to identify areas where "levelling the playing field" will not promote development in line with underlying competitive advantage, and to implement appropriate policies and programs'.[79] In particular, there was growing support for some form of positive government intervention to facilitate the development of new generic technologies such as biotechnology, where Australia had a great deal of world-class research, and information technology, where Australia had a massive trade deficit. The government might, for example, try to strengthen the technological infrastructure, assist with the diffusion of the new technologies, particularly to smaller businesses, and encourage cooperative research endeavours on projects too expensive for any one firm to undertake alone. Free marketeers were willing to support interventions which clearly supplemented market outcomes, especially when such policies were aimed at improving whole industries rather than individual firms—or where they generated positive externalities for the economy as a whole—and where government financial assistance required matching expenditure by private firms. There was, too, a case for export assistance, both financial and informational, to help small and medium size firms especially to identify export opportunities, notably in Asia.

There was some agreement that the government needed to intervene to improve the rate of savings, although the IC was less disposed to be critical of the banks and the private capital market. The issue of what use to make of the superannuation funds fell in the too-hard basket. By the time of *One Nation* (Chapter 7), Treasury had given in, reluctantly, to business demands for an accelerated tax depreciation scheme to promote investment, and to several small measures to assist with the provision of venture capital and to facilitate the commercialisation of promising research ideas. Treasury and the IC were very reluctant to entertain the idea of offering tax inducements to attract foreign multinationals to Australia. They were not convinced that the benefit of so doing outweighed the costs. They were also unenthusiastic towards *The Global Challenge*'s arguments that the Partnerships for Development scheme should be extended and strengthened. The report argued there were further opportunities for Australian firms to become involved in a number of high-tech areas which were dominated by a handful of companies—aerospace, computers, pharmaceuticals and telecommunications. The government should try, in conjunction with relevant businesses, to put together development packages which might encourage 'global scale' industries to locate some portion of their production here. The long-term benefits for Australian technology, via the linkages argument, could be substantial.[80]

However, at the point where reacting to market failure changed into proactive policies to promote industry development, Treasury and the IC became more cautious, emphasising risks and costs. They were generally opposed to the government exercising its own economic judgment, preferring firms to act in the context of market disciplines. Thus they opposed any extensive use of governments' procurement powers to consolidate the market share of domestic firms.[81] They were unhappy with one-off interventions to assist 'strategic exporters' like Kodak,[82] and remained cautious towards the argument that the government could help create the factor conditions on which the competitive advantage of high-tech firms depended. They were hostile to suggestions that Australia use tariffs deliberately to enable domestic industries to acquire a competitive advantage. Not unreasonably, Treasury wanted some assurance that any assistance would benefit the economy overall as well as its direct recipients. However, Treasury might not be opposed in principle to a policy by which the government tried to target weaknesses in the product chain of a given industry, leading from production to marketing, and then offered appropriate forms of assistance to redress such weaknesses with a view to strengthening the performance of the industry or sector overall.[83]

There were three important points which did separate the middle way from the neo-classical approach. The first was their respective interpretations of market failure. Government intervention could be justified to redress the latter, or to provide positive externalities to an industry or society. However, Treasury and the IC were invariably the slowest to recognise that a market failure had occurred, their usual assumption being that 'the market works best'. This distanced them conceptually from those who saw market imperfections as a routine rather than an extraordinary event, and for whom selective interventions by government were thus the norm rather than the exception. Here there was a philosophic difference between those who thought the market should by and large be left alone as much as possible, and those who thought it either could not or should not be.

Second, there was a prime difference over the nature and aims of macro-economic policy. Those arguing for a middle way were very conscious of Australia's persistent deficit and mounting debt. Their view was that Australia had to do everything possible to both increase exports and reduce imports. There was a case for assisting industries which could reduce the import bill. There might even come a time for selected import quotas. It was also foolish to risk losing industries if the result was more imports. This perspective was quite different from Treasury's, which believed, apparently, 'that the reduction of [the] deficit is not an appropriate goal for economic policy . . . the market will provide any adjustment that is necessary by bidding down the exchange rate for the Australian dollar'.[84] For Treasury the ultimate determinants of macro-economic policy were properly market forces rather than government decisions. One should not worry too much about rising imports of manufactures because, ultimately, the market would make the necessary adjustments[85], although such 'adjustments' could well affect Australians' collective standard of living adversely. Similarly, there would come a time when 'the market' would penalise firms or others who borrowed unwisely.

Many people found this approach hard to understand, especially those who thought that one of the prime purposes of government was precisely to formulate policies which did *not* leave the nation's overall well-being at the mercy of market forces. The pure neo-classical approach to the twin problems of deficit and debt seemed to involve not only high risk but an element of social irresponsibility too. Here the great majority of business leaders thought Treasury's approach too cavalier. The middle way was very much an argument on behalf of establishing a stronger control over Australia's destiny.

Nonetheless, in 1992 it did seem that Treasury no longer believed in an active macro-economic management strategy, i.e. it no longer thought it possible or desirable to use the conventional tools of macro-economic policy (monetary, fiscal, wages and exchange rates) to loosely control the level of economic activity, or 'drive' the economy in one direction rather than another. Increasingly it was pinning its hopes on micro-economic reform and competition policy to create an intrinsically stronger economy. This was, then, another major philosophic difference between those who favoured a definite industry policy as a way of consciously shaping the pattern of economic development, of achieving certain intended outcomes, and the government's central economic advisers, who did not seem to find this approach feasible or, indeed, desirable.

The third difference concerned planning. The case for some degree of planning was implicit in all those among business leaders who called for a 'Vision' or a five or ten-year strategy statement modelled on Asian examples. It was stated more explicitly in *Vision 10* by the Manufacturing Council of Victoria. The middle way basically expressed the desire for a more conscious and coordinated approach to long-term industry planning and economic development. Business in general favoured developing a national strategy which could inform the policies of different industries and mobilise collective effort in the community for structural reform. Ideas of strategic and/or sectoral planning were supported by many in the Labor movement. Planning, however, was probably the one word which most aroused the hostility of those whose belief in the free market went beyond arguments about structural reform or industry policy, and who held ideologically inspired views about the respective spheres of states and markets.

Treasury and the IC might accept some of the schemes for assisting industry, but the basis of their opposition to 'picking winners' or to various forms of intervention was informed by a distaste for planning and all it was thought to entail. It was an opposition to allowing any government to think that it could actually *make* economic policy, as distinct from freeing up the market to take care of the crucial policy decisions for it. Here was the most fundamental philosophic difference between the two approaches. On the one hand were those who thought Australia had reached the point where, for reasons of social as well as industrial policy, the state had to re-assert a collective social responsibility to ensure that henceforth development occurred in a manner compatible with the nation's declared priorities and values. On the other were those, in the bureaucracy and the Opposition, who believed that 'free markets' were a superior means of achieving human progress, and who therefore opposed calls to improve the institutional capacity of the state. This was an argument about the proper province of government, or state v. market. By 1992 those who believed in something like a middle way, who feared to trust the market completely with their destinies, had to produce a reconceptualisation of the possible and desirable relations between state and market. Failing that, the argument over industry policy had gone as far as it could, and the neo-classical proponents were not inclined to budge any further. The only way out of the impasse that threatened was to change the ruling paradigm. This was the unresolved issue in Mr Keating's support for social democratic values: was he prepared to change that paradigm and rely a little more on the state in the 1990s to steer the process of structural reform?

7
The impact
of globalisation

The government's change of emphasis

In 1990, both before and after the March election, there were
growing signs of ministerial divisions over economic and industrial
policy. Several ministers, notably Mr Dawkins, Senator Button,
Mr Kerin (and Barry Jones), expressed reservations as to the
wisdom of the neo-classical agenda, and made muted calls for
the government to do more to assist business. This earned them
the displeasure of Mr Hawke or Mr Keating or both. Indeed,
the policy and political debate in this period would fill a small
thesis. Suffice to say that by early 1992, with unemployment
rising and several economic indicators set to 'danger', there were
sufficient reasons for cabinet to feel impelled to change the policy
mix somewhat. There were signs that several ministers (and the
party) were dissatisfied with Treasury advice which for some
months had assured the government recovery was imminent and
all it had to do was 'hold its nerve and everything would come
right'.[1] In January the Prime Minister, Mr Keating, met business
leaders in all states and was receptive to their calls for measures
to improve tax depreciation on capital investment, reduce interest

rates and fast-track major development projects. The government now announced itself willing to override bureaucratic opposition to such measures. *One Nation* in February represented a substantial shift from the tenor of Mr Hawke's industry policy statement in March 1991. Although it sometimes read rather like a propaganda statement,[2] it was the nearest thing yet to an embryonic industry policy. It provided an overview of the reform process, while the government formally acknowledged the relevance of business inputs to policy.[3]

In fact, *One Nation* contained a number of items previously urged by business groups, notably an accelerated tax depreciation scheme to place Australia on a more competitive footing with Asian countries. Investment in capital assets such as plant and equipment could now be written off at a faster rate against tax, with the largest benefits reserved for longer-life assets. For example, assets with effective lives of 13 to 20 years could now be written off in 7.5 years compared with 11.1 previously. The government also agreed to accelerate the write-off available for certain kinds of income-producing buildings. It announced it would supplement these depreciation changes for a limited period by introducing a 10 per cent development allowance for investment projects with a total capital cost of $50 million or more, completed within a tight time-frame, and which could demonstrate that they were internationally competitive according to certain designated criteria. The government said it was thinking of projects in areas such as food, fibre and mineral processing, pulp and paper, tourism, waste and environmental management technology, scientific and medical equipment. It accepted the complaint that small and medium-sized firms found it difficult to obtain capital for R and D. It proposed to offer tax concessions to investment companies willing to allocate funds to established small and medium firms. Such funds would be called Pooled Development Funds and were meant to provide patient equity capital for those companies resident in Australia whose total assets were less than $30 million.

It also accepted that the private sector in Australia was not sufficiently adept at picking up and developing the inventions and ideas produced by the CSIRO and the universities. It proposed to set up an Australian Technology Group (ATG) to assist with the commercialisation of research. This would initially be a government-owned company but future privatisation was possible. The ATG would have a one-off capital base of $30 million; act as a small, commercially-focused company; help to identify research with commercial potential, principally from the public sector; safeguard intellectual property rights for Australians while promoting their export potential; and provide seed money for promising research ideas. The government also proposed further help for export promotion: it would provide $5 million over three years to AUSTRADE to open new offices in the Asia-Pacific region. It would treble the size of the three-year Export Access program (from $4 to $12 million) which was meant to provide expertise to small firms thinking of exporting. It hoped this would increase the number of participating firms from 250 to 700. The government also announced substantial extra funding for both the Development Import Finance Facility and the Performance Bond Facility.

It announced a $2 billion spending program, over three years, for infrastructure improvements. This included money to advance the National Highway System and for selected national arterial projects; and to establish at long last a standard gauge rail network throughout Australia. Responding to business criticisms of the time taken to approve new investment projects, the government foreshadowed a Major Projects Facilitation Unit within the PM's Department to help expedite the approval process. (This was set up in March under Laurie Brereton.[4]) Other initiatives included tax benefits for small business and the tourism industry; more money for the Tourist Commission to promote Australia overseas; a lower wholesale sales tax on sub-luxury cars; further help for the domestic computer industry; financial assistance for structural adjustment in both the TCF and the rural sector; measures to promote greater competition in aviation, the electricity generation and supply industry and the finance sector; and in response to *Fightback!*, substantial personal income tax cuts to be introduced in two stages, from 1 July 1994 and 1 January 1996.

One Nation was followed by a slight but significant change in the government's stance on tariffs. Mr Keating had previously implied that Labor would lower tariffs as far as possible, conceivably to zero. In the wake of the Wills by-election reverse in April, Mr Keating indicated that Labor would not go beyond the levels announced by Mr Hawke in March 1991. Another significant change came in May when the Treasurer, Mr Dawkins, announced changes to the composition and role of the Industry Commission. Henceforth the IC would be based in Melbourne to keep it more in touch with business. Its terms of reference would be changed to require it to consider how to overcome impediments to the growth of promising export industries. It would be asked to cooperate with industry in targeting areas where Australia enjoyed a comparative advantage which might be converted, through appropriate policies, into a competitive advantage in world markets.[5] This implied a more proactive role for the Commission and one which seemed to go beyond its hitherto strict application of neo-classical principles. Certainly the shift in its rationale was received with hostility by free market devotees. The IC was also given a new head, Mr Bill Scales, formerly the chairman of the Automotive Industry Authority, known for his strong but pragmatic support for tariff reform.

The August budget contained further industry initiatives. It provided an extra $75 million over three years to assist exporters entering new markets, plus a new working capital guarantee facility for export-oriented firms short of working capital. The government decided to extend indefinitely the 150 per cent tax concession for R and D, and increased the funding for CSIRO. It had previously announced further financial assistance for structural assistance in both the TCF and rural sectors, and expedited spending on roads. Together with its increased spending on education and training, the government was clearly taking a more proactive approach in the interests of stimulating growth and creating jobs. It had also shown itself receptive to most of the main policy proposals coming from the business sector in 1991. However, it would not commit itself to an overt industry policy: the language and framework assumptions of *One Nation* and the budget remained strongly free market oriented. The underlying tension between the government's main theoretical approach and its de facto industry policy was more clearly exposed in 1992.

In the run-up to the election the government announced further measures calculated to assuage business criticisms. Mr Keating delivered *Investing in the Nation*, which announced that a Labor government would cut the company tax rate from 39 to 33 cents in the dollar while reintroducing quarterly payments for company tax. This brought Australia more into line with south-east Asian countries. The Reserve Bank would try to facilitate bank lending to small and medium business. While the statement also contained increased social spending, Mr Keating stressed that 'if we are to reduce unemployment, the revolution in our economy must continue'. Senator Evans released *Australia in Asia*, which listed eighteen initiatives to help Australian businesses improve their export performance in Asia. These would cost the government $60 million over four years. During the campaign the government was keen to stress its receptiveness to new ideas. Afterwards, however, Mr Keating chose Mr Griffiths as Industry minister in preference to Mr Crean or Senator Richardson, whom he regarded as too favourable towards interventionist policies.

The government in two minds

Between December 1991 and March 1993 the government was moving towards greater intervention in the market: its spending initiatives effectively acknowledged that a market economy could not be left to run itself. 'Market failure' was a more frequent or pervasive occurrence and not just an isolated or one-off phenomenon. And yet, in the area of industry policy especially, the government still adhered theoretically to the premise of non-intervention unless absolutely necessary. No doubt the government feared Opposition accusations that it had deserted the true faith and subordinated long-term structural reform to short-term electoral expediency. Nevertheless, it was finding it more difficult to reconcile its previous commitment to neo-classical principles with pressures for greater intervention. Increasingly it was coming to inhabit a theoretical no-man's-land.

As 1992 progressed, and within official policy-making circles at least, the neo-classical position appeared to be losing, if not the initiative, then certainly the dominance its proponents had enjoyed between 1987 and 1991. Although several scathing critiques appeared[6], it was still far from clear what might take its place. The critics, from both left and right, were united more by a sense of what they were against than what they were for. Opponents of 'economic rationalism' lacked a coherent sense of alternative strategy. The government faced demands from all quarters that it do something to counter unemployment, even if this meant reneging on 'economic fundamentals'. But these demands were motivated usually by short-term thinking: free market radicals were not altogether wrong in claiming that calls for intervention and assistance contained a potential to divert the process of structural reform. There was a certain danger that the reaction against economic rationalism would go too far: the original problems to which such rationalism was a response were not yet resolved. Using competition as the main spur to raise efficiency was overall the right course. It was just that the meaning, or the operational realities, of competition were more complicated than textbook models usually allowed. But the government found it hard to distinguish between conceivably legitimate calls for specific forms of intervention from, say, manufacturing councils, from the background noise of persons clamouring for a policy change. Without a clearer sense of what it was doing, it felt it could not abandon the basic premises on which its policy was still notionally based. It would not risk a formal commitment to interventionism, or even an industry policy, for fear this might produce worse long-term outcomes for the economy. It preferred to stick with the language of 'market failure'. Meanwhile, free marketeers hardened their positions in the face of criticism, which exasperated their opponents further.

What the government required was a clearer sense of how to legitimise its shift towards greater intervention other than by using appeals to social justice. In the case of industry, it needed a greater theoretical justification for explicitly shifting the basis of policy from free market concepts towards something else that involved a more proactive role for the state. The government (not to mention its advisers) had to be persuaded of the need to think differently about the nature of economic development—specifically, industrial and manufacturing development, in the contemporary global context. And for both electoral and intellectual reasons this was a very difficult move to make in Australia in 1992 and 1993. As Chapter 1 foreshadowed, once one rejected the case for the minimal state it was much more difficult to say what a proactive or interventionist role for the state actually meant. If one thought the government had a significant responsibility to help create a productive or an export culture, then what were the limits to government intervention, political as well as economic? Or if one thought Australia required a nationally coordinated program of economic development and social reconstruction, virtually a national plan, this went beyond a proactive role for government. Conceivably it involved an element of *dirigisme.*[7] How did this square with Australia's past record and the current commitment to encouraging competition and open markets? Could one have a strong, more interventionist state and a fully competitive market economy?

There were difficulties here: the case for intervention was not self-evident. One did not want to recreate old problems. To reject economic rationalism as a sufficient framework for policy was the beginning not the end of the matter. What was needed was a fresh conceptualisation from which one could derive criteria for working out a different, preferred relationship between state and market. In Australia in the early 1990s—and more widely in the cultures of Anglo-American liberalism—viable conceptual alternatives to free market thinking were strangely lacking. These had to be constructed (or reconstructed). Again, this was the government's special difficulty: making a policy shift that could be presented as a step forward, i.e. neither a loss of nerve nor a U-turn, meant first knowing how to change the premises on which policy was based.

This problem is the focus of Chapters 7 and 8. The rest of this Chapter argues that what is happening in and to the global economy supports the points made by manufacturers: a durable modern economy is, not completely but increasingly, built around a strong tradeable goods sector; establishing this now requires a more sophisticated set of policies than those advocated by pure free traders. It does justify selective forms of intervention, including some degree of protection in order to build up over time the strength and competitiveness of domestic industries. Governments do have a proactive role to play in helping to construct a favourable trading and exporting environment. This should not be construed as a step backwards, but as a necessary response to the realities of globalisation. The aim is still to build a more competitive and self-reliant economy, but the emphasis is on building: the requisite changes will not happen by themselves.

In several respects, this approach is more an extension from, rather than a denial of, neo-classical principles. However, it does change one key assumption: government should no longer be seen in negative terms as an unwelcome intruder in market processes. Rather it embodies, on behalf of the community, a residual, strategic responsibility to chart the nation's overall economic development, to help construct and sustain a viable economy. What goes is the notion that the market can and should be left to develop according to its own logic or momentum, with the government confined to maintaining the minimum legal order and dealing with specific and limited cases of market failure. While one accepts that markets usually provide the best means of handling complex questions of choice and resource allocation in modern societies—and therefore the scope for market activities should be kept as wide as possible—one also recognises that 'the market economy' is a construct whose own workings and outcomes require continual assessment to ensure they are consistent with other social values and the long-run national interest.

Chapter 8 develops this argument by suggesting that a social market economy is a more fruitful concept in today's world than a purely free market economy. It provides a means of resolving the kind of unhelpful dichotomies which are created by viewing the market too much in isolation from its wider environment.

The change to a global economy

Chapter 3 noted that world trade grew rapidly post-war while the strongest economies became export-based. National wealth came increasingly from trade, especially from trade in manufactures. Australia's problems stem from failing to respond more quickly to these changes. What also matters, however, is the dynamic process of economic and technological change which lies behind the trends in world trade. In the last decade or so, the international economy seems to have gone one stage further and turned into a truly global or interlinked economy. This is more than a change in scale. It can be argued that globalisation embodies qualitative changes in both the nature of world trade and manufacturing production, thereby creating a novel situation with which firms, policy-makers and theorists are struggling to come to terms. The concept of competitive advantage and strategic trade theory are two particular responses. Together, globalisation and such responses to it contain important implications for the policy debate in Australia.

There are different ways of conceptualising the nature of the change which has occurred, and the selection of salient phenomena depends as usual on one's theoretical vantage-point. However, there is a fair degree of agreement among various authors that the idea of national territorially-defined states trading with one another within a conceptually distinct international economy is outmoded. Instead, the kind of economic linkages which now exist, not only between countries but even more between transnational firms and their component units in different countries, has produced a truly global economy. In some respects, this is a new version of world systems theory[8], but for most commentators the type of political economy involved is more complicated, and the interactive relations between both states and firms defies any single, clearcut theoretical explanation.[9]

According to several authors the key features of globalisation include major changes to the structure of international finance allied to the revolution in communications technology, which has made it virtually impossible to control the flow of money and other information across national borders: such things 'are now easily transformed into electronic blips that move through the atmosphere at the speed of light'. Globalisation is an effect of the truly global web of communications which has taken shape over the last ten years or more, the threads of which are 'computers, facsimile machines, satellites, high-resolution monitors and modems—all of them linking designers, engineers, contractors, licensees and dealers worldwide'.[10] Globalisation is also the effect of a series of technological breakthroughs achieved over the last ten to twenty years in microchips, computers and electronics, in information technology, in the areas of materials engineering and superconductors and in the development of 'programmable automation' and the spread of computerised production processes in industry and manufacturing. The impact of such changes, combined with a very much higher rate of technological diffusion, has seen the rapid spread of high-tech manufacturing on a global scale. Any country whose population either has or can acquire the skills and capacities to utilise the new process technologies—and, moreover, has the creative ability to adapt them to yield a new range of products—can compete effectively with long-established industrial economies.

Globalisation thus refers especially to the spread of increasingly high-tech manufacturing industry to many countries throughout the world, partly as a result of developing countries trying to build industrial economies and improve their share of world trade, and partly as a result of transnational firms relocating their operations in other countries either to exploit particular production opportunities or to gain access to new or better markets. Globalisation refers to the emergence of systems of production which increasingly transcend national boundaries, and it refers to a growing, worldwide struggle for markets, especially markets for high value-added goods and ETMs. In Thurow's terms, it marks a shift from 'niche competition'—where countries usually specialised in different areas of manufacturing and traded one another's goods which tended to complement each other's consumer and industrial markets—to 'head to head' competition, where the developed nations are increasingly engaged in a race to secure a dominant position in key strategic industries which have a global dimension, notably microelectronics, biotechnology, the new materials science industries, telecommunications, civilian aviation, robotics and machine tools, computers and software. Such industries are 'strategic' because their products are either crucial to the viability of a modern industrial economy, or central to the material living standards of its population. Wealth in the global economy derives increasingly from achieving a position of strength in these or similar high-tech industries. The struggle for wealth, for competitive advantage, also begins to look very much like a zero-sum game. Countries which are excluded from the development of such industries simply cannot generate the same wealth as the more successful. Countries, therefore, and not just firms, are competing to attract and sustain such industries. Competition takes the form of identifying and providing the particular factor conditions on which the competitive advantage of the latter depends. 'Industry policy' is simply the term which describes the steps required to develop a competitive advantage in the global economy, in global markets, for one's key wealth-producing industries.

Globalisation is also very much identified with the growth of a vast international market for all kinds of consumer goods and for the technology, skills and equipment with which to design and produce these goods. Ohmae, for example, suggests that the core feature of globalisation is the level of interconnectedness which now exists between three especially powerful economic areas—North America, Japan (and east Asia), and the European Community. These comprise an economic triad.[11] The linkages between their industries have grown so close, and their overall consumer profiles are so similar, that they form one interlinked economy. In the mid-1980s they made up a single uniform market of around 700 million people. The struggle for markets between the capital and consumer goods industries within this economic triad provides a catalytic accelerator to high-tech competition around the world. Japan, America and the four largest European economies (Germany, France, the UK and Italy) accounted for roughly 45 per cent of global production. Increasingly, economic success for any aspiring country depends on gaining access to Triad markets and to the host of design and product innovations these economies generate. Because national prosperity depends more and more on sharing in world trade in manufactured goods, especially ETMs, no country which aspires to be a developed or first world society can afford to be marginalised from the Triad. To be cut adrift from the leading economies would not only mean loss of markets: it would mean falling behind in the race for innovation. Economic success in the global economy depends on both being exposed to and having access to the latest breakthroughs, ideas and skills generated elsewhere. It depends on being forced to improve all aspects of one's performance under the stimulus of competition, matching 'international best practice' in productivity, quality, reliability and service.

Across the Triad the goal of production is to create and market a product which, by virtue of its features or reliability, will be accepted as a highly desirable quality product by customers everywhere. The brand-name is crucial to this process, but increasingly the success of the brand in international markets depends on its reputation as a desirable product. Everywhere, in cars, electronics, footwear, clothing, watches, alcohol, china, glassware, soft drinks, fountain pens, etc., the power of the brand-name determines market success. The emphasis on brand alone is scarcely new: what is comparatively recent is the growth of much larger consumer markets for all kinds of sophisticated products. Rising competition has generated steady improvements in reliability and quality. Many more people can afford relatively expensive items; faced with the cornucopia of the international supermarket, consumers everywhere have become much more discerning about what they will accept. So the goal of producers is to create (or assist in creating) the 'best' (or branded) quality item for a specified market. Such niche markets, especially if they span different countries, can yield very high returns.

For Reich, globalisation entails a shift from high volume to high value production and the development of a 'global web' of enterprises.[12] (See also the discussion of intra-industry trade, below.) The origins of this shift lay in the effects of rising levels of global competition on the profitability of established national corporations, especially in America. By the 1970s the latter found themselves under attack from competitors in Japan and Europe. In basic industries like steel and cars, and consumer durables generally, the older corporations found they could no longer rely on secure profits generated by mass-producing standard items for sale in traditional mass markets. Their competitors too often undercut them on price and quality. Increasingly, threatened firms responded by identifying and producing for the unique needs of particular customers.[13] These included both consumers and other producers who required inputs or services of one kind or another which were tailor-made for their own increasingly specialised operations. Rising competition in the domestic market heightened the firms' incentive to find markets for their own more specialised or more highly differentiated products overseas. It also increased the incentive to relocate overseas to take advantage of lower labour costs and to have better access to raw materials or markets. The shift towards customer-centred production also brought with it a heightened sense of the huge profits to be made by 'adding value' to production, by giving new weight to such factors as design and innovation, quality and reliability.

> [The new] businesses are profitable both because customers are willing to pay a premium for goods or services that exactly meet their needs, and because these high-value businesses cannot easily be duplicated by high-volume competitors around the world . . . The new barrier to entry is not volume or price; it is skill in finding the right fit between particular technologies and particular markets.[14]

This shift was further accentuated from the late 1970s by astonishing developments in science and technology, notably in computers and electronics, plastics and material engineering, lasers, information technology and, most recently, biotechnology. These developments not only greatly extended the range of products which could be sold throughout the Triad (and the potential size of the new markets for value-added goods was often staggering)[15], they also revolutionised the processes of production themselves, greatly increasing their flexibility and capacity. Rapid advances in microchip and computer technology produced a new generation of computer-driven machine tools and equivalent advances in automation, including robotics. The computer revolution also generated a seemingly endless supply of new products and services for Triad markets.[16]

The overall result was the rapid appearance during the 1980s of a new kind of manufacturing industry which was less labour or materials intensive than before, and which relied much more on the application of specialised, often theoretical, knowledge to production together with the creative manipulation of new technologies by a more highly-skilled labour force in the constant search for new ideas and products. Technology, all forms of science-based specialised knowledge, became the crucial factor of production.[17]

As Reich explains, the market dominance of the old-style corporation, geared to mass production, was based on its ability to organise and control vast resources and impose predictable routines on disciplined armies of production workers. The modern manufacturing corporation, partly to reduce fixed costs as far as possible and partly to take full advantage of new production technologies, has become increasingly decentralised. It has contracted out many of the products and services it used to handle internally to an intricate network of 'contractors, sub-contractors, licensees, franchisees, partnerships and other temporary alliances'. It has become, increasingly, 'a facade behind which teems an array of decentralised groups and sub-groups continuously contracting with similar diffuse working units all over the world'. It has become 'an enterprise web'—a complex amalgam of independent profit centres, spin-off and spin-in partnerships, and licensing arrangements. Each corporate web has become part of a more complex global web through which the quasi-autonomous entities of the major corporate networks set up their own design, project or production teams to develop particular products for particular markets. There is no longer, Reich avers, any such thing as a distinctively 'national' corporation. The latter may exist as a 'strategic centre', but corporations are now so decentralised and make so much use of one another's units, services and products that, for example, the idea of a car or electronics company, whether in America or Japan, producing a national product in and for its own national market is a misnomer. Products have become 'international composites', assembled at one or more spots from components made by a variety of firms in many locations, both domestic and overseas. Famous trademarks 'adhere to services and products that are cobbled together from many . . . sources outside the firm'. The car industry provides some of the best examples—by 1990 Chrysler (US) directly produced about 30 per cent of the value of its cars; Ford about 50 per cent; GM bought half its design and engineering services from 800 different companies—but the same pattern is evident everywhere.[18]

In the modern high-value enterprise, the most important people tend to be those who can identify new opportunities, invent new products or overcome technical barriers to production—plus the 'strategic brokers' who can manage the interface between theoretical knowledge, technical application, product development, financial services and marketing. What counts in a highly competitive environment is creative ability and quick response: being able to come up with a new or better product and then upgrade it—or shift to a new product entirely—ahead of one's competitors. What matters most is the ability to appropriate and exploit specialised knowledge:

> The key assets of high-value enterprise are not tangible things, but the skills involved in linking solutions to particular needs, and the reputations that come from having done so successfully in the past. No single group . . . 'controls' this enterprise as the high-volume enterprise was controlled . . . Power depends not on formal authority or rank but on the capacity to add value to enterprise webs. Problem solvers, identifiers, or brokers exercise leadership by creating ways in which others can add value as well.[19]

More and more the true worth of the high-value enterprise lies in the brains and skills of its employees. Intellectual capital either has or is overtaking physical capital as the key asset of the corporation. This may seem truer of the emerging science-based industries, but it also applies to traditional ones:

> In 1920, more than 85 per cent of the cost of an automobile went to pay routine labourers and investors. By 1990, these two groups received less than 60 per cent, with the remainder going to designers, engineers, stylists, planners, strategists, financial specialists, executive officers, lawyers, advertisers, marketers and the like.[20]

Some general implications

The globalisation of business, which can only be sketched here, reinforces a number of familiar points: for nations the major sources of wealth-generation in the global economy lie, in general, with the development of value-added industries, and more specifically, by being able to participate in the expansion of the new science-based high-technology industries—pharmaceuticals, telecommunications, computers and information technology, specialised medical and scientific equipment, aerospace or environmental waste management. Because no developed society can survive without these and many other manufactured products, and because the potential costs or rewards can make a great difference, for better or worse, to a nation's balance of payments, governments in virtually all industrial societies now take an active, strategic interest in trying to facilitate links between their own domestic firms—including offshoots of multinationals—and the global networks in some at least of these new industries. This may mean trying to attract or build firms in areas where the government and/or others think it feasible to either exploit an existing advantage or facility, or develop one in the foreseeable future. Or it may mean encouraging partnership arrangements between local firms and international companies.[21] The overall goal is to ensure that the nation's manufacturing sector remains actively abreast of the speed of technological change worldwide and able to participate in some significant ways in the global projects and inter-firm networks which are of rising significance in the world economy. The aim of such intervention is to avoid the risk of marginalisation, of becoming a spectator rather than a player.

The level and type of competition which characterises Triad markets underlines the importance of R and D and the processes of invention, innovation and product development.[22] These processes, especially in the science-based industries, are long and costly. A company has to be prepared to sink large sums of money in basic research and experimentation in searching for a product which may yield sizeable, even multi-billion dollar, returns. Access to patient capital, being willing to take the very long-term view, becomes more important. Again, modern manufacturing tends to be highly technology-dependent: all of it has been affected, in greater or lesser degree, by the rapid diffusion of (mostly expensive) new technologies. The latter provide a crucial competitive edge but the cost of building a pulp mill, a car plant or a fully-automated factory is very high. This situation also has certain implications for intervention.

A company planning a large investment to supply some portion of a Triad market will usually have several near-equivalent locations in different countries to choose between. Its decision will depend partly on the availability and cost of raw materials, capital and equipment, and on wage levels. Increasingly it will also depend on a variety of factors which can either be created or improved by deliberate policies developed by government and industry together. For example, a firm would assess the quality of the labour force—its levels of skill, motivation, discipline—and not just wage levels alone; the level of industrial disruption; the adequacy of infrastructure and communications; the level of corporate taxes and the presence of tax concessions for investment; the real cost of capital; price stability; market security; the cost of environmental restrictions; financial and political stability. For many manufacturers competing for Triad markets the decision on where to invest or locate does not depend simply on a straightforward response to current market signals. It reflects a strategic synthesis of several different kinds of information and a projection of trading conditions well into the future. It may anticipate the evolution of technologies or politico-environmental constraints as yet unknown. Because globalisation forces companies to think strategically, to take account also of geo-political factors, governments need to think and behave strategically too, devising policies more likely to attract wealth-generating firms than repel them.

The rise of high-tech industries and the greater use of sophisticated technical equipment on the shop-floor reinforces the importance of education and training. The overall quality of the labour force now matters more. The sources of competitive advantage lie more and more with innovation, with creative design or specialised engineering services, total quality control and after-sales service, clever marketing and continuous attention to product development and productivity. Science-based industries depend especially on the ideas and imagination of their employees, but elsewhere too the pursuit of quality and productivity depends on encouraging employees' identification with, and commitment to, the enterprise and its products. The shift towards higher levels of education and technical expertise further implies that the organisational methods of mass production have become outmoded. As Reich argues, the high-value enterprise not only requires different talents but encourages the progressive decentralisation of authority and initiative to workers at all levels of the organisation. High-tech industry reinforces the shift towards flatter, more flexible team-based systems of working: the stress lies on encouraging all workers either to eliminate faults or to add value to production wherever possible.[23] This has certain implications for those who would reform the workplace: the aim is not to cut organised labour down to size but to create a more responsible and responsive labour force.

Five points especially should be stressed. First, the nature of competition and capitalism is changing. In Reich's terms we are moving away from the heyday of the daring individual entrepreneur and the single firm towards an era of 'collective entrepreneurialism'. Increasingly, what matters is teamwork, cooperation and collective effort, both within the firm itself and even among firms. In Australia Johnston describes it thus:

> There is an increasingly close interaction between firms in the development, production and use of goods and services. Arms-length marketing, strict buy-sell relationships and perfect competition are, particularly in technology-based trade, increasingly the exception rather than the norm. To a significant extent, goods and their related services are increasingly inseparable and are produced, marketed, and need to be comprehended, as a package . . . [For a variety of technical reasons] cooperation has emerged as an increasingly important form of competition. This . . . can take many forms, ranging from inter-firm alliances to multi-firm consortia which may or may not involve government support or approval . . . Inter-firm cooperation appears to be greatest where technological change is rapid, where there are large economies of scale in research, production or

marketing, where technologies have system-like characteristics, and where internationalisation is rapid. Such strategic alliances have an increasingly important role in access to required 'complementary capabilities' for innovation, production and marketing in many industries.

Under these conditions, the firm is no longer to the same extent the dominant active unit of economic activity . . . As a consequence, innovation and international competitiveness are no longer simply part of a discontinuous and competitive process between firms. They are the product of structure, systems and interacting organisations.[24]

In a growing number of areas the component processes of capitalist production systems are less and less like those presented by neo-classical models of the firm. Technology, rising competition and globalisation in general are propelling advanced economies—or rather, the successful ones—in broadly communitarian directions (see Chapter 8). They are also encouraging new forms of collaboration between business and government to develop new production structures which rely much more on 'collective' rather than individualist 'entrepreneurialism'.[25]

This leads directly to the second point: competitiveness in modern manufacturing depends less and less on the conventional factors of production, even including technology, and more on such things as the capacity for innovation, the quality and reliability of the product and the organisation's own internal effectiveness, including its ability 'to learn and to implement appropriate action faster than its competitors'.[26] Here there is increasing scope for firms and government to act together to design not only a better environment for business, but more intelligent forms of organisational life.

Third, globalisation involves a double process of competition, between states as well as firms: one has to take account of the changing nature of the modern state as it too reacts to the global forces undermining both its own sovereignty and domestic cohesion:

. . . states are now competing more for the means to create wealth within their territory than for power over more territory. Where they used to compete for power as a means to wealth, they now compete more for wealth as a means to power—but more for the power to maintain internal order and social cohesion than for the power to conduct foreign conquest or to defend themselves against attack. The implication is that national choices of industrial policy and efficiency in economic management are beginning to override choices of foreign or defence policy as the primary influences on how resources are allocated.[27]

Meanwhile, 'as firms harness the power of new technology to create systems of activity linked directly across borders, so they increasingly concentrate on those territories offering the greatest potential for recovering their investments'. States concerned with the viability of their social and production structures are drawn ineluctably into the firms' rivalries and calculations. Smaller, poorer or more vulnerable states face 'increased barriers to entry in industries most subject to global forces of competition'.[28] 'States are being drawn willy-nilly, into a new game with more complex rules and far greater demands on the skills of public servants.'[29] Stopford and Strange discuss the implications at length, but one clear conclusion is that the emergence of what 'could be described as a New Form of Production'[30] has created not only a highly complicated bargaining situation between states and firms; it has also, along with the dynamic impact of technological change, created a situation of radical or 'generic uncertainty'[31] which has gone beyond the textbooks, requiring a rethinking of some basic issues in international political economy, and also made it somewhat naive to pontificate on trade and industry policy from the unalloyed standpoint of pure free trade theory.

Fourth, even while saying that Australian firms have to come to terms with this new world of uncertainty, one must also allow for the fact that globalisation embodies socially destructive tendencies. It can accentuate the inequalities of wealth within society and between nations. It places further stress on social relations already strained by the dynamic forces of industrialism and capitalism:

> All that will remain rooted within national borders are the people who comprise a nation. Each nation's primary assets will be its citizen's skills and insights. Each nation's primary political task will be to cope with the centrifugal forces of the global economy which tear at the ties binding citizens together—bestowing ever greater wealth on the most skilled and insightful, while consigning the less skilled to a declining standard of living.[32]

One may well feel disturbed at the implications. Globalisation does seem to make the whole world into a giant market. Conceivably it represents the triumph of business civilisation and/or consumerism. It not only diminishes the significance of national borders but undermines the powers of elected governments to determine policy within their own borders. Knowing this reinforces the point that, in seeking to integrate with the global economy, governments must also provide strategies to safeguard social cohesion and public order. No government can afford to relinquish its collective responsibility in this regard. To say 'let the market decide' in the face of the dynamic changes released by globalisation would be an act of gross social irresponsibility. (The Liberals might well ponder that point.)

Fifth, the way in which states are responding to the impact of globalisation is clearly eroding the rules which have underpinned the international trading economy since 1945 and which have facilitated the huge growth in trade and wealth which has occurred. This is, of course, an ironic and potentially tragic situation: the very success of those rules has helped produce new circumstances which may well destroy them, thereby leading to the beggar-my-neighbour kind of protectionism which the rules were designed to prevent. This situation creates a special dilemma for Australia, whose economic wellbeing as a relatively small trading economy is linked very closely to the maintenance of free trade: How far should Australia try to speak and act according to the liberal model of the good international citizen when the major players in the global economy are moving under the pressure of economic necessity in a very different and quasi-protectionist direction? To retreat from the 1980s commitment to free trade and open markets would not be in Australia's long-term interest. Yet neither can Australia afford to play by a set of rules which, whatever their intrinsic importance, have been discarded by the major players themselves. At the time of writing it is unclear whether this has actually occurred, although there is a good deal of evidence in the literature on globalisation to suggest that it has. The current quite rapid deterioration in trading relations between the three major zones of the Triad lends further support.

Although Australia's trade policies are not the focus of this book, one point might be made in passing. The more aware one is of the kind of dynamics present in globalisation, especially of the forces driving the major states to act to defend their own resource bases, production structures and social cohesion, the less likely it seems that the neo-classical perspective on the 'proper' relations between states and markets is an adequate framework from which to develop fresh policies. What is different about the kind of global economy which has now emerged is the increasing pressures on states to act to shape or direct—or to override—'market forces' in order to secure the integrity of their entire social systems (or regime stability). The stakes are much higher than some free market economists, concerned primarily to optimise conditions for free markets, may realise. Globalisation has conceivably replaced military rivalries with economic ones, but the integrity or autonomy of the individual nation-state is the real bottom line, not the relative efficiency of markets *per se*. Some variant of managed trade, and some degree of protectionism, might well seem less attractive than free trade to neo-classical economists. Politically, however, it may be a suitably realist strategy for the 1990s.

Intra-industry trade

This section explains the further significance of Reich's 'global web' of enterprise.

The significance of Multi-National Corporations (MNCs) has been evident for some time. In the early 1980s half of the largest economic units in the world were nation-states, and half were MNCs.[33] The latter have more often had a bad press but in the global economy the activities of multinational manufacturing firms have acquired a more positive importance.[34] If such a firm locates some part of its production in another country, it generates export earnings and employment for its host. It brings with it new technology and expertise, access to overseas production and distribution networks, and it has a useful demonstration effect on domestic suppliers. Such firms can assist with global integration.

An increasing proportion of international trade now occurs in the form of intra-industry trade, i.e. trade between firms in the same industry, or even trade between branches of the same firm located in different countries. A country's percentage share of intra-industry trade provides a further indication of how well integrated it is in wealth-generating global trading networks. Table 7.1 illustrates once again Australia's fairly marginal position.

The growth of intra-industry trade in manufactures runs counter to the policy advice generated by the theory of comparative advantage, which advises nations to specialise in products where factor endowments provide a comparative cost advantage. In fact, with the steady convergence of economic conditions among leading industrialised nations, the resource base available

Table 7.1   Intra-industry trade as a percentage of total intra-OECD trade

	1965	1970	1975	1980	1985	1987
Canada	27	37	40	42	47	50
USA	24	32	34	35	37	39
Japan	13	19	17	19	19	21
Australia	6	5	7	8	9	12
NZ	2	4	6	10	13	16
France	39	46	50	51	50	52
Germany	37	44	47	50	50	52
Italy	31	38	38	40	41	43
Sweden	28	35	35	42	41	43
Switzerland	33	38	41	49	49	50
UK	27	35	41	46	45	48
OECD average	28	35	38	41	41	43

Source: From Reserve Bank Discussion Paper No. 9110, reproduced by Alan Wood in *The Australian*, 5 February 1992

to firms varies little between many countries. Capital and technology are highly mobile. Differences in labour costs have greatly diminished and more expensive labour can be offset by building more highly automated plants. With the shift away from manufacturing that is materials or labour intensive towards that which is knowledge intensive, countries now find it easier to develop strong manufacturing industries despite an apparent lack of relevant factor endowments. Japan is the obvious example. However, the pattern in many countries with similar resource bases has been to try and establish themselves in lucrative markets for high value goods by developing the kind of special skills and facilities mentioned in the previous section; i.e. strength in modern manufacturing to an increasing degree reflects national decisions to create a comparative advantage in a given industry or product, rather than accepting the limitations imposed by one's given factor endowments.

The phenomenon of firms as well as countries trading with one another has developed *pari passu* with the globalisation of business described by Reich and Ohmae. There are various causes, notably the impact of technology yet again and the effect of the interlinked economy on company strategy.[35] Many of today's manufactured products incorporate so many different technology-based components—and the rate of technological innovation and diffusion is now so rapid—that most companies can no longer maintain a lead in, or even remain abreast of, new advances in relevant fields. The result is that they make increasing use of one another's specialised knowledge and products. Companies in electronics and computers supply each other extensively with products, while specialised component manufacturers exploit economies of sale by making the same (or very similar) parts for competing famous brand items. Huge companies like IBM and General Electric trade among their affiliate firms around the world. Car manufacturers also supply one another extensively with engines and parts.[36] At the point of distribution, too, one company may decide to license an overseas competitor to distribute its product in particular countries, offering reciprocal facilities itself—an arrangement common in the pharmaceuticals industry.

Globalisation provides large companies with an incentive to establish plants in more than one of the major zones of the Triad. This is attractive to industries organised for large-volume production to whom the economies of scale available by selling worldwide are especially important. A company will try to maximise sales of a standard product (or components) throughout Triad markets in order to lower the average cost of production. Since the zones are widely separated, it may be cheaper to set up another plant overseas rather than trying to supply the world from just one base. Plants often supply one another with component parts. Japanese car firms recognised early the advantages of building assembly plants within the zone they were supplying, modifying models to suit the requirements of customers in different countries. Companies may also choose to locate a new plant overseas to pre-empt the possible imposition of trade barriers by countries in another zone. Many Japanese and American companies established European plants prior to the EC countries establishing a free trade zone of their own in 1992, protected by tariff and non-tariff barriers. Large companies may try to develop quasi-autonomous operations in all Triad zones to offset the problems caused by severe and unpredictable currency fluctuations in an era of deregulated financial markets. In many industries, notably cars, the individual firms have acquired extensive cross-holdings in each other's operations.

The overall result is the 'global web' which Reich describes so vividly. Global firms operate increasingly through a series of web-like relationships with other firms in the industry on a world-wide basis. National economic boundaries and national economic units have less and less meaning. Indeed, the concept of trade is itself changing. This is best described in Reich's own words:

> By the 1990s, most 'trade' no longer occurred in arm's length transactions between buyers in one nation and sellers in another, but between people within the same web who are likely to deal repeatedly with each other across borders. Such cross-border links now comprise most international trade among advanced economies. Less than half of America's declining trade balance in the 1980s was due to imports of *finished* products . . . Most of the imports were *parts* of such items, plus the engineering, design, consulting, advertising, financial and management services which would find their way into them. In fact, in 1990 more than half of America's exports and imports, by value, were simply the transfers of such goods and services *within* global corporations (*emphasis added*).[37]

Globalisation has produced a confusing, not to say extraordinary, situation whereby 'foreign' firms operate routinely in one another's domestic 'territories', so much so that it is often difficult to determine the 'true' nationality of corporations. 'American-owned firms are researching, designing and fabricating some of the highest of their high technologies in Japan, while Japanese-owned firms are doing ever more of their complex work in the US.'[38] IBM in Japan employs 20 000 Japanese and over the past decade supplied three times more revenue to the Japanese government than Fujitsu.[39] In 1990 40 per cent of IBM's employees lived outside America while 'American-owned corpo-

rations employed more than 100 000 Singaporeans . . .
Singapore's largest employer was General Electric . . . Major
American firms were among Taiwan's largest exporters'.[40] By
comparison, again by 1990, more than 20 per cent of the output
of American-owned firms was produced by foreign workers
outside the US and that percentage was rising rapidly. Foreigners
owned more than 13 per cent of America's manufacturing
assets—including half of all American-based companies involved
in consumer electronics—and employed 8 per cent of America's
manufacturing workers.[41] The American experience was repli-
cated, to varying degrees, in other countries.[42]

This is a situation which has again gone beyond the textbooks,
in both politics and economics. The main point here is that the
phenomena collectively dubbed globalisation have given rise to a
trading environment which, in the case of modern high-tech
manufacturing especially, is diverging in significant ways from
the account of reality provided by the original conceptual apparatus of free market theory. How one operates and how one
succeeds in the global economy requires a fuller and more
sophisticated strategy than that acknowledged by (pure) neo-classical economists. What manufacturers (and others) are saying is
that the world has changed so much that it is no longer enough
to try and respond to these new curiosities simply by re-jigging
or fine-tuning the original model. The curiosities are not the
exception: they are the new reality. If one is serious about
integrating with the global economy—developing firms with global
reach; developing strategic exporters; trying to take advantage of
markets for ETM products—then one has to come up with a
different understanding of the problems, a fresh conceptualisation
of theory which will yield better policy prescriptions than the
existing free market paradigm does. This too is a major reason
for thinking more deliberately about an industry policy.

Strategic trade theory

Two main points emerge from accounts of globalisation. First,
trading conditions in the real world have diverged from the
assumptions which underpin the neo-classical analysis of how
markets work, and are continuing to diverge still. That analysis
is grounded in a general equilibrium model which posits a natural
tendency in free markets towards equilibrium results (or mutually
satisfying outcomes for the players involved) assuming that
certain conditions for perfect competition are met, notably ready
access by the players to markets and information, and free
movements in and out of markets as the players respond rationally

to price signals. But in markets for high-tech manufactures especially, oligopolistic competition is the norm and market imperfections abound. Market entry for newcomers may be extremely difficult, given the costs of entry and the strength of established players. Conventional profit-maximising strategies, based on a direct response to 'objective' market signals, may not provide sufficient information on whether or not to invest heavily in a product or plant when its actual viability involves an 'over-the-horizon' assessment. Approaching the global economy from the perspective imparted by a general equilibrium model may also be problematic, given the rate of technological change, the growing struggle for markets, and the ensuing responses of other nation-states. The neo-classical model regards political intervention in market forces as highly undesirable, but other governments may (and do) see things differently, and may be more prepared to develop defensive strategies to defend themselves from the impact of globalisation. A policy response predicated almost wholly on a sense of how markets alone will or should behave, and which ignores nation-states as economic players in their own right, may turn out to be disastrously beside the point.

The second and related point is that success in high-tech manufacturing does not depend solely on the conditions recognised by the theory of comparative advantage, i.e. the ready availability of one or other of the conventional factors of production (labour, capital or raw materials). The resource base available to producers now varies little between many Triad countries. And, the competitive success of knowledge-intensive, high-value manufacturing depends very much on things like R and D, innovation and creativity, world-class infrastructure and continuously boosting productivity levels. So the more the world economy turns to trading products that are knowledge-intensive, and the more competitive advantage hinges on things other than given factor endowments, the more scope there appears for governments to intervene to improve the resource base or provide the enabling conditions likely to attract and/or advantage globally competitive industries within its own territory.

Strategic trade theory represents a significant though cautious response by some free market economists (and others: see further below) to these two points. It illustrates an emerging shift of emphasis, a sense that free market theory does not have all the answers. Free trade 'can never again be asserted as the policy that economic theory tells us is always right'. It may not be *passé* but 'its status has shifted from optimum to reasonable rule of thumb'.[43] Strategic trade theorists have also been influenced by the example of Japan and other Asian newly industrialised countries which have intervened in the market place to assist the development of strategic industries (see also below).

Strategic trade theory recognises that oligopolistic conditions are frequently the norm in modern industries, therefore economic theory should take more account of the strategies adopted by firms to win and/or consolidate market share. Its main insight or proposal is that a government may be able to use the range of resources at its disposal—production or export subsidies, tax concessions, tariff or non-tariff barriers—to influence the decisions made by firms engaged in oligopolistic competition. Such intervention may encourage a domestically-based firm to undertake production in an area where it would otherwise have judged the costs or uncertainties too great to proceed. The long-term benefits will then benefit the nation as well as the firm.

For example, given the overall start-up costs in a high-tech industry, and the risks posed by technological diffusion, a firm may not proceed unless it has some form of guarantee in regard to future markets, the rate of return on its investment, or overall cost-sharing arrangements, which only a government can arrange. The government may want at the same time to encourage the growth of a particular industry, because it thinks it important to the nation's long-term development and security. 'Strategic', then, has two interrelated meanings: it can refer to industries which are thought to have a general importance for the entire manufacturing sector, whose development contributes to building up the industrial base as a whole; and it refers to the deliberate use of plans or strategies—usually by government and an industry together—to improve the long-term competitive strength of key industries.

Strategic trade theory does not, however, license wholesale intervention. Its more specific aim is, usually, to improve the share of the domestic market enjoyed by a domestic firm (or firms) in order to provide it with a capacity to export at lower prices. Where the cost structure of a given firm reflects clear economies of scale (i.e. the marginal cost of each unit produced declines as output rises, up to a given point), then the larger the volume of domestic production, the lower the possible price of exports. In an industry with reasonable export prospects, this could provide a case for some initial protection and/or guaranteed purchases by the public sector. Once an industry has gained a price advantage overseas, it may then be in a position to expand more rapidly in foreign markets.

This is a general argument for providing government assistance, including protection and export subsidies, to help a domestic industry steal a lead on its competitors. This argument can be reinforced by considering the special circumstances of the emerging science-based industries. Here there is often a long lead time in R and D and/or product development plus high start-up costs. There is also a steep learning curve involved, i.e. getting established requires high initial commitments in both time and skill as well as money. So on all counts, being first in the field can confer a significant advantage. Science-based industries especially are characterised by 'learning-by-doing', i.e. the longer its involvement, the better a firm gets at innovation, design, solving problems, meeting and anticipating market demands—and the greater the lead it can build up over competitors, who may then be reluctant to enter the field at all. A firm which acquires significant market strength in this way can consolidate its position further by exploiting economies of scale. A series of cumulative advantages makes a firm, once established, hard to dislodge. This is the rationale for a government to intervene to buy time for a domestic industry to build up its skills and develop a significant competitive advantage. By concerted action, a government and an industry can develop the skills, infrastructure, plant, networks and experience which together amount to a position of strength that inhibits competitors.[44]

Strategic trade theorists conclude therefore that in the global economy free trade will not always produce the best outcome for a given country: 'There is some reason to believe that a government, by supporting its firms in international competition, can raise national welfare at another country's expense'.[45] This theory also implies that in several areas the government can intervene in the strategic calculations made by firms, and so influence the choice of products in which a country chooses to specialise; it can also bypass limitations to production which might follow from a too-literal interpretation of comparative advantage theory. However, strategic trade theorists are also clear that intervention always entails risks: it may send the wrong signals to firms and encourage rent-seeking behaviour. It is difficult to determine in advance whether it will result in a net addition to national welfare because it consumes resources which might have been better used elsewhere—and it is always difficult for a government to assess the flow-on effects of intervention on other industries. Intervention should be directed at an industry rather than a particular firm. It should be justified in terms of promoting the export-competitiveness of a given industry (although this might also cover import replacement at home). A final risk was that by creating a stronger export-oriented industry one might end up benefiting consumers elsewhere rather than at home. In the eyes of pure free market theorists, such risks constitute a sufficient reason for not intervening.[46] Strategic trade theory recognises, however, that some form of intervention may

be strategically appropriate under certain conditions. To that
extent it represents a step away from an absolute respect for
market outcomes.

The theory of competitive advantage

Michael Porter's theory of competitive advantage provides a more
direct challenge to the classical theory of comparative advantage.
It is a call for a paradigm shift in economics in response to the
radical changes occurring in international trade and competition.
There is a need for a theory which looks at what nations and
firms actually do in order to be competitive. 'We need to know,
very simply, what works and why. Then we need to apply it.'
The classical theory of comparative advantage does not do this:
'it has been overshadowed in advanced industries and economies
by the globalisation of competition and the power of new
technology'. It is not entirely wrong but it is much more relevant
to resource-based industries and trade in semi-processed foodstuffs and minerals.

> A new theory must move beyond comparative advantage to the
> competitive advantage of a nation. It must reflect a rich conception
> of competition that includes segmented markets, differentiated prod-
> ucts, technology differences and economies of scale. A new theory
> must go beyond cost and explain why companies from some nations
> are better than others at creating advantages based on quality features
> and new product innovation. A new theory must begin from the
> premise that competition is dynamic and evolving.[47]

Porter's theory is in no way an argument for protectionism
although it acknowledges a role for selective forms of government
intervention. It stresses the importance of domestic competition
and the ultimate desirability of free markets. It is presented as
a middle way between free markets and interventionism and is
another argument for modifying the ideological opposition of
neo-classical theory to intervention.

The starting point for this theory is once again the significance
of innovation and product development: innovation in a variety
of aspects is the key to competitive success. Innovation may be
big and bold but is more likely to occur through a series of
small insights and advances. Either way, it requires unusual effort
and dogged determination on the part of a firm. An advantage
gained has to be defended through relentless improvement via R
and D and strategic marketing. The key question is: Why are
companies from certain nations better at the ruthless pursuit of
product innovation than others? The answer lies in Porter's
diamond of national competitive advantage (Figure 7.1): four

reinforcing sets of attributes which comprise 'the playing field that each nation establishes and operates for its industries'.

The factor conditions emphasised by comparative advantage theory is only one of the four. The supply of large quantities of capital is still important but labour and raw materials are less so because 'companies can access them easily through a global strategy or circumvent them through technology'. For manufacturing, the crucial feature is factor creation: 'competitive advantage results from the presence of world-class [firms] that first create specialised factors and then continually work to upgrade them.' The absence of suitable labour or raw materials can force a determined company to innovate to overcome such restrictions: 'a disadvantage in a static model of competition can become an advantage in a dynamic one'. The emphasis lies on creating factor advantage: 'the stock of factors that a nation enjoys at a particular time is less important than the rate and efficiency with which it creates, upgrades and deploys them in particular industries.'[48]

- *Demand conditions.* This refers to the presence of sophisticated and demanding buyers in the home market who pressure companies to meet high standards and to upgrade into more advanced products. World-class firms are most likely to emerge where domestic circumstances force them to upgrade, creating more sophisticated products which can then be sold overseas.

Figure 7.1   Porter's diamond of national competitive advantage

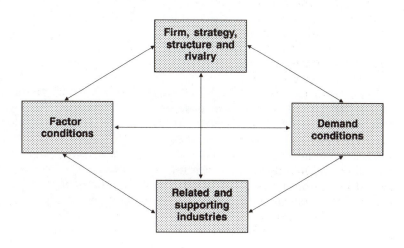

- *Related and supporting industries.* A geographic cluster of related and supporting industries can raise the competitiveness of each through the cross-fertilisation of ideas and local competition. A cluster can build up a highly favourable concentration of skilled personnel, research facilities and relevant infrastructure. (The Italian footwear cluster provides one graphic example.)
- *Firm strategy and rivalry.* Domestic rivalry between strong local firms 'creates pressures on companies to innovate and improve . . . to lower costs, improve quality and service'. Such rivalry can be magnified by geographic proximity, e.g. by two towns making similar goods, a common occurrence in Europe. Firms which have to fight for success at home are toughened for international competition, and more willing to venture overseas. Particular countries also develop organisation and management styles best suited to their own culture and to the requirements of particular industries.

Competitive advantage is maximised where all four attributes are present. The points of the diamond, once established, tend to become self-reinforcing. Domestic rivalry plus geographic concentration have great power together to transform the diamond into a system. Moreover:

> Competitive industries are not scattered helter-skelter throughout the economy but are usually linked together through vertical (buyer-seller) or horizontal (common customers, technology, channels) relationships . . . One competitive industry helps to create another in a mutually-reinforcing process. Japan's strength in consumer electronics, for example, drove its success in semiconductors towards the memory chips and integrated circuits these products use. Japanese strength in lap-top computers . . . reflects the base of strength in other compact, portable products and leading expertise in liquid-crystal display gained in the calculator and watch industries.

Implications for government

This is a strong argument on behalf of markets and competition: 'ultimately, only companies themselves can achieve and sustain competitive advantage'. Domestic rivalry is the catalyst which drives the process of innovation and product development. Firms which become dependent on government assistance or protection are most unlikely to be competitive. However, this is not an argument for the self-sufficiency of market forces either. Too much market theory, like too much protection, 'would lead to the permanent erosion of a country's competitive capabilities'. Governments can help to create the right cultural and institutional conditions to stimulate companies to pursue competitive advantage. Although governments cannot themselves create competitive industries, they can serve as catalyst and challenger, pushing companies to take new initiatives or to raise their performance. Since the viability of the state depends increasingly on the strength of the manufacturing sector, the government must provide directions, or a strategic vision, for the latter's development: it must help establish the cycle of innovation and improvement and facilitate the appearance of the diamond.

The government's role should be pragmatic rather than ideological. Since nations pass through stages of competitive development, a government's role and policies—and the balance between market forces and interventionism—will change accordingly. At certain times a government may have to intervene financially to help create the particular combination of factor conditions required by an industry, or to chart the development of particular industries and select policies likely to promote their competitive advantage. These may include some level of protection, tax concessions or export assistance—but again, those should be directed towards an industry rather than single firms, and their overt goal must be to develop outward-looking, globally competitive firms. The government's contributions fall into five categories.

- *Strategic vision.* This includes long-term planning for national development, setting production, productivity or export targets for firms; encouraging technological change, R and D and domestic competition; advising firms of global trends, providing information on opportunities and coordinating the efforts of firms in different sectors.
- *Infrastructural assistance.* This includes developing both social and physical infrastructure facilities to world-class standards. A government may encourage education, research and development in areas where the country already has resources or skills which can be made to yield a stronger competitive advantage.
- *Promoting sustained investment.* Since modern manufacturing is usually capital intensive, governments should act to facilitate domestic capital formation by policies to encourage or favour savings, and reduce the cost of investment to firms by offering attractive tax depreciation measures. The government should actively foster long-term productive investment in the country.
- *Enforce strict product, safety and environment standards.* Stringent standards force companies to 'improve quality, upgrade technology, and provide features that respond to consumer and social demands. Easing standards . . . is counterproductive'. Tougher regulations can create a competitive

edge. Companies that respond positively can develop products capable of export to other environments.

- *What governments should not do.* They should not act in ways likely to shield firms from having to confront tough choices on how to improve their own competitiveness. They should encourage domestic competition by breaking down monopolies, whether public or private, and outlawing collusive behaviour. They should ensure that clustering does not preclude rivalry. Where appropriate, a government must endure the political pain of necessary structural change. It must be prepared to phase out industries which cannot contribute to developing the diamond, and must not bail out uncompetitive industries for purely electoral reasons. The long-term goal is to build up those industries which can compete, either overseas or, in certain cases, in the home market.

Implications for the overall argument

Neither Porter's theory nor, for that matter, strategic trade theory, provide the complete alternative to neo-classical theory. Porter's book is more an account of the factors that seem to have helped certain firms in certain nations acquire their competitive advantage. It does not provide a neat set of instructions which a country like Australia can simply apply directly: it does not apply readily to resource-based industries. However, insofar as trade in certain categories of manufactured goods is likely to provide more enduring sources of wealth in the future than trade in commodities, countries wishing to participate in this trade would be well advised to address the sources of competitive advantage suggested by Porter and others. In particular, they should attend to the factors which promote technological creativity and innovation, organisational responsiveness and the rapid commercialisation of research.

The work described in this Chapter does suggest that international political economy is now less straightforward—and globalisation is a more complicated phenomenon—than neo-classical theory tends to recognise; it therefore requires a more considered response than a flat commitment to the virtues of free markets. In terms of the three points mentioned at the end of Chapter 6 which separate the neo-classical position from the middle way, the ideas discussed above tip the balance of the argument towards the middle way. A narrow definition of, and circumscribed responses to, market failure is not enough. An economic policy which has no higher ambition than simply trying to stay afloat in the face of globalisation is likewise insufficient. Governments need to be proactive rather than reactive because globalisation is both double-edged and entails 'generic uncertainty'. One cannot go with the flow because no-one knows quite where the flow is going. Some degree of foresight, strategic planning or collective response is required. It is a time to be improving both the quality of government and the institutional capacity of the state, especially in regard to economic development and industrial policy, rather than dismantling it holus-bolus in the name of small government.[49]

Governments have to take a broader and more active approach to wealth creation. They have to do more to assist the emergence and/or building-up of industries which can either make a substantial export contribution, or reduce the need for imports, in the next 5 to 10 years or so. This need not involve large amounts of government money in direct assistance, but it does mean looking systematically at, and either encouraging or spending money on, R and D and innovation, infrastructure and facilities, education and training, especially in science (pure and applied) and engineering. It means encouraging resource-based industries to move further along the value chain in pursuit of greater value-added products, and helping to eliminate weaknesses in the production-to-marketing chain of other manufacturing industries.

Such actions should not present a major obstacle to neo-classical economists, although some change of attitude is required in Australia. A narrow cost-accounting approach to industrial policy (the mindset of the alleged 'feral abacus') has to go. The government, in cooperation with business and academic research bodies, has to make more of an effort to identify and encourage new technologies, and actively explore and facilitate their commercial development. Both have to accept a greater element of risk. Barely a month goes by without the press announcing a major breakthrough or invention by Australia's scientific community, accompanied usually by a call for further funding or commercial support. Some of these at least must have potential. Australia hardly seems short of possible areas in which to develop world-class industries—in several areas of medical science, not only bio-technology; in environmental management, with the emphasis on anti-pollution and waste disposal equipment; in food processing and in engineering and construction, both oriented to Asia; in the specialised use of metals; information technology, even aerospace or micro-machines. The obstacle is only partly money. It is also the mindset which believes that it should be left to the individual scientist or single firm to wrestle with all the obstacles in the way of developing, patenting and marketing an invention. One should not offer assistance because that would be to undermine their independence and make them too receptive to handouts. The competitive market can best determine the viability of the product.

This attitude is too much a reaction to the past. Competitive success in the science-based industries depends more on encouraging cooperative research and collective effort, with the government offering active assistance, whether financial, legal or information, to facilitate the research process and product development. The bottom line in the neo-classical perspective is that the government should stand apart from the market and from the economic activities of firms. The perspective which informs the middle way is that success in key areas of modern manufacturing goes to those countries best able, by designing appropriate institutions, to mobilise the combined efforts and resources of private and public sectors to promote the growth of those industries jointly agreed to be of long-term strategic significance for the nation's economy.

It is time to relax the mindset which has shaped policy over the last five years or more and to get other ideas onto the agenda for discussion. That mindset was very much a response to Australia's past, especially to the evidence of government failures and the costs of protection-all-round. It was and still is informed by a strong regard for the greater potential benefits of free trade. Yet the desire to reduce the role of the state in the market also reflects, in some part at least, assumptions which belong to a previous historical era. In the 1990s it no longer seems either sensible or desirable to maintain a rigid line of division between state and market, or to assert that strong markets require minimal states. Increasingly, even in America and Britain and more strongly elsewhere in Asia and Europe, the trend is to inquire how the state can best contribute to developing the competitive advantage of domestic firms, and how it can orient the development of the economy in response to the perceived pressures arising from fiercer global competition. Outside Australia it is less a question of minimising the state and the possibilities for state intervention and more a matter of asking what kinds of selective intervention are now required to build or sustain a competitive market economy, one which will also prove durable in the face of rising global pressures. In this context an ideologically-conditioned hostility to the state and state intervention can obstruct the kind of theoretical and practical adjustments now required for Australia to build a stronger and a more secure economy.

Globalisation has produced a new era of ultra-competitive trading states. Modern states are competing actively for new sources of wealth, for economic rather than (for the most part) military advantage. States are vying with one another to form

strategic relationships with MNCs in order to defend and
strengthen their own production structures. Nearly all would-be
developed nations either have or are acquiring industrial policies
aimed at consolidating or securing access to the emerging range
of knowledge-based high-tech industries. There is a growing
recognition, even in America, that the speed and dynamics of
technological change make some form of strategic planning, or
planning for the market, essential: that governments do have to
make a more determined effort to steer change and the economy
in a certain direction, and to actively pursue investment and
industrial development strategies which anticipate global change.
To rely too much on market processes in the current era is to
increase the risk of marginalisation.[50]

The mindset which has prevailed in some quarters in Australia
has so far prevented a proper appreciation of these trends. The
IC in particular has been so keen to see Australia placed on a
different developmental trajectory, so keen to prevent any return
to the past, that it has over-emphasised the virtues of free market
policies alone while paying too little attention to the context in
which, and the means by which, they have been implemented
elsewhere. In the disputed area of east Asia, for example, there
seems little doubt that one major reason for the industrial success
of countries like Japan, South Korea and Taiwan has been their
deliberate creation of freely-functioning product markets, plus
strategies for integrating those markets with international markets.
The IC is correct up to a point to advocate similar policies for
Australia, and to emphasise the costs and risks attached to a
more overtly interventionist approach.[51] However, what the IC
in its report passes over is precisely how those 'free markets'
and internationally competitive industries were deliberately created and built up. The story is a good deal more complicated
than the IC allows. A strong argument can be made that the
industrial success of those countries was achieved only partly
through their pursuit of efficient resource allocation via the
unfettered price mechanism, and owed rather more to the role
of the state in deliberately guiding or governing the way in which
their respective market economies developed.[52] The latter were
more the creation of the state than the 'natural' outcome of
market forces. What was especially decisive in the case of the
east Asian countries was

> the use of state power to raise the economy's investible surplus;
> insure that a high proportion is invested in productive capacity within
> the national territory; guide investment into industries that are
> important for the economy's ability to sustain higher wages in the
> future; and expose the investment projects to international compet-
> itive pressure whether directly or indirectly . . .[53]

Governments there used 'a mixture of incentives, controls and mechanisms to spread risk, and to . . . govern market processes of resource allocation so as to produce different production and investment outcomes' than would have occurred with free market policies alone.[54] The latter were important, but their importance derived from the overall strategy, the pattern for development, laid down by the state. Whereas neo-classical economists like to argue that countries like Japan or South Korea would have done even better with less intervention or state involvement, Wade argues persuasively that it was precisely the framework, the coordination, the strategic direction provided by the state which made the crucial difference—especially in generating higher than expected levels of productive investment, and seeing that such investment flowed systematically into designated sectors. Again, this is not an argument on behalf of 'interventionism' against free markets: the various forms of intervention were often of limited duration and were directed to building up strong, outward-facing industries. It is an argument for thinking that 'governed markets' will produce more durable results than 'free markets':

> . . . The difference between what happened in East Asia and experience elsewhere does not lie in the discovery of industrial policy instruments not known elsewhere. Many other nations have at one time or another tried most of the policy tools used in East Asia. What differentiates their efforts, above all, are a consistent and coordinated attentiveness to the problems and opportunities of particular industries, in the context of a long-term perspective on the economy's evolution, and a state which is hard enough not only to produce sizeable effects on the economy but also to control the direction of the effects, which is a more demanding achievement.[55]

The 'governed market' approach draws on and develops from the model of the developmental state.[56] It provides a sophisticated critique of neo-classical thinking which on the one hand explains why one cannot explain east Asian successes in terms of economic liberalisation alone, but on the other makes it clear that indiscriminate state intervention is not the answer either. Success has been due to a particular combination of state directives and incentives and market processes. Wade's account therefore illustrates the practicalities of 'planning for the market', the difference between making winners as distinct from simply picking them[57]; the importance of designing specialised institutions for promoting collaboration between industry, banks or other savings sources and government[58]; and the role of quasi-corporatist strategies for mobilising community support for sustained economic reforms. (The latter two points also tally with the experience of West Germany and other European countries.[59])

In his last chapter, Wade lists ten policy prescriptions to promote industrial and economic development in the current era, and these too can be read as supporting the case for the middle way.[60] While his points go a little further than the ideas of Porter or Krugman, they agree very closely with the position of Lodge and other theorists of globalisation (notes 9 and 50). Overall, the literature surveyed in this Chapter makes it clear that in nearly all leading industrial nations, some kind of deliberate industry policy, involving especially 'national strategies built around close cooperation between business and government to gain world market share in selected industries'[61], is seen as a necessary and inevitable response to the competitive pressures released by globalisation. Australia should take special note of the forms of 'strategic planning' used elsewhere, especially attempts to increase the 'investible surplus' and direct it into long-term productive investment, and the use of specialised consultative and long-term planning forums linking government, business and labour.

Overall, Australia should investigate the concept of the governed market and the supporting model of the developmental state. Indeed, what is required here is for policy-makers to revisit (or even visit) the literature on other industrial success stories, trying to set aside the preconceptions or blinkers imposed by an over-rigid or ideological adherence to the tenets of classical liberal political economy. It is time to recognise that the relationship between state and market has entered a new phase under globalisation, and neo-classical theory requires some updating. It is not enough to treat state and market, or interventionism and free trade, as binary opposites. A different configuration is required, and this has to be constructed by each country to suit its own economic profile, culture and circumstances. It would help a good deal to approach this task with a relatively open mind.

8

The social market model

Searching for social democracy

Labor won the 1993 election in large part because Mr Keating
cast his opponents as extreme economic radicals while claiming
Labor was the more moderate, centrist party whose mission was
to reconcile the economic imperative of structural reform with
policies to address unemployment, inequalities and poverty. The
argument was good enough to defeat the Coalition on the day.
The question after the election was: Could Labor carry it out?
In particular, how much substance was there to Mr Keating's
social democratic rhetoric? The prime minister certainly had a
dream of Australian nationhood in which republicanism and
making Australia an integral player in the Asian–Pacific region
rather than an outpost of Europe were integral elements, but
how far did his social vision extend to the area of structural
reform? To what extent did he entertain any new ideas or policies
for reconciling his own free market preferences with other social
and political values? In the month after the election the evidence
was not encouraging. While many people—outside Canberra at
least—thought it was time to rethink the premises and parameters

of the neo-classical agenda, Mr Keating seemed reluctant to make more than marginal changes to existing policies. The big questions in the debate about where Australia was going, or what kind of society Labor would create, were still without answers.

For example, to what extent were Labor and Mr Keating still prepared to leave the future security of Australia's economy and people simply and solely to the free play of market forces? Were they really willing to question the efficacy of the advice proferred by their principal economic advisers, or to shrug off the mindset imposed by the neo-classical free market paradigm? Did the government think that Australia's current highly vulnerable situation might have something to do with the tenor of the economic advice offered by Treasury for the last ten or twenty years? Were they willing to entertain new ideas?[1] For example, were they and their advisers prepared to start looking seriously at the example of how other more successful economies were organised and run? Would they accept, as the previous Chapter suggested, that Australia had something to learn from the model of the developmental state, corporatist styles of economic planning, strategic trade theory or notions of managed capitalism? Would they now acknowledge that the time had come to involve the state rather more in strategic planning, to emphasise its steering capacity in regard to structural reform, and to start building the institutions and developing the institutional relationships between the private and public sectors which existed in Germany or Japan, rather than maintaining a rigid separation between the two? Would ministers acknowledge that the particular and peculiar circumstances of Australia—its isolation, geography and terrain, climate and demography—strongly implied that relying on market forces could not guarantee sustainable development or national security? That the public sector had always played a central role in Australia's national development and it was still most unlikely, even with higher productivity and a much more open economy, that the private sector alone could resolve three of the major problems facing the nation—renewing and upgrading the infrastructure, generating jobs and reconciling the current emphasis on economic growth with Australia's fragile and often ravaged environment?[2]

One could continue: How far did the government perceive that the economic challenges of the 1990s differed in significant ways from those of the 1980s? That 'integrating with the global economy' was becoming increasingly more problematic as the major economic powers adopted defensive strategies to cope with the impact of globalisation and ever-sharper competition for markets? That 'head to head' competition meant the steady erosion of the liberal trading system which in turn necessitated some modification to rhetoric and policies predicated on the continued viability of 'free trade'? When Mr Keating espoused 'social democracy', was he prepared to accept that there was, indeed, a middle way between pure market theory and protectionism: that selective interventionism was not necessarily bad, that some measure of protectionism might be necessary in the particular circumstances of a given industry, and that a more definite industry policy was necessary to maintain the competitive advantage of domestic firms in the face of globalisation? How sympathetic was he to the manufacturers' point that in the 1990s industry and government needed to collaborate, in a different way from the past, to build a more durable trading economy? That to persist with unalloyed free market theory in the face of the phenomena collectively labelled 'globalisation' could well prove a recipe for disaster? In the weeks following the election, there was little sign that the fifth Labor government was either able or willing to give positive answers to such questions. Accordingly, there seemed to be more shell than substance to Mr Keating's use of the term 'social democracy'.

Despite the government's avowed concern for the unemployed, it was not clear either that it could or would do much to alleviate the social costs of restructuring. While lowering unemployment of course depended on restoring economic growth, which was the government's chief priority, those who most wanted Labor to re-establish its credentials as a social democratic party had three important concerns. They hoped Mr Keating especially would show some awareness of them:

- The necessary contemporary emphasis on individual self-reliance and the importance of engaging in productive work should not obscure the fundamentally social nature of organised production (or, indeed, of human productive life). Wealth creation depended partly on individual efforts and partly on social cooperation and the availability of social and physical infrastructure. Certainly, individuals should be rewarded for their efforts, but a Labor government should also be responsible for levying taxes at a rate sufficient to maintain the infrastructure at the level required to sustain production, and for ensuring that the structure of incentives and rewards in society did not develop inequities which could undermine not only an individual's willingness to work but social cooperation itself. Critics from the left called on the government to redress inequities in the distribution of wealth and income, to maintain spending on the social wage and to accept a greater collective responsibility for assisting the victims of structural change. Their underlying point was that the current stress on individual responsibility should not go so far as to threaten the communitarian values on which, in the last analysis, a viable industrial economy depended.[3]

- The current appeal to individual self-interest (or the philosophy of possessive individualism[4]) was not a sufficient basis on which to ground social cohesion and public order. This was more a moral than a pragmatic argument: a liberal democratic society was supposed to be, in principle, a moral community, i.e. a free voluntary association of moral equals who, because of their formal status as human (rational and moral) beings, enjoyed certain rights in common: notably, rights to political and legal equality, equitable treatment and respect for their intrinsic human dignity. Too great a stress on self-interest, or on motivating individuals to follow their own private or selfish desires in the hope of greater material rewards, would undermine their regard for one another as moral beings. Therefore policies to maximise the creation of wealth should be modified to make them compatible with the other social values and principles which helped to legitimate this society as a distinctive kind of association.

- Policies for structural reform had to take account of the need to mobilise broad-based community support if they were to be implemented successfully. The previous consensus for reform was unravelling. There had to be a greater degree of substantive communication between rulers and ruled than either party had yet achieved. What was required was a social vision couched in moral as well as economic terms, and the ALP had not really provided this either. Mr Keating's references to social democracy did not come to terms with these concerns.

By the first half of 1993 the common thread which linked many of the government's critics was their desire to qualify, in varying degrees, its commitment to the free market, to economic individualism and economic rationalism. There was a pervasive sense in the community that Australia had reached an important fork in the road: it was time to replace a rigorous commitment to the neo-classical agenda with a different policy mix. Mr Keating had appeared to promise this at the election, but was his rhetoric simply a clever electoral ploy? Those attracted to the social democratic goal wished above all to create a more balanced relationship between state and market, and between individual and collective responsibility. This was the main challenge facing Labor: how to reverse the bias against the state; how to bring the state back into the structural reform program as an important player without sending the wrong signals to the currency markets or the special interests; how to reconcile a continued commitment to bringing about a more open and efficient economy with a legitimate role for the state as both an active structural support for the market itself and the body responsible for steering national development in certain designated directions.

Those most critical of the free market approach were clear on the type of policies they wanted: systematic efforts to lift national savings substantially and direct these into developing both the infrastructure and productive assets in general; policies to discourage overseas borrowings, perhaps by eliminating tax concessions for them or subjecting them to special approval processes; a plan for long-term industrial development, involving better efforts to identify and develop those sectors where Australia stood a realistic chance of developing a competitive advantage overseas; a stronger regard for import substitution policies and a willingness to implement both tougher anti-dumping measures and the kind of non-tariff barriers used extensively by nearly all other industrial nations; plus a stronger commitment to tackling income inequalities (the concentration of wealth in fewer hands) and to increased spending on the social wage.[5] These, and other more specific industry policies[6] all presumed a greater role for the state and a more balanced relationship between state and market.

To move in the direction desired by the Labour movement, to make some headway in the direction of social democratic values, the government required a different conceptual map. While it had some idea of where it wanted to get to, it lacked precise directions on how to get there from its present position. It did not want to leap into the unknown—its pursuit of a 5 per cent growth rate was enough of a gamble—and it was well aware that the strongest calls for changing the free market agenda usually came from those for whom economic rationalism and/or free market capitalism represented the work of the devil. What it needed was some sense of how to evolve a different policy mix out of its existing program: how, by making a series of related, incremental adjustments to current policies, it could actually advance towards a social democratic society while still preserving the integrity of structural reform.

The government did not wish to be seen to be looking or moving backwards: the intellectual traditions on which it might have drawn were all currently compromised to some degree—socialism by its association with excessive statism; Labourism by its association with protectionism-all-round and the mores of rent-seeking; even social liberalism was compromised, though to a lesser degree, by its entanglements with the policies and practices on which the previous Australian Settlement had been based.[7] What Labor required was a new synthesis of ideas which retained the centrality of the market—because, in intellectual, electoral and policy terms, that remained a central feature of its agenda—but which placed the market in a conceptual framework which gave a greater importance both to the state and to other social and moral values. This Chapter suggests that the idea of a social market could provide such a framework. It provides a way of drawing together many of the threads which have run through the discussion to this point. Most of all, perhaps, it shows how one can reconcile a strong commitment to a market economy with a legitimate role for the state as a necessary adjunct to, and support for, the market. Conceivably, the concept of a social rather than a free market offers Labor the map it requires to progress further in the direction of a social democratic society. It is an idea which has a certain appositeness in intellectual and electoral terms at the current time. And because it permits more than one interpretation of the relative importance attaching to 'state' as opposed to 'market', it may not be unattractive to the political right (see further below). It may, then, be of some use in recreating a consensus for reform.

Before discussing this idea, however, there are two themes mentioned in previous chapters which require a separate emphasis, as they contribute to the argument for adopting the idea of a social market, as both a bridge towards, and a component of, social democracy. The first concerns the importance of communitarian and corporatist values, and the second the trade-offs which have to be made between economic and political development.

The emphasis upon community

Why is one country more successful than another in achieving sustained growth or developing globally competitive firms? Perhaps because of the impact of its central value-system. Or because ideology itself can provide a source of comparative advantage.[8] (The role and authority attributed to the state in a given society may provide a further advantage.[9]) Lodge and Vogel suggest that some ideologies are better adapted than others to dealing with the effects of globalisation. In particular, countries with distinctly communitarian value systems, especially Japan, Germany and other Asian and European societies, have adapted more successfully to the heightened pace of international competition because 'the commitment of many parts of their societies to work together has given them [greater] flexibility in devising new institutions and procedures, and in using new technology'.[10]

By contrast, the strongly individualistic cultures in Anglo–Liberal countries like America, Britain and Australia have sanctioned adversarial behaviour and attitudes which undermine social cooperation and prevent the development of concerted adaptive strategies.

The latter cultures place too much emphasis on self-interest or private advantage. They lose sight of the need to define and pursue long-term community needs. The economic and property rights of the individual to acquire wealth overshadow the individual's duty to assist with the development of society. The public interest is defined too much as the sum of individual interests. There is little or no explicit emphasis given to ensuring that free market competition will actually serve the national interest: that problem is 'solved' by invoking the invisible hand. There is too little distinction made between the desire for gain and genuinely productive economic activity. The market is conceptualised too readily as a source of struggle: relations between individuals, groups, or business and government are seen too much as relations of opposition and antagonism. Such norms prevent the kind of social coordination, institutional collaboration and strategic planning required to cope with the effects of globalisation:

> . . . some elements of the Lockean tradition . . . make adaptation involving large portions of the public difficult. Contracts and the legal procedures surrounding them, the concern for the parts rather than the group or nation as a whole, and the assumption that everything will turn out well if each individual pursues his or her own self-interest, do not provide a framework that enables governments to adapt easily to [new global conditions].[11]

On the other hand, communitarian societies, especially Asian ones, emphasise that wealth creation depends on collective effort focused through carefully-designed procedures and institutions. 'Communitarian nations can expect that individual firms, managers, employees and ordinary citizens will all give great weight to the nation as a whole'.[12] In Japan, 'large businesses in basic industry are seen as essential for the nation and are therefore given a legitimacy greater than that given smaller companies that produce only for Japanese consumers'. The prevalence of communitarian norms and expectations help to cement effective working relationships within firms and between business and government. In Japan, fierce rivalry between firms

> takes place within the framework of the government and sectoral associations which define the scope and nature of activity and permit and even encourage some co-operation between firms in R and D, setting standards, market segmentation, pollution control and the like.

It is considered that this effort at 'managed competition' brings . . . communitarian benefits for the entire sector.[13]

The effectiveness of strategic planning grows out of the communitarian ethic: comparative advantage is 'created by the nation through collective action following the dictates of a national strategy laid down by government in close collaboration with business and labour'.[14] Communitarian societies stress social duties as well as rights, collaboration as well as competition, group loyalty and holism ahead of naked individualism. They are more inclined to link wealth creation to national development and to value savings and productive investment accordingly. They are also more favourably disposed to a planning and developmental role for the state.

Competitive success in the global economy has gone to nations able to mobilise their societies to act in a concerted and disciplined manner, which have created the kind of 'collective entrepreneurialism' conducive to the growth of knowledge-intensive industries. It is not enough to copy particular policy tools used successfully by such nations unless one can also create to some degree the social and organisational context which made them so effective: 'pragmatic innovation without ideological renovation is not sufficient'.[15] The Anglo–American societies should grasp therefore that laissez-faire values are out of place in the modern era: effective adjustments to globalisation require 'a higher level of domestic coordination' than is possible under 'rugged individualism'. This implies especially taking a more positive view of the state, trying to instil teamwork within the firm, and encouraging collaboration or partnership at all levels of society. It is of course true that the communitarian ethic has its downside as well. The history of Germany and Japan shows that communitarian cultures can develop particularly unpleasant regimes. One should therefore not overdo the superiority of communitarian over individualistic norms. The point is a more specific one. In the global economy of today, extreme individualism is an obstacle to competitive success, and countries like Australia should not overdo the appeal to economic individualism as the motive force of structural reform.

The importance of communitarian values extends to the potential significance of corporatist-style political arrangements. The latter appear to work rather better in societies where communitarian values are generally stronger than individualistic. In social rather more than liberal democracies, corporatist methods have often helped to provide the consensus required to implement economic and labour policies during times of economic difficulty, including structural change.

Briefly, social corporatism refers to a style of policy making which relies heavily on negotiating ongoing agreements between those in charge of the state, and the representatives of principal (or 'peak') producer groups, especially business and labour.[16] Typically, the government will try to engineer a 'social contract' between the major organised interests within society, offering concessions to win their active cooperation. The main area in which this occurs is usually the intersection between economic (especially prices and incomes) industrial and social policies, where trade-offs have to be negotiated between capital and labour in order to minimise confrontations. Corporatism is a strategy for constructing agreements on broad public policy goals, obliging interested groups to contribute to the development of policy, and sometimes to assist with its implementation. It is an attempt to reinforce the government's grant of electoral consent, especially when it feels compelled to make policy which affects directly the distribution of social costs and benefits—or the distribution of national income between capital and labour. In the 1980s the Accord between the Labor government and the ACTU, and the earlier economic and tax 'summits', were examples of a quasi-corporatist approach.

Corporatism has received a mixed press from academics. In the 1970s it seemed that in countries like Germany, Austria and Scandinavia corporatist techniques had helped to produce better economic results than in non-corporatist societies. As Dow argues, a number of European countries, and Japan, have achieved rather lower levels of unemployment and usually lower levels of inflation than Anglo-Saxon countries utilising neo-classical methods.

> Good economic performance, especially over the past seventeen years, has depended on institutional arrangements labelled corporatist. The literature from political sociology that has criticised corporatism for its violation of liberal or parliamentary niceties therefore seems to have missed the point. Such arrangements have been effective at maintaining the security and living standards of the subject populations; liberal institutions have not.[17]

In the 1980s it appeared for a while that the kind of economic individualism (or supply-side economics) practiced by Reagan's America and Thatcher's Britain was producing comparable or better results. Their success now seems to have been short-lived. As America and Britain fell into increasing disarray after 1989, neo-corporatist strategies have re-emerged as a useful means of mobilising the consensus required to sustain substantial structural change over a period of years. In Europe there appears to be a rising sense that some form of neo-corporatism is preferable, and is perhaps the only way to manage the dynamic forces unleashed by technological change and the globalisation of business. The alternative is to bow before 'market forces', to leave individuals and firms to find their own salvation in the market place—an approach which contains more than a whiff of social darwinism.[18] Societies which do not make a conscious effort to protect their own social integrity in the face of global economic forces could well experience serious social dislocation.[19]

The choice of strategy by which to pursue or facilitate structural reform is thus a crucial one. Strategies which set out to build alliances across the capital–labour divide, which set out to encourage teamwork, partnership and cooperation, and which include a deliberate focus on reducing unemployment, may well reduce social conflict and dislocation, producing stronger societies in the longer term. The European experience with corporatism is reinforced by the way the state in east Asia has acted to maximise communitarian values for national economic ends.[20] In both cases the emphasis has generally been on managing capitalism by political means: the market has more often been given a substantial but relative autonomy, not complete autonomy.

Economic versus political development

Liberal democracies, of which Australia is one, are curious, hybrid societies. They are organised according to the principles of both democracy and the market. Resources are allocated through both the political and the economic systems. The two contain differing and sometimes conflicting sets of values and have different functional requirements. Political stability depends on maintaining a balance between the two.[21]

Liberal democracies appear well-integrated so long as the productive system works reasonably well. If that system falters underlying tensions will rise to the surface—production requirements versus distributive values, individualist versus communal values, or arguments over the role and size of the state. This is what has been happening in Australia in the 1980s. The rising awareness of economic vulnerability has led to policies to shore up the market economy. But the emphasis given to the latter's functional requirements—to 'the culture of production'—threatens to undermine the values on which democratic institutions are based—moral equality, equity or fairness, respect for human dignity, among others. In other words, the policies adopted for structural reform have made explicit the awkward question which is always latent within the structure of a liberal democracy: Which set of values, those of democracy or those of the market, are the more important? Or, how should this society be organised? Neo-classical economists think the real question is: What is the proper role of the state in a market society? Political scientists and others think it is: What is the proper role of the market in a democratic society?

Democratic institutions and values and free markets are arguably both part of our idea of a developed society. Much of the time, the two enjoy a close, even symbiotic, relationship. However, circumstances do arise, as now, where the two conflict, and where the pursuit of economic and political development do not go automatically hand-in-hand—as the 'benign theory of development' held by many neo-classical economists assumes they do.[22] Trade-offs are necessary between the two, notably between efficiency and fairness, or growth and social cohesion. The critics of extreme economic rationalists are really making precisely this point: a wealthier society will not necessarily be a better one if inequities increase, or if the costs of growth are shared unequally. And the manner in which structural reform is pursued should be compatible with the integrity of democratic institutions or we could all suffer an eventual loss of civil and political freedoms. Market freedom is not the only freedom there is.

It is not just the economy that is vulnerable: society is too. As unemployment approaches the one million mark, over one-third of those have been out of work for one year or more (there were just 1900 long-term unemployed in 1974). There are now 680 000 Australian children growing up in homes where neither parent has a job. At the height of the recession, every day another 500 children under the age of 14 joined the total.[23] Reliable estimates put the number of Australians living on or below the poverty line at around two million, one-third of whom are children. This includes, of course, many of the unemployed. Whereas Australia was one of the most egalitarian of industrialised nations in 1970, it now appears to be one of the least.[24] The concentration of wealth in society appears to be increasing: the top 1 per cent of wealth owners own about one-quarter of the nation's private wealth. The richest 10 per cent own more than half the nation's private wealth, while the poorest 30 per cent of the population own none.[25] Meanwhile, at the end of 1991, 1.4 million Australians received welfare benefits in the form of unemployment, single parent or disability pensions.[26] The number of recipients had doubled in ten years. Three in ten Australians owed more than they owned. The number of people waiting for public housing had grown from 125 000 in 1983 to 200 000 in 1991 (federal funding had been halved since 1986). The Burdekin Report estimated there were 20–25 000 homeless children in the major cities. Poverty levels were also severe among many rural and Aboriginal communities. Between half and three-quarters of the farmers were technically bankrupt.[27]

In a population of 17 million, in what is still a relatively wealthy country, these figures represent a social disaster. They also give the lie to the Liberals' presumption that Australia is, embryonically, a nation of rugged individuals just waiting for the call to arms. Rugged individuals there may be. There are also 2.54 million people suffering from a classified disability of one kind or another, including 72 000 people with Alzheimer's disease.[28] (This does not include the occupants of hospital beds.) As the population ages, the incidence of senile dementia and cancer will increase. 'Social infrastructure' acquires added meaning in the light of such figures.

They also mean it is far from fanciful to talk about 'two nations' or an underclass. This in turn raises the question as to whether Australia is developing into a society in which social tensions, the growing gap between rich and poor, will militate against the meaningful survival of democratic values and institutions. Mancur Olson has warned that history provides numerous examples of countries where structural change or economic intensification caused social and political instability. His argument made three points: the determined pursuit of growth may create a new category of socially marginalised persons whose political behaviour can be unpredictable; there is no certainty that new economically powerful elites will be especially sympathetic either to the people beneath them or to democratic norms; even though structural change may produce greater overall wealth, in political terms the gains realised by the gainers may not be sufficient to offset the losses of the losers; social conflict can result.[29] Given Australia's current social profile, it might be wise to bear his points in mind.

On current trends, what will our society look like in ten or twenty years time? What community of interest will exist between those at the top and those at the bottom of the social pyramid? Will the growing numbers at the bottom of the social heap, especially among the young, be willing to believe in the rhetoric of democracy, in give and take, in rotating majorities, when their circumstances suggest they are something less than equals? What permanent stake will such people have in the social order?

To cope with these issues we need a broader concept of development than the neo-classical perspective alone provides. The economic imperative has to be placed in social perspective. Greater scope for market forces, given the nature of globalisation, could well accentuate the social problems that exist now. We need to provide distributive mechanisms to ensure that a certain percentage of the wealth available from a stronger economy (i.e.

an increase in the social surplus) is used to meet objective human needs. In pursuing greater wealth we do not want to set in motion structural changes in society which, by affecting behaviour and attitudes, may threaten stability or the legitimacy of existing institutions. A viable market economy assumes the existence of a just and secure public order. Maintaining such an order and, indeed, preserving democratic values requires separate consideration. A market economy may be a necessary condition for a pluralist democracy to develop, but it is certainly not a sufficient condition.

The overall challenge therefore is to reconcile the central concerns of the economic reformers with the valid points of their critics. We are looking for a conceptual framework which can accommodate the drive for a stronger market economy and preserve those other social values—especially the key concept of 'moral community'—which help to legitimate the public order. This is the contribution of the social market model. In the current context it can, perhaps, provide the switch to send the intellectual current flowing in a different direction. The social market model is the product of a compatible intellectual tradition, having been formulated in post-war Germany to deal with problems very similar to those facing Australia now. It is consistent with Australia's central structural reform initiatives. It also contains a strong communitarian and corporatist emphasis. It offers a way to develop a coherent alternative to the pure free market approach which subsumes the case for the middle way. It also provides a fruitful approach to the central problem: how to achieve a more balanced relationship between state and market.

The social market economy

This concept originated on the political right in post-war West Germany. Its component ideas informed the Christian Democratic program throughout the 1950s, and were adopted implicitly by the Social Democrats after 1959. The right and the left disputed the relative importance of market and state, but the term very largely shaped the policy consensus and institutions on which the reconstruction and the prosperity of the new Germany were built.

The concept was developed by the Ordo-Liberals, who were part of the Freiburg school of liberal political economists who opposed the economic and social policies of the Third Reich. Their goal in 1945 was to bring about an economic recovery while countering any renewed threat to individual liberties posed by an over-powerful state. They thought a market economy provided the best prospects for growth, while a vigorous competition policy would prevent concentrations of private economic power similar to those that had bedevilled pre-war Germany. Their perspective was liberal in that they began with a firm commitment to the principles and practice of the free market. They believed the price mechanism was the most efficient way to allocate scarce resources between competing values. Free markets maximised freedom of choice for buyers and sellers, and contributed to sustaining the civil and political freedoms on which the market itself depended.

The social market, however, signified a combination of free market ideas and the need for continuous social adjustment. One of its key exponents, Alfred Muller-Armack, did not want 'a market economy left to its own devices, but a consciously and indeed socially guided market economy', where 'social' included moral values and legal norms.[30] He wished to erect, on the basis of a market economy, 'a multi-form and complete system of social protection'. Other Ordo-Liberals disputed the proper relationship between market and social policy, but the key feature of the social market economy was precisely this attempt to develop a socio-economic system which represented a middle way between laissez-faire and collectivism.

The Ordo-Liberals saw free markets as human constructs which took differing forms in different cultures. Unlike Hayek and the contemporary Austrian school, they did not believe that the order found in a free market society was the result of natural or spontaneous social evolution. Neither did they believe that market economies embodied a long-run self-correcting process; they were accordingly sceptical of the *modus operandi* of general equilibrium analysis. Markets had to be managed to make them compatible with other important social values, notably human dignity and the rule of law. Care was also needed to see that the market evolved in a manner compatible with the nation's long-term economic security and the cultural integrity of the nation itself. The Ordo-Liberals therefore wanted to find a middle way between, on the one hand, an idealised (and often abstract) form of liberal political economy which held that unrestricted markets provided the high road to progress; and on the other, left-wing opponents of market capitalism who thought such a system would inevitably bring about its own collapse. The Ordo-Liberals stressed the realm of contingency, experiment and practice against the theoreticism they found in both extremes. The proper extent of market freedom or state power could not be decided in advance, according to *a priori* principles. Their relationship was an empirical matter to be decided by human agents at successive points in time.

The Ordo-Liberals agreed that the scope of the market should be encouraged, but rejected the laissez-faire position. As Karl Schiller later put it, 'the market as much as possible, and planning as much as necessary'. They did not see market freedom or market forces as self-sufficient: such 'freedom needs to be supplemented by carefully considered rules and institutions . . . Trust in freedom must be accompanied by a distrust of forces that abolish freedom or interfere with it'.[31] The state, by upholding the terms of a democratic constitution and the rule of law, had to check private economic power, insist on business morality, and prevent economically short-sighted behaviour. The law and the state, not the invisible hand, ultimately protected the community from the anti-social consequences which could result from giving too much rein to market forces. The Ordo-Liberals, then, believed in a constitutional state whose functions and responsibilities were broader than the nightwatchman state favoured by classical liberals. They saw the market fitting within a public order structured by principles derived from the law and moral philosophy, as well as from economics. Their ideas reflected a synthesis between Anglo-Saxon liberalism, with its emphasis upon the freedom of the individual and individual rights, and elements of European social and political theory which stressed instead the importance of community, conceptions of social solidarity, and reserved a stronger role for the state as an agent of order and development.[32]

The social market economy is based as much on ethical principles (derived in some part from the tradition of German idealist philosophy, especially Kant, and perhaps even more from Catholic social thought) as on Anglo-Saxon political economy.[33] Its founders were as much concerned with developing 'a good society' based on substantive values such as respect for human dignity, moral equality and regard for human potential, as with maximising market freedoms and economic growth. Ordo-Liberals generally saw the latter as a means to other ends: the wealth generated by the market should not be appropriated by individuals alone but used in part to build a better society. Concern for social justice was integral to this approach and contrasts with that of more overtly individualistic societies which, following Hayek, have more and more privileged the individual's private pursuit of his or her own 'good' and delegitimised collectivist attempts to regulate or structure relations between individuals in the name of higher goods like justice or social equality.[34] While the social market position begins by emphasising that the market economy offers potentially the best means of optimising the supply of goods and services to its citizens, it also emphasises, simultaneously, three other principles.

First, full respect for the dignity of the individual citizen.

Article 1 of the German constitution states: 'The dignity of man (sic) is inviolable. To respect and protect it is a commitment of every institution of the state.' The constitution also guarantees specified human rights, the rule of law, political pluralism, the separation of powers, the federal structure and the supreme court. The constitution as Basic Law draws on the German doctrine of *Rechsstaat* and establishes thereby a normative framework for political and policy debate which is held in high regard in Germany.[35] This helps establish that in a self-consciously democratic state the market economy must be made to work in a manner consistent with the value placed formally on the dignity of the person, and on the in-principle commitment to the right of every person to live a fully human existence. The deeper implication is that although the market is valued for its productive potential, it requires a deeper justification than simply its capacity to generate more goods and services. It, too, requires its own moral justification: it has to contribute to fulfilling the set of legitimating values on which the whole society is based. Certainly, as everyone these days is well aware, market forces can promote democratisation, but they can work against it too. The relationship between the two is a contingent rather than a necessary one. There is no automatic regulator to maintain the 'correct' balance: that has to be worked out by human agents, politically.

Second, the principle of solidarity, or encouraging among people at all levels of society—family, neighbourhood and workplace—a firm sense of being partners in a common enterprise, or social partners. The German approach to the social market 'recognises the importance of mobilising solidarity within the market' by encouraging both collaborative behaviour among business actors and workers and 'a strong ethic of public service' among private as well as public sector organisations.[36] A firm commitment to encouraging price competition is quite compatible with encouraging cooperative rather than adversarial behaviour patterns. Or, the social market is an attempt to situate the desirable attributes of market competition within a communitarian rather than an individualistic value system.

The major practical example of solidarity or social partnership is probably the idea of co-determination. This refers to the institutionalised participation of workers—specifically, union members—on the supervisory boards of directors of all medium-sized and large firms. By law every company and every state agency has an elected board on which unions can have up to 50 per cent representation (in companies with more than 2000 employees) although management normally retains a casting vote. The main idea is to provide workers with a detailed understanding of the affairs and competitive position of their enterprise, and to develop their sense of common interest and responsibility through participation. There is also an extensive system of elected works councils in German firms which have extensive powers over social and personnel matters, while wages and related conditions of employment are determined by free collective bargaining at enterprise level, between employers and representatives from one of Germany's seventeen federated unions. The concept of social partnership has further applications in the way the German social security and insurance systems are organised. In another context, it is embodied in the very close liaison which has been institutionalised between the German banking system, firms and both levels of the federal system.

Third, the principle of subsidiarity, which means delegating responsibility for action or policy to the level deemed most appropriate in society, beginning with the individual and the family. Subsidiarity acknowledges that a coherent and well ordered society depends on the different levels and units within it accepting a certain degree of responsibility to look after their own affairs and wellbeing, being able to call on the resources of the next level only when their own are clearly inadequate. Thus individuals and families are personally responsible for organising their own lives; this includes a stress on self-help. Voluntary organisations exist to support the family, while beyond them are state agencies which ultimately provide a comprehensive system of unemployment, medical and accident insurance to support individuals in recognisably difficult circumstances. The German system is intended to be interlocking and systematic: it is conceptualised and organised as a 'hierarchy of solidarity' which starts at the level of private responsibility and 'rises through different stages right up to the level of the federal budget'.[37] According to this system there is no conflict in principle between individual responsibility and collective social responsibility: the two co-exist as different expressions of the principle of subsidiarity.

Similarly, the state is portrayed in positive rather than negative terms: it is the body which historically has played a crucial role in facilitating the growth and expansion of free market societies and coping with the effects of social and technological change on existing institutions, notably the family. Because market capitalism is a dynamic agency of change, and because it creates not one guaranteed route but different possibilities for human social evolution (negative as well as positive), the state should be seen as a necessary steering mechanism: it is through political decisions made and enforced at the level of the state that the community (in principle) decides the way in which the market should develop. It is neither feasible nor desirable for the state to stand aside from market forces: the latter have to be managed to produce socially desirable results: 'The question is not whether or not the state should act in economic life. The question is when, where and under which conditions the state should act'.[38] The state has four primary functions, directed towards creating a durable market economy. The first two are quite familiar to free market economists; the others illustrate the social and political dimensions.

- To establish a secure juridical framework for market exchange; to enforce voluntary contracts; to define and protect property rights; to punish physical harms and fraud; to guarantee free choice of occupation; and to establish the framework conditions required for the fair and efficient operation of capital, employment or insurance markets.
- To limit or supplement the market where necessary. This means, broadly, dealing with the effects of market failure, e.g. dealing with monopolies, eliminating restrictive trade and work practices, and promoting competition. This may also include encouraging (or compelling) firms to develop in ways which they would not have done if left alone (raising productivity, expanding into other markets); providing tax depreciation schemes or other financial incentives to induce firms to develop long-run productive capacity (by investing in new plant and R and D) likely to benefit the nation in the future; providing facilities to improve the overall competitiveness of domestic firms (better infrastructure; a more highly-skilled labour force); and providing public goods such as a sound currency, policing and defence. It also includes safeguarding consumers' rights and coping with negative externalities, the adverse impact of (unpriced) private economic activity upon society or the environment. This point may also include a long-term steering function for the state: it has to anticipate how the market will develop in the future, what needs or challenges have to be met, the effects of technological change, or the behaviour of other economies and societies.
- To ensure that the market system is politically acceptable. The key point here is that 'those who value the market . . . must be concerned to keep its support system in good repair'.[39] The long-run viability of the market depends on having social outcomes that are broadly seen as fair. Therefore, a government may find it necessary to intervene in the market to prevent or redress outcomes widely regarded as unjust. It may need to intervene to protect people against the unintended consequences or the excesses produced by free markets. This means especially that a balance must be struck

between encouraging market-efficient outcomes and ensuring social cohesion: 'certain market outcomes may be efficient and yet be socially unacceptable, and thus weaken the system which produces them'. Advocates for non-intervention as well as intervention should have regard for the full range of social costs and benefits their policies might entail.

This may mean, in particular, compensating under-privileged or under-resourced groups, or taking action to lessen significant disparities in resources and power on the ground that the emergence of 'two nations' is a potential threat to social cohesion and political order. The government may also intervene in the market to provide social insurance, e.g. for health or old age pensions, where it thinks that private insurance is either too costly or inadequate. The social market position also regards mass unemployment as fundamentally unjust, a severe indictment of a market economy, a potential delegitimising factor. The pursuit of full(er) employment is seen as a significant social objective. Work is a personal right, not just a commodity.

- To see that the development of the market is compatible with the continued pursuit of democratic institutions and values. While markets work best in an open society where individual responsibility, personal freedom and social trust exist, such enabling conditions have to be reproduced by political means. They do not necessarily flow from free markets alone: the social relations on which effective markets depend cannot be taken for granted. The state has to judge whether 'the market' is developing in a manner consistent with the cultural fabric of society and with the other values which help to legitimate it.

The precise relationship between state and market has to be adjusted in response to change. However, the relationship is ambiguous. German theorists themselves disagreed over how far the state should intervene in the economy either to promote market competition or to secure a greater degree of income redistribution and equality. Clearly, one may choose to privilege the market ahead of the state and vice versa.[40] The Christian Democrats and the Social Democrats disagreed on that point. The balance between state and market may tilt according to which set of social and political values are uppermost at a particular time, and there is a good deal to be said for a formula which allows electoral shifts to resolve the inevitable theoretical disagreements. The great merit of the social market idea in Germany was that after massive destruction it provided a flexible consensus within which rebuilding the nation and economy proceeded rapidly and successfully. At this moment Australia requires just such a consensus in order to mobilise collective support for restructuring.

Implications for the left

The attraction of the social market is that it combines strong support for the virtues of open and competitive markets with a legitimate role for government as the guarantor of social and political order, entitled to intervene in economy and society to promote the long-term viability of each. It conceptualises state and market as partners, not opponents. It provides a means of bypassing the kind of binary oppositions which are endemic in Anglo-Saxon liberalism. It emphasises that a democratic market society rests on ethical as well as economic principles, and the two sets of principles have to be developed concurrently—which is the challenge for politics. It picks up an earlier Weberian perspective: neither the state nor the market alone is sufficient to sustain individual freedom in bureaucratised industrial societies: each both checks and supplements the other.

The concept may be attractive to anyone who has qualms about a full-bore commitment to free market principles. In England it was taken up by Sir Keith Joseph in the 1970s, by David Owen for the Social Democrats in the 1980s, and most recently, if implicitly, by Neil Kinnock. In Australia, given the problems facing the ALP, it may be of more use to that party. It is a matter of persuading a majority on the left that the ideas one finds in the social market are not only in accord with the communitarian values of social liberalism and social democracy which predominate in the ALP, but also provide an electorally attractive response to the circumstances of the 1990s.

Fundamentally, the left in general has to come to terms with two points: first, strategies for human emancipation which made the state responsible for articulating and enforcing a central value-system, and which saw it replacing the market in economic life, too easily degenerate into unpleasant forms of statism. Longstanding liberal suspicions of state power are historically well grounded. Second, the market is here to stay—at least for the foreseeable future. There is no alternative 'big idea' available. This means taking a constructive rather than a negative approach to it. It means recognising that markets can widen the scope for choice and individual freedoms, and provide a countervailing power to the state: that competition and the pursuit of enlightened self-interest have positive features as well as negative: that there is some substance to the idea of an invisible hand through which competition between numerous buyers and sellers can limit the power of each and produce collective outcomes which are in the public interest.

For those on the left critical of the ALP's policies in office, the basic message is: 'There is no way back.' Given the overall circumstances of globalisation, as well as the particular circumstances now facing Australia, the left has to relinquish any lingering preference for replacing the price mechanism with command principles. There is widespread agreement among all OECD nations that markets handle the problems of resource allocation in huge, complex societies better than governments: that market systems are most capable of delivering the kind and the scale of goods and services which most people desire. Therefore as many economic activities as possible should be handled via markets. Having said this, however, one should add there is more than one way of organising a market economy. The central question for the 1990s is not 'Is the market good or bad, and if bad, what could replace it?' but 'What is the most appropriate constitutional and political setting for the market, in this culture at this particular time?' The issue is how best to combine market freedoms with social balance and political order.

The left overall has to accept the central thrust of economic liberalisation and restructuring. Raising productivity, eliminating all kinds of structural rigidities, pursuing workplace reform via award restructuring and enterprise bargaining, etc., is the only route open to Australia. Structural reform cannot be confined to the private sector: the necessary emphasis on competition policy and micro-economic reform means confronting the known inefficiencies of government business enterprises and asking 'How can essential services be provided to the community or business as efficiently as possible?' This means accepting the logic behind corporatisation and, in selected instances, privatisation. This is not now, perhaps, so much of a problem: thinking within the Labour movement has clearly been moving in this direction.

For some, however, legitimising the market as an integral component of a free and prosperous society requires substantial sacrifice. It means giving up long-standing socialist opposition to the private ownership of the means of production and legitimising the profit motive. It means reconceptualising the significance of 'public ownership': neither it nor the idea of a mixed economy can stand any more as a bridgehead or a half-way house on the road to a socialist society. It also means shifting one's position on social equality: avowed socialists have always emphasised substantive equality, or equality of outcomes. In a market society, the emphasis falls instead on equality of opportunity and access while accepting that outcomes will reflect differences in skill and talents. However, a social market economy is very much concerned with trying to equalise the resources which people 'bring to market' at the start of their working careers. Where free market liberals usually require formal equality of opportunity—or equality before the law—the social market model, like social democrats, would add 'equalising social conditions'. This has important policy consequences. For example, it would mean a more deliberate effort to minimise the inequalities transmitted from one generation to the next by taxing the inheritance of personal wealth through death duties. It would also mean greater emphasis on provision of educational opportunities, since level and quality of education has a major impact on subsequent life chances. The social market approach views education, on both social and economic grounds, as a collective right as well as an individual good, whose cost should be met substantially if not entirely by the state. And now more than ever, a developed society requires as much money as possible to be spent on education and training.

Certainly, some on the left will find the emphasis on the market either exaggerated or over-idealised. Drawing on the German experience, three points should be made. First, that model retains an emphasis on compassion and social justice. It acknowledges that the market alone cannot guarantee social outcomes which the great majority of society would regard as just or fair. Therefore income distribution cannot be left to the market alone: there is scope for the state to intervene in the market to compensate those who cannot hold their own in the market unaided by providing reasonable unemployment benefits, retraining and social security assistance, pensions and health benefits. There is also scope for a minimum incomes scheme. The social market, unlike the thrust of contemporary free market thinking, does not see welfare spending as an unnecessary diversion of resources to the ill-deserving, or as an obstacle to economic growth. The perspective is instead that collective responsibility for social misfortune must supplement individual responsibility in systematic ways: that the way to create a productive and creative workforce is not to threaten people with market forces and the consequences of failure, but to emphasise the individual's responsibility to look after him/her self and family while providing adequate security against disaster—and considerable state assistance to retrain in order to re-establish oneself in the workforce.[41] The social market thus tries to strike a balance between the duty to work and rights to compensation and assistance when something beyond the individual's control goes wrong. The German experience seems to show that one can have both a strong commitment to market principles and a sizeable state, including a large welfare sector.[42]

Second, although the basic reward principle in any market society will produce income inequalities, the significance of these may be lessened if the state is able to increase its spending on the social wage. As Whitlam put it, 'The quality of life depends less and less on the things which individuals obtain for themselves . . . from their personal incomes and . . . more and more on the things which the community provides for all its members from the combined resources of the community.'[43] The citizen's real standard of living depends on such things as the availability of preschool and childcare facilities, access to quality education or retraining, clean air and water, good roads, parks, cultural and recreational facilities, i.e. proper access to the services and facilities which contribute much to a decent standard of living. The social market approach implies that developing the social infrastructure available to all citizens—including a comprehensive range of social services—has now become a more important and a more feasible goal than pursuing outright social equality. In the kind of environment in which most Australians live there are a variety of ways in which governments can improve individuals' quality of life—sometimes by inducing the market to act, sometimes by providing services themselves, or by requiring private actors to desist from certain activities. The underlying principle, which stands opposed to the pure free market approach, is that in a relatively wealthy society, the state is entitled to appropriate a significant portion of the social surplus and apply it to developing facilities for the community as a whole.

Third, this approach takes a constructive but by no means uncritical approach to the market economy. It attaches a high priority to the benefits the latter can provide but recognises its downside too. The profit motive combined with the force of self-interest provides obvious possibilities for individual aggrandisement, greed and anti-social behaviour. Social market theory recognises explicitly that the material values privileged by a free-market consumer-oriented society have to be qualified and, in practice, regulated to make them compatible with the ethical principles which also help to legitimise a pluralist democracy. This too has policy implications. The state is entitled to respond to avarice or greed by placing a high marginal tax rate on very high incomes, or by utilising capital gains or wealth taxes. The social market model accepts that wealth generation involves social dimensions—cooperation and infrastructure—as well as individual effort. The state is entitled to reclaim some part of this wealth for the community, and to reclaim more from those who have done best in society; that is, the principle of collective social responsibility—or the stress on society as a social partnership—implies strong support for a progressive tax scale. And while accepting that some inequalities are inevitable, the state's concern for social cohesion and integration may cause it to intervene to ensure that inequalities fall within a socially acceptable range, or that the privileges which wealth can buy do not clash grotesquely with society's legitimating principles.

Once again the overall aim is to give as much scope as possible to free market processes while denying them complete autonomy and ensuring that they work in a manner which contributes to the long-run strength and cohesion of the society of which they form part.

Labor and the left may find it worthwhile to look further at the German experience. This does not mean trying to copy it wholesale but rather to gain insights from a parallel exercise in reconstruction and nation-building. There are some suggestive affinities: the theory and practice of co-determination, and the comprehensive system for education and training, are very relevant to current Australian strategies for workplace and union reform, which also mesh with the recent recommendations by the Finn and Carmichael reports for developing vocational education schemes. The German model also makes clear the link between economic and political reform. The energy and commitment to rebuild Germany derived in large part from national support for, and identification with, the cultural values and principles expressed through the Basic Law which provided the normative framework within which the program for economic modernisation was constructed.

Implications for the right

It is true that the term 'social market' signifies less a single precise philosophy and more a bounded spectrum of positions. The stress placed on the market or the state can vary according to the values of the party in power. This means that the concept is accessible, in principle, to the Liberal party. Indeed, the language of 'moral community' in *Fightback!* suggests the Opposition still contains members who might be happier with a social market emphasis than the current economic individualism. The Opposition's special problem is that it has become over-identified with one strand of liberal thought, which the Dries have mistakenly identified as the embodiment of classical liberalism. In fact, liberalism has always been a richer but more internally complicated body of thought than many of the current exponents of 'classical' liberalism acknowledge. The founding fathers of the neo-classical perspective, including Adam Smith, were more

aware of the social and moral aspects of community than are
some of their contemporary descendants.[44]

The recurrent problem with neo-classical liberalism is that it
tends to place too much emphasis on 'the presocial self, a solitary
and sometimes heroic individual confronting society, who is fully
formed before the confrontation begins'.[45] This encourages liberal
individualists to conceptualise society as no more than the sum
of its individual parts, held together by voluntary agreement and
contract. It also leads them to value the market as the institution
which apparently maximises the freedom of rational agents to
pursue their own interests in a variety of ways. This in turn
leads them to devalue the state as a potential opponent of freedom
and to treat it as a necessary evil, there only to uphold the order
required by the market. While liberal individualism does give rise
to many ideas of permanent value, it is doubtful if the purist
account of the preferred relations between individual, market and
state really provides a sufficient basis for maintaining a durable
society. Arguably, too many aspects of human life and association
are overlooked.[46]

If the left has to come to terms with the case for markets,
the right in Australia also has to get the market in perspective,
to stop treating it as a panacea for all social problems. The
economic 'solutions' propounded by the Liberals do not stand
alone: they are not as inherently rational or obvious as Dr Hewson
seems to think they are. They are the tip of an ideological iceberg
whose social and political ramifications are a great deal more
complicated. The Liberals have to rediscover the concept of
collective social responsibility; society cannot be broken down
into a series of contractual relationships between individuals or
firms intent on maximising their own rewards without doing
damage to the cooperative and communitarian relations which
sustain both society as an association, and organised production
itself. The Liberals also have to bring the state back in: there is
simply no guarantee that the market, through the invisible hand,
will produce outcomes that are consistent with the long-term
good or development of society. It *may* do so, and from time
to time it certainly does, but the existence of the business cycle
(to name only one such example) suggests that it does not always
do so. Some degree of management or guidance is required: the
state must retain some responsibility for assessing social and
economic trends and deciding what policies may be required to
produce either socially desirable results or the requisite production
structure, five, ten, or even twenty years ahead. To leave
outcomes wholly to market forces is socially irresponsible: because
markets are a potent source of wealth and change, the rules
which govern them must, to some degree, be crafted and

monitored by political actors to produce outcomes in the national interest. The market is, after all, a social construct; ultimately its viability will depend on the skills of those actors, and not on a hidden hand.

Notes

Chapter 1: The challenge for Labor

1. M. Gordon, *A question of leadership: Paul Keating, political fighter*, University of Queensland Press, St Lucia, 1993.
2. E.g. David Kemp, 'Defeated by fear, smear and cynicism', *The Australian*, 18 March 1993.
3. G. Barker, 'Keating stakes claim to social democracy', *The Age*, 16 January 1993.
4. *The Australian*, 1 March 1993.
5. G. Barker, 'After the Triumph, where to for Labor?', *The Age*, 27 March 1993.
6. Cf. Paul Kelly, *The end of certainty: the story of the 1980s*, Allen and Unwin, Sydney, 1992, esp. ch. 34.
7. E.g. G. Barker (note 5) wrote: Paul Keating 'sees the future and its possibilities in vibrant and sharply focused colours . . . he sees himself and his "new generation" Labor team leading Australia to greatness in the 21st Century if it can stay focused on a clear vision of where it wants to go. He is, one senior Labor MP said, "looking to establish his position in history and searching for an ideology within which he can package his ideas". Another shrewdly observed: "Paul's a bit of an aesthete: he's interested in policy that feels right, that has style and finesse. That's what he is looking for." '
8. Kelly, *End of certainty*, ch. 1: the Australian Settlement, or the governing consensus on which Australia was founded and which

informed development for most of this century included five main ideas: the White Australia policy (formally abandoned in 1965–66); Industry Protection, Wage Arbitration, State Paternalism, and Imperial Benevolence.

Chapter 2: The background

1. *Australian exports: performance obstacles and issues of assistance*, Report of the Committee for review of export market development assistance (the Hughes report) AGPS, Canberra, 1989, p. 8.
2. Tim Duncan and John Fogarty, *Australia and Argentina: on parallel paths*, Melbourne University Press, Melbourne, 1984, p. 104.
3. B. Schedvin, 'The Australian economy on the hinge of history,' *The Australian Economic Review*, First Quarter, 1987.
4. Susan Strange, *States and markets*, Pinter, London, 1988, p. 62: 'the sum of all the arrangements determining what is produced, by whom and for whom, by what method and on what terms'.
5. See H.V. Emy and O.E. Hughes, *Australian politics: realities in conflict*, Macmillan, Melbourne, second ed. 1991, pp. 23–7.
6. *Australia's foreign debt: choices for the future*, National Summit on Debt, Business Council of Australia, Melbourne, 1990. Also comments by J. Stanford in J. Stanford (ed.), *Industrial policy in Australia and Europe*, AGPS, Canberra, 1992, p. 52.
7. E.g, comments by Sir Arvi Parbo, 'Snake oils and bears in the cave', *Australia and World Affairs*, No. 11, Summer, 1991. This number also reprints 'An Expression of Deep Concern' from nine other leading business figures.
8. Brian Loton, 'Advance Australia—where?' (1989 Sir Robert Garran memorial oration), *Australian Journal of Public Administration*, vol. 49:3, 1990. Loton also made sharp criticisms of Labor's lopsided policies late in 1992, *The Australian*, 20 October 1992.
9. A point emphasised by Alan Wood, 'How Labor lost business', *The Australian*, 20 October 1992.
10. See esp. John Carroll, 'Economic rationalism and its consequences', in John Carroll and Robert Manne (eds), *Shutdown: the failure of economic rationalism and how to rescue Australia*, Text Publishing, Melbourne, 1992.
11. Attributed to Rolf Gerritsen, 'Authority, persuasion and Exchange (revisited): The public policy of internationalising the Australian economy', IPSA working paper, Canberra, September 1992.
12. Ralph Evans, 'The *Global Challenge* report and the clash of paradigms', in M. Costa and M. Easson (eds), *Australian industry: what policy?* Sydney, Pluto Press, 1991.
13. Sir Arvi Parbo wrote an open letter to the press (1 October 1992) to make this point, and was supported strongly by chief executives from six leading companies (*The Australian*, 2 October 1992).
14. A point made frequently in press reports. See also Stanford, 'Industrial policy'; Greg Whitwell, 'The triumph of economic rationalism: the Treasury and the market economy', *Australian Journal of Public Administration*, 49:2, 1990.
15. Evans, 'The *Global Challenge* report'; Carroll, 'Economic rationalism'.
16. See e.g. Lester Thurow, *Head to head: the coming economic battle among Japan, Europe and America*, Allen and Unwin, Sydney, 1993;

J. Stopford and S. Strange, with J. Henley, *Rival states, rival firms; competition for world market shares*, Cambridge UP, Cambridge, 1991.

17. Evans, 'The *Global Challenge* report'.

18. See P.N. Junankar and C.A. Kapuscinski, *The costs of unemployment in Australia*, EPAC Background paper No. 24, AGPS, Canberra, December 1992: if the unemployment rate in 1991–92 had remained at 6.5 rather than 11.4 per cent, the nation's GDP might have been 6 per cent or $23 billion higher. The paper also models the social costs arising from unemployment.

19. See e.g. Helen Hughes, 'The possible dream', *Weekend Australian*, 13–14 March 1993.

20. In 1988, Australian social security transfers as a percentage of GDP was 9.3 per cent compared with the OECD average of 14 per cent. On a broader definition of social (welfare) expenditure Australia has always been in the bottom half of OECD countries, and often close to the bottom. See esp. F.G. Castles, *Australian public policy and economic vulnerability*, Allen and Unwin, Sydney, 1988.

21. See also David Denemark, 'Social democracy and the politics of crisis in New Zealand, Britain and Sweden', in M. Holland and J. Boston (eds), *The fourth Labour government*, Oxford University Press, Auckland, second ed., 1990.

22. Saulwick-Age polls in May 1992 revealed that two-thirds of respondents doubted the ability of either party to govern well, *The Age*, 12 May 1992.

23. J. Brett, 'The end of the parties', *Arena Magazine*, No. 1, October–November 1992; H.V. Emy, 'From liberalism to conservatism? changing political alignments in the 1990s', *Quadrant*, December 1991; B.A. Santamaria, 'Whither Australia?' *Australia and World Affairs*, No. 11, Summer 1991; Boris Frankel, *From the prophets deserts come: the struggle to reshape Australian political culture*, Arena Publishing, Melbourne, 1992.

24. For background see Emy and Hughes, *Australian politics*, chs. 5 and 6.

25. Whitwell, 'The triumph of economic rationalism'.

26. Marian Sawer (ed.), *Australia and the New Right*, Allen and Unwin, Sydney, 1982; Ruth Levitas (ed.), *The ideology of the New Right*, Polity Press, Cambridge, 1986.

27. M. Pusey, *Economic rationalism in Canberra: a nation-building state changes its mind*, Cambridge University Press, Melbourne, 1991; Carroll and Manne (eds), *Shutdown*; P. Vintila, J. Phillimore and P. Newman (eds), *Markets, morals and manifestoes: Fightback! and the politics of economic rationalism in the 1990s*, Murdoch University Perth, Institute for Science and Technology Policy, 1992; S. Rees, G. Rodley and F. Stilwell (eds), *Beyond the market: alternatives to economic rationalism*, Pluto Press, Sydney, 1993.

28. i.e. the point at which production for trade in increasingly distant markets began to outpace production for more immediate consumption.

29. Cf. Lester Thurow, *Dangerous currents: the state of economics*, Oxford University Press, Oxford, 1983.

30. cf. Geoff Dow, 'The economic consequences of economists', *Australian Journal of Political Science*, 27:2 1992.

31. cf. J. Stopford and S. Strange, *Rival states, rival firms*.

32. Cited by Stanford, 'Industrial policy', p. 50.

33. Loton, 'Advance Australia—where?'; *Australian manufacturing and*

industry development: policies and prospects for the 1990s and into the 21st century, ACTU, Melbourne, 1990.

34. Whitwell, 'The triumph of economic rationalism'; B. Dyster and D. Meredith, *Australia in the international economy*, Cambridge University Press, Melbourne, 1990; also Dow, 'The economic consequences of economists'.

35. L. Haddad, 'The rise and fall of planning: a global perspective', *Australian Journal of Public Administration*, 49:2, 1990, esp. p. 99.

36. Karl Schiller, cited by D.T. Charles in Stanford (ed.), *Industrial policy*, p. 34.

37. Australian Industries Development Corporation.

38. Economic Planning and Advisory Council; Australian Manufacturing Council.

39. A. Cox (ed.), *State, finance and industry*, Wheatsheaf, Brighton, 1986.

40. cf. J. Stewart, 'Industry policy and why Australia needs one', *Canberra Bulletin of Public Administration*, No. 59, August 1989.

41. G.C. Lodge and E.G. Vogel (eds), *Ideology and national competitiveness: an analysis of nine countries*, Harvard Business School, Boston, 1987.

42. Also, Thurow, *Head to head*; Dow, 'The economic consequences of economists'.

43. cf. M. Olson, 'Rapid growth as a destabilising force', *Journal of Economic History*, 23:4, 1963.

44. The governor of the Reserve Bank, Mr B. Fraser, called for a White Paper, similar to the 1945 document on post-war reconstruction, to define Australia's long-term economic priorities, and to 'outline a sound, stable and credible policy framework to assist longer-term decision-making, and to help create a constituency for change that is not driven by crisis situations', *The Australian*, 1 December 1992.

Chapter 3: Structural problems

1. D. Horne, *The lucky country*, Penguin Books, Melbourne. 1964; D. Horne, *Money made us*, Penguin Books, Melbourne, 1976; C. McGregor, *Profile of Australia*, Penguin Books, Melbourne, 1968; R. Conway, *The great Australian stupor*, Sun Books, Melbourne, 1971; M. Walsh, *Poor little rich country*, Penguin Books, Melbourne, 1979; F. Hilmer, *When the luck runs out*, Harper and Row, Sydney, 1985.

2. P.D. Wilde, 'Economic restructuring and Australia's changing role in the world economic system', in F.E. Ian Hamilton (ed.), *Industrialisation in developing and peripheral regions*, Croom Helm, London, 1986; R.E. Caves and L.B. Krause (eds), *The Australian economy: a view from the north*, Allen and Unwin, Sydney, 1984.

3. Caves and Krause, *Australian economy*, p. 5; 1987 figure from H.V. Emy and O.E. Hughes, *Australian politics: realities in conflict*, Macmillan, Melbourne, second edition 1991, p. 13.

4. A.L. Lougheed, *Australia in the world economy*, McPhee-Gribble, Melbourne, 1988; B. Dyster and D. Meredith, *Australia in the international economy*, Cambridge University Press, Melbourne, 1990.

5. An American magazine (*Money*, October 1991) ranked Australia as having the second highest standard of living in the world behind

the United States. Countries were rated on such criteria as health care, employment opportunities, house and car ownership, tertiary enrolments and holidays (*The Age*, 6 October 1991). Japan's income per head is roughly 80 per cent higher than Australia's, but if one takes account of cultural and environmental factors which are not readily quantifiable, the suggested gap between the two virtually disappears. Australians have more leisure time, live in less cramped conditions, have ready access to many recreational facilities which are in short supply and expensive in Japan, and enjoy high quality food and wine at prices well below those in Japan. I. Castles, 'Living standards in Sydney and Japanese cities—a comparison', in Kyoko Sheridan (ed.), *The Australian economy in the Japanese mirror*, University of Queensland Press, Brisbane, 1992. Note too that only 42 per cent of Japanese homes are sewered against 90 per cent in Australia.

6. From a report by the Australian Federation of Construction Contractors and the Australian Local Government Association, summarised in *The Weekend Australian*, 1–2 February 1992.

7. *The Age*, 3 May 1991; *The Australian*, 22 June 1992.

8. *OECD Economic survey of Australia, 1992* reported in *The Australian* and *The Age*, 1 May 1992.

9. H. Kahn and T. Pepper, *Will she be right? The future of Australia*, University of Queensland Press, Brisbane, 1980.

10. See esp. C.B. Schedvin, 'The Australian economy on the hinge of history', *The Australian Economic Review*, First Quarter, 1987.

11. R. Higgott, 'The politics of Australia's international economic relations', *Australian Journal of Political Science*, Vol. 26, No. 1, 1991, p. 5.

12. From R.G. Gregory, 'How much are Australia's economy and economic policy influenced by the world economy?' in F.G. Castles (ed.), *Australia compared: people, policies and politics*, Allen and Unwin, Sydney, 1991, p. 104.

13. *The Age*, 2 June 1986.

14. *The Australian*, 18 December 1991 and 5 February 1992.

15. *The Age*, 20 September 1991.

16. *The Age*, 14 January 1992.

17. P. Drucker, 'The changed world economy', *Foreign Affairs*, Vol. 64, No. 4, 1986, p. 769.

18. F.H. Gruen, 'How bad is Australia's economic performance and why?', Discussion paper 127, Centre for Economic Policy Research, ANU 1985, p. 31.

19. *The global challenge: Australian manufacturing in the 1990s*, Final Report of the Pappas Carter Evans and Koop/Telesis Study, Australian Manufacturing Council, Melbourne, July 1990, p. 18.

20. Note especially Robert Reich, *The work of nations*, Vintage Books, New York, 1992; Kenichae Ohmae, *The borderless world: power and strategy in the interlinked economy*, Fontana, London, 1990.

21. Drucker, 'Changed world economy', p. 773.

22. Reich, *Work of nations*, p. 83.

23. *The global challenge*, ch. 1.

24. Ibid. ch. 1. In fact, if one grouped Australia's exports of semi-processed goods in the resources rather than the manufacturing sector, then the trade gap in consumer products and all forms of industrial equipment is around $35 billion annually (p. 128).

25. See P. Ewer, W. Higgins and A. Stevens, *Unions and the future of Australian manufacturing*, Allen and Unwin, Sydney, 1987, ch. 3.
26. K. Anderson and R. Garnaut, 'The political economy of manufacturing protection in Australia', in C. Findlay and R. Garnaut (eds), *The political economy of manufacturing protection: experiences of ASEAN and Australia*, Allen and Unwin, Sydney, 1987.
27. M. Olson, 'Australia in the perspective of *The rise and fall of nations*', Centre for Economic Policy and Research, Discussion Paper 109, ANU, 1984.
28. See R. Stewart, 'Industrial policy', in Randal G. Stewart and Christine Jennett (eds), *Hawke and Australian public policy: consensus and restructuring*, Macmillan, Melbourne, 1990.
29. *Australia and the northeast Asian ascendancy*, AGPS, Canberra, 1989.
30. Cited by R. Garnaut in *The Australian Quarterly*, Autumn, 1991, p. 16.
31. See also F.G. Castles, 'Australia and Sweden: The Politics of Economic Vulnerability', *Thesis XI*, No. 16, 1987; *Australian public policy and economic vulnerability*, Allen and Unwin, Sydney, 1988.
32. Caves and Krause, *The Australian economy*, p. 13.
33. E. Luard, *The management of the world economy*, Macmillan, London, 1983, p. 67; *Australian Exports* (The Hughes Report), p. 9.
34. Dyster and Meredith, *Australia in the international economy*, p. 254; *The Age*, 28 March 1991.
35. *Developing Australia's national competitiveness*, Business Council, Melbourne, 1991, p. 45.
36. *Australian exports*, p. xix and p. 9.
37. P.J. Drake and J.P. Nieuwenhuysen, *Economic growth for Australia: agenda for action*, Oxford University Press and CEDA, Melbourne, 1988, p. 7.
38. Dyster and Meredith, p. 291.
39. Details from *The global challenge*, ch. 1.
40. From M.T. Daly and M.I. Logan, *The brittle rim: finance, business and the Pacific region*, Penguin Books, Melbourne, 1989, ch. 1.
41. Association of South-East Asian Nations: Indonesia, Malaysia, Philippines, Singapore, Thailand.
42. *Brittle rim*, ch. 1; *Global challenge*, ch. 1.
43. *Brittle rim*, ch. 1; Drake and Nieuwenhuysen, *Economic growth*, p. 8.
44. *Australia and north-east Asia in the 1990s: accelerating change*, Department of Foreign Affairs and Trade, AGPS, Canberra, 1992, p. 165.
45. *The Australian*, 10 April 1992 (special survey).
46. *Australia and north-east Asia*, p. 13.
47. *Australia and the northeast Asian ascendancy* (the argument was restated with fresh data in *Australia and north-east Asia*).
48. *Australia and north-east Asia*, p. 49.
49. *Global Challenge*, p. 8.
50. *Australia and north-east Asia*, p. 53.
51. *The Age*, 30 April 1991.
52. Dennis Muller in *The Age*, 21 and 27 April 1992. A Saulwick Age poll found that 69 per cent of respondents believed Australia was basically separate from Asia while 54 per cent welcomed and 40 per cent opposed investment from Asia. Another poll revealed a substantial minority (36 per cent) did not consider any of Australia's eight major Asian neighbours to be trustworthy.

53. Cited by Brian Loton, 'Advance Australia—where?'

54. *The Australian*, 29 January 1992 (feature article).

55. H. Hughes, 'Australia and the world environment', in J. Scutt (ed.), *Poor nation of the Pacific: Australia's future*, Allen and Unwin, Sydney, 1985, p. 3.

56. The following pages draw on Emy and Hughes, *Australian politics: realities in conflict*, chs. 1 and 2. For more current detail see, e.g., *Student Economic Briefs* prepared by David Clark and published annually by the *Australian Financial Review*; INDECS, *State of play: the Australian economic policy debate*, published annually by Allen and Unwin, Sydney.

57. From Dyster and Meredith, *Australia in the international economy*, p. 252, 270.

58. Mr Dawkins, quoted in *The Age*, 5 May 1992; Treasury, *Economic round-up*, Summer 1991, pp. 10–11.

59. Ross Garnaut, 'The end of protection and the beginnings of a modern industrial economy: Australia in the 1990s', *Australian Quarterly*, Autumn 1991.

60. *Economic round-up*, Summer 1991, p. 11.

61. Australia's gross debt is considerably larger at $203 billion. However, Australians also invest and own assets in other countries which generate property income for Australia. Net debt refers to the amount owing after allowance has been made for the income generated by Australians' overseas investments.

62. See e.g. 'Current account adjustment: options for the 1990s', Economic Planning Advisory Council, Council Paper No. 50, Canberra, May 1992.

63. Bureau of Industry Economics, 'Manufacturing enterprises investment and other strategies for growth', Discussion paper 8, Canberra, 1990, p. 9.

64. See e.g. Peter L. Daniels, 'Australia's foreign debt: searching for the benefits', *Economic Papers*, Vol. 11, No. 1, 1992.

65. In September 1986 both Moody's and Standard and Poor downgraded Australia's credit rating from AAA to AA1. In August and September 1989, they downgraded it again to AA2, putting Australia into the third rank of international borrowers. This marginally increased the cost of borrowing. Several state governments and their public utilities were similarly downgraded because of their unacceptably high levels of indebtedness.

66. INDECS, *State of play 6: the Australian economic policy debate*, Allen and Unwin, Sydney, 1990, p. 116.

67. Treasury, *Economic round-up*, Summer 1991, p. 8. *The Australian*, 5 March 1993.

68. Glenda Korporaal, 'Australia's foreign debt: the killer boomerang', *The Age*, 11 January 1991.

69. It fell from 8.7 per cent of GDP in March 1989 to 5.46 per cent in December 1991. This was the lowest point ever recorded in 32 years of quarterly statistics. *The Age*, 19 March 1992.

Chapter 4: Labor and structural reform

1. For further details, see e.g. B. Galligan and G. Singleton (eds), *Business and government under Labor*, Longman Cheshire, Melbourne, 1991; H.V. Emy and O.E. Hughes, *Australian politics: realities in*

conflict, Macmillan, Melbourne, second edition, 1991; C. Jennett and R.G. Stewart (eds), *Hawke and Australian public policy: consensus and restructuring*, Macmillan, Melbourne, 1990; P. Ewer et al. *Politics and the Accord*, Pluto Press, Sydney, 1991.

2. From a report in the *Bulletin*, quoted by Coleene Anger in the *Australian Journal of Public Administration*, Vol. 49, No. 3, 1990, p. 250.

3. M.A. Keating, 'The nature and significance of overloaded government', *Australian Journal of Public Administration*, Vol. 43, No. 1, 1984.

4. Anger (ibid.) p. 250.

5. J.S. Dawkins, 'Privatisation and deregulation: myths and practicalities', *Journal of Australian Political Economy* 20, October 1986.

6. *The Australian*, 7 September 1992.

7. 'Micro-economic reform', Economic Planning and Advisory Council Paper No. 42, May 1990, p. 3. For further detail, see P. Forsyth (ed.), *Microeconomic reform in Australia*, Allen and Unwin, Sydney, 1992.

8. *Annual report of the Industry Commission, 1989–90*, Canberra, 1990, pp. 3–6.

9. *Annual Report of the Industry Commission*, 1990–91, Canberra 1991, pp. 9–10, 12, 25–6.

10. Ibid. p. 9.

11. Ibid. pp. 9–10.

12. Ibid. p. 15.

13. *The Age* and *The Australian*, 1 and 2 June 1992.

14. Interstate Commission, *Waterfront investigation: preliminary finding and discussion papers*, AGPS, Canberra, 1989.

15. *The Weekend Australian*, 26–27 October 1991.

16. *The Age*, 10 April 1989.

17. Waterfront Industry Reform Authority, Final Report, October 1992. Other data from *The Australian*, 26–27 and 30 October 1991; 13 and 26 February 1992.

18. Cabotage means that coastal shipping must be licensed and, whenever possible, coastal trade carried in Australian controlled and crewed ships. The government established the Shipping Industry Reform Authority in mid-1989. This has overseen several reforms, including crew reductions through redundancy packages, and a more flexible use of the permit system. See generally, Industry Commission, *Annual Report, 1990–91*, Appendix 1, pp. 52–58.

19. The four were: the 'Australian Nation principle': issues of national importance to be resolved cooperatively with reference to the social, political and economic imperatives of nationhood; the 'subsidiarity' principle: responsibility for regulation and allocation of public goods should be devolved to the greatest extent consistent with the national interest; the 'structural efficiency' principle: micro-economic reform in the private sector should be mirrored in the public; and the 'accountability' principle: the structure of intergovernmental arrangements should promote democratic accountability. *Intergovernmental News*, Vol. 4, No. 1, November 1991.

20. The best known critics of the centralised system, and the strongest exponents of a fully deregulated labour market, were the members of the H.R. Nicholls Society, formed in early 1986. See e.g. *Arbitration in Contempt: Proceedings of the H.R. Nicholls Society*, The

H.R. Nicholls Society, Melbourne, 1986; the Society published an annual volume of proceedings, as follows: *Trade union reform* (1986); *The light on the hill* (1987); *Back to basics* (1988); *In search of the magic pudding* (1989); *No ticket no start* (1989); *The legacy of 'the hungry mile'* (1989).

21. There are many examples of this in the references cited in note 19. See also J. Hyde and J. Nurick (eds), *Wages wasteland*, Hale and Iremonger, Sydney, 1985; R. Blandy and J. Niland (eds), *Alternatives to arbitration*, Allen and Unwin, Sydney, 1986.

22. See e.g. H. Stretton, 'The quality of leading Australians', *Daedalus*, Vol. 114, Winter 1985. Also EPAC Council Paper No. 45, 'Improving Australia's International Competitiveness,' Canberra, 1991.

23. See F. Stilwell, *The Accord . . . and beyond*, Pluto Press, Sydney, 1986; P. Ewer et al., *Politics and the Accord*.

24. *Politics and the Accord*, p. 32.

25. Ibid. p. 31.

26. *The Age*, 20 March 1990.

27. *The Age*, 20 April 1991.

28. Ibid.

29. *The Age*, 22 April 1991.

30. The IRC also disagreed with the ACTU's view of how to consolidate minimum rates of pay. It was prepared to accept that some workers, or some classifications, might receive less money following an efficiency review.

31. Shane Green, 'An offside umpire is Labor's loss', *The Australian*, 18 March 1992; Geoffrey Barker, 'The IRC: facing death by a thousand cuts', *The Age*, 24 March 1992.

32. *The Australian*, 22 June 1992.

33. *The Age*, 1 August 1992.

34. So too was the Australian Chamber of Manufactures. Its industrial relations director, Mr Barry Watchorn, said: 'One would need to feel fairly optimistic with the unions to say that [they would encourage productivity agreements] regardless of any need to do so. There's any number of unions who regard the whole process of productivity and efficiency improvements and the processes they have to go through as a vast and unpleasant imposition.' *The Australian*, 22 June 1992.

35. Business Council of Australia, *Enterprise-based bargaining units: a better way of working*, Joint Study with the Industrial Relations Study Commission, Melbourne, 1989.

36. *The Age*, 21 March 1990.

37. *The Australian*, 14 January 1992.

38. *The Age*, 27 February 1992.

39. *The Age*, 29 July 1992.

40. Toyota stipulated single union coverage before it would proceed with a new $500 million motor vehicle plant in Melbourne's west. The ACTU agreed, and also agreed to single union coverage for the workforce of Optus, the second telecommunications carrier; and a $2 billion Compact Steel Mill to be built in Western Australia.

41. *The Weekend Australian*, 14–15 March 1992 (special article).

42. EPAC Council Paper No. 45, 'Improving Australia's international competitiveness', listed a dozen such cases. Major agreements were in place at Tubemakers, Rheem, Email, ICI, Toyota, Ford, BTR Nylex, BHP Steel and AMECON, among others. In 1990, the Shepparton Preserving Company set a major precedent in winning

approval to vary the length of the working day and lower special allowances in order to stay in business. In March 1992 a similar benchmark deal was approved by the IRC at the Southern Cross Machinery factory in Toowoomba. In June the IRC approved the reduction of 50 federal awards in the meat industry to three minimum rates awards covering about 20 000 employees.

43. *The Age*, 29 July 1992.
44. *Industrial Relations and Management Newsletter*, Vol. 8, Issue 11, December 1991.
45. Shane Green, in *The Australian*, 29 October 1991.
46. *The Australian*, 22 April 1993. During the campaign, Mr Keating also announced that wage increases negotiated with the ACTU under Accord Mark VII were conditional on the progress made towards the government's target of 500 000 new jobs by 1996.
47. B. Graetz and I. McAllister, *Dimensions of Australian society*, Macmillan, Melbourne, 1988, pp. 151, 156.
48. *Foundations for the 'clever country'*, Australian Vice-Chancellors' Committee, Report for the 1992–94 Triennium, Canberra, March 1991.
49. *Higher Education, a policy statement*, AGPS, Canberra, 1988; *Higher Education: quality and diversity in the 1990s*, AGPS, Canberra, October 1991.
50. *The Age*, 19 June 1991.
51. *The Bulletin*, 5 May 1992.
52. Ibid.
53. From a speech by Mr Keating, *The Australian*, 21 July 1992; also Tim Duncan, 'The changing face of the workforce', *The Weekend Australian*, 18–19 July 1992.
54. The report by the Taskforce on Pathways in Education and Training, in Victoria, chaired by Mr Ivan Deveson, April 1992.
55. *Young people's participation in post-compulsory education and training*, Report of the Australian Education Council Review Committee, chair: Mr Brian Finn, AGPS, Canberra, July 1991.
56. *The Australian vocational certificate training system*, Report by the Employment and Skills Formation Council (National Board of Employment, Education and Training), chair: Mr Laurie Carmichael, AGPS, Canberra, March 1992.
57. See esp. L. Carmichael, 'Group solution to work problems', *The Australian*, 2 June 1992. By late 1992, the commonwealth had accepted that education in seven key areas of competence should be a compulsory feature of all post-compulsory education in Australia, although it was not clear whether that included universities or not. The Mayer Committee was appointed to recommend appropriate descriptions for the seven. Its summary report, released in March 1993, met increasing criticism.
58. *The Australian*, 28 July 1992. The government also announced a Landcare and Environment Action program to be introduced over 3 years to employ 6000 young people at a cost of $135 million.
59. The unions also agreed to support lower wages for people working on public job-creation schemes.

Chapter 5: The Liberal alternative

1. Quotations drawn from *Fightback! It's your Australia,* a shorter version of the main document.
2. For more background, see Emy and Hughes, *Australian politics,* ch. 2 and ch. 5, esp. pp. 202ff.
3. Who rules the kingdom determines the religion of the people.
4. The Dries (or economic rationalists) believed strongly in small government and the virtues of free markets. The Wets were more cautious in supporting the free market and tolerated a more substantial role for governments.
5. In October 1991 Mr Costello and Mr Howard both made speeches stressing that economic rationalism was not a stand-alone philosophy: 'Politics is about the kind of society we have and the kind of people we are. The breadth and reach of the vision of a political party must always go above and beyond its economic dimension.' Mr Howard, *The Australian,* 29 October 1991.
6. For a strong critique, see P. Vintila, J. Phillimore and P. Newman (eds), *Markets, morals and manifestoes: Fightback! and the politics of economic rationalism in the 1990s,* Murdoch University, Institute for Science and Technology Policy, 1992.
7. Notably, for families earning up to $50 000 p.a. there would be no tax payable on up to $2000 interest on new savings.
8. Wholesale taxes were estimated to add $1 billion to total business costs. Payroll tax had risen from 3.5 per cent of wages in 1970 to 7 per cent of wages and all benefits by 1991. It raised at least $5.5 billion for the states.
9. K. Davidson, 'Tax cuts a luxury we cannot afford', *The Age,* 17 September, 1992; F. Castles, 'Public expenditure and the culture of dependency' in P. Vintila et al. (eds), *Markets, morals and manifestoes.*
10. See esp. E. Savage and G. Jones, 'A distributional analysis of the *Fightback!* tax proposals', in *Markets, morals and manifestoes.*
11. See esp. Brian Howe, 'Social justice—visions and strategies', in D. Kerr (ed.), *Reinventing Socialism,* Pluto Press, Sydney, 1992.
12. *The Australian,* 23 October 1991.
13. *The Age,* 15 June 1991.
14. G. Barker, 'The self-made man and the Ferrari syndrome', *The Age,* 29 August 1991.
15. A point nicely illustrated by Dr Hewson's not wholly rhetorical question during his budget reply speech: 'What's wrong with working 7 days a week, 365 days a year?' (20 August 1992).
16. A Saulwick Age poll found that 49 per cent of respondents preferred direct employer–employee negotiations; 22 per cent preferred a system in which trade unions negotiated with employers, without recourse to the IRC; 22 per cent preferred a system in which the IRC decides (*The Age,* 15 July 1992). A Newspoll found nearly two-thirds of respondents would prefer to negotiate pay and conditions directly with their employers rather than have a trade union act on their behalf. (*The Australian,* 29 July 1992).
17. In a speech to a New Zealand audience, he said: 'When I look at New Zealand, I draw a number of particular conclusions from your experience . . . you can't move too quickly or do too much in my view. The longer you drag the adjustment process out, the more pain you inflict on people. Indeed, you can avoid almost all that

pain . . . if you move decisively and carry your constituency with you. You can't tinker. It is really a big bang approach to policy.' *The Age*, 21 May 1992.

18. E.g. *The Age*, 24 January 1992.
19. *The Age*, 25 January 1992.
20. *The Australian*, 5 May 1992.
21. *The Age*, 23 May 1992.
22. This was well put by John Mathews, 'Competitive edge is on the line', *Australian Financial Review*, 22 October 1992: '. . . the productivity paradox at the heart of the coalition's industrial relations policy. By *maximising* the freedom of choice of *individual* employers, they in effect *minimise* the freedom of choice of the *country as a whole* to shift itself onto a high-wage, high-skill, high-productivity trajectory' (original emphasis). Note also Bill Kelty, 'Award-winning system gives workers a fair go', *The Australian*, 31 August 1992.
23. For example, in early 1991, waterfront reform was going very slowly. In addressing the National Press Club in March 1991, Dr Hewson foreshadowed that an Opposition government would use troops if necessary to bypass resistance on the waterfront.
24. E.g. Glenn Milne, 'The worms in Hewson's rose', *The Australian*, 7 February 1992: 'Hewson is a rigidly ideological political leader absolutely committed to imposing his supply-side, free market blueprint on Australia . . . Some colleagues who have sat through private meetings with the Opposition leader describe his inability to tolerate policy deviation in the interests of pragmatism as "frightening". Also G. Barker, 'Zealot of the market-place', *The Age*, 14 August 1991.
25. Interviewed by Michelle Grattan in *The Age*, 13 February 1992.
26. In October 1991 Dr Hewson made a strong attack on ACOSS, which Mr Julian Disney, the council's economics spokesperson, dismissed as a 'farrago of ignorance, nonsense and prejudice', *The Age*, 5 October 1991; J. Disney, 'Hewson's poor show strains charity', *The Australian*, 16 October 1991; in February 1992, a similar row ensued when Dr Hewson accused the ACF under Mr Toyne of pursuing 'a partisan political agenda'. *The Weekend Australian*, 8-9 February 1992.
27. E.g. *The Australian*, 20 February 1992.

Chapter 6: The industry policy debate

1. See e.g. 'Competing on World Markets', EPAC Discussion Paper 90/08, December 1990.
2. Cf. J. Stewart, 'Industry policy and why Australia needs one', *Canberra Bulletin of Public Administration*, No. 59, August 1989.
3. Cf. D. Kerr (ed.), *Reinventing socialism*, Pluto Press, Sydney, 1992.
4. Tony Cole, interview in *The Age*, 13 December 1990.
5. Ibid. See also annual reports of the Industry Commission.
6. Also J. Stanford (ed.), *Industrial policy in Australia and Europe*, AGPS, Canberra, 1992.
7. See R. Stewart, 'Industrial policy' in C. Jennett and R. Stewart (eds), *Hawke and Australian public policy: consensus and restructuring*, Macmillan, Melbourne, 1990.
8. For details, see Stanford (ed.), *Industrial policy*, pp. 40–2; B.

Galligan and G. Singleton (eds), *Business and government under Labor*, Longman Cheshire, Melbourne, 1991; B. Galligan and A. Capling, *Beyond the protective state: the political economy of Australia's manufacturing industry policy*, Cambridge UP, Sydney, 1992.

9. D.T. Charles, 'Common themes between Australian and European industrial policy', in Stanford (ed.), *Industrial policy*, p. 34.

10. See R. Stewart, 'Industrial policy', in Jennett and Stewart (eds), *Hawke and Australian public policy*.

11. Ibid. pp. 125–6.

12. See, generally, 'Science, technology and industrial development', EPAC Discussion Paper 91/08, September 1991.

13. Stanford (ed.), *Industrial policy*, p. 45.

14. Ibid. p.47.

15. See, generally, *Australian exports: performance, obstacles, and issues of assistance*, Report of the (Hughes) Committee for Review of Export Market Development Assistance, AGPS, Canberra, 1989.

16. See especially its *Annual Report for 1989–90*, ch. 4.

17. Many of the IC's reports upset the industry group affected, notably the car industry, electronics, telecommunications and the electricity supply industry. The common complaint was the excessive theoreticism of IC reports, plus wilful misunderstanding of the problems an industry faced.

18. *The Australian Business Monthly*, June 1992, published a survey of 189 'key business executives': 56 per cent said even the complete abolition of tariffs would have no impact on their businesses, 40 per cent predicted tariff cuts would cause cuts in investment and employment, 4 per cent expected an increase in investment, 53 per cent thought free trade would best serve Australia's long-term interests, 41 per cent disagreed. Only 22 per cent thought unilateral tariff reductions responsible. Business generally thought the parties expected too much from tariff cuts. *The Bulletin*, 5 May 1992.

19. The following is based generally on *The global challenge: Australian manufacturing in the 1990s*, Final Report of the Pappas Carter Evans and Koop/Telesis Study, Australian Manufacturing Council, Melbourne, July 1990; *Developing Australia's National Competitiveness*, a report by Access Economics for the Business Council of Australia, Melbourne 1991. Also, R. Evans, 'The *global challenge* report and the clash of paradigms', in M. Costa and M. Easson (eds), *Australian industry: what policy?* Pluto Press, Sydney, 1991. S. Bell, 'The travails of industry policy in Australia', *Australian Quarterly*, Autumn, 1991.

20. *The Global challenge*, p. 10.

21. E.g. a mineral sand like zircon, fetching $300 a tonne, when fused at high temperatures with alumina, produces refractory (brick) cruciforms which sell for $2500 a tonne. Cruciforms are used to make glass-factory ovens where they produce substantial energy savings. The Australian mineral sands firm Consolidated Rutile in 1992 entered a partnership with a French-based multinational, specialising in industrial ceramics, to produce cruciforms, mainly for Asian markets. *Business Review Weekly*, 17 January 1992.

22. *The Global challenge*, p. 105. *The Australian*, 30 May 1992 (advertisement by the AMC).

23. The Asian food market is expanding at 22 per cent a year and is predicted to be worth $150 billion by 2000. In July 1992 the government announced a $12.7 million plan to promote Australia

as a supplier of clean, safe, high quality foods to Asia. Currently the processed food industry exports about $2.3 billion of produce a year (and employs about 170 000 people or one-sixth of the manufacturing workforce). The industry hoped to raise this to $7 billion by the end of the decade. *The Age* and *The Australian*, 20 July 1992.

24. *The Global challenge*, p. 107.
25. Ibid. p. 108, for other examples.
26. Industry Commission, *Export of education services*, (Report No.12) Canberra, 1991, pp. 36–9.
27. AMC figures, *The Australian*, 16 May 1992.
28. A Report by Tourism Workforce 2000 (*The Australian*, 13 July 1992), a federal government study, forecast that employment growth in tourism would be three times the rate projected for employment generally, and would generate 209 000 new jobs by 2000. Demand for multilingual staff would triple by the end of the decade to 97 000.
29. *The Global challenge*, p. 21.
30. Ibid. p. 22.
31. Stephen Cohen and John Zysman, *Manufacturing matters: the myth of the post-industrial economy*, Basic Books, New York, 1987.
32. Ibid. p. 18–19.
33. Ibid. p. 22.
34. *Vision 10*, a Ten Year Vision Statement produced by the Manufacturing Council of Victoria in May 1992, cited research by the National Institute of Economic and Industry Research to claim that for any 100 jobs created in Victorian manufacturing, an additional 147 jobs are created elsewhere in Victoria. Australia-wide, that figure rises to 185. p. 10.
35. Ibid. p. 49.
36. Major companies relocating in Asia included Ansell (a subsidiary of Pacific Dunlop, and the world's largest condom producer), Email, Plessey, STC, HyQ (electronics), Amcor (partially), Memtec, Kambrook and Philips (both partially), Black and Decker, Adidas, Eastcoast and Country Road (partially). In the year to November 1990 the number of manufacturing jobs fell by 47 000 (including TCF). *The Sunday Age*, 31 March 1991, 19 January 1992. A survey of NSW manufacturers in 1992 found 2 per cent had gone offshore and a further 8.5 per cent were considering moving. Having been encouraged to invest overseas, one study found that projected direct Australian investment in manufacturing overseas would rise from around $7 billion in 1989 to $20 billion by 1999. Earning from overseas investments would double to $1.5 billion a year, but at the cost of domestic employment. *The Weekend Australian*, 8–9 August 1992.
37. Jack Nasser (Ford) in *The Weekend Australian*, 19–20 September 1992.
38. *The Global challenge*, pp.70; 183; also, James P. Womack, D.T. Jones and D. Roos, *The machine that changed the world: the story of lean production*, Harper Perennial, New York, 1991.
39. *Developing Australia's national competitiveness*, ch. 3, p. 30; *The Global challenge*, ch. 4; Economic Planning and Advisory Council, Council Papers No. 45 and No. 47, January and April, 1991, both dealing with improving Australia's competitiveness.
40. *The Global challenge*, ch. 1, p. 14: only a small minority of firms

took seriously re-training, reskilling and the use of new management practices, e.g. Pacific Dunlop, Tubemakers (Newcastle), BHP Coated Products (Westernport, Vic.), ICI (Botany Bay), Holdens (Elizabeth), Southern Aluminium (Bell Bay). *The Age*, 20 April 1992, cited a study showing productivity gains among 12 leading manufacturers of around 8–12 per cent, 1989–91, on average.

41. *Australia's national competitiveness*, pp. 15, 38–40.
42. Bill Dix, quoted in *The Sunday Age*, 14 April 1991.
43. *The Sunday Age*, 5 May 1991 (report on the Australian Workplace Industrial Relations survey by Ross Gittins).
44. *The Age*, 27 July 1991.
45. *The Age*, 3 May 1991.
46. *The Sunday Age*, 5 May 1991.
47. *Australia's national competitiveness*, pp. 23–6.
48. *Australian exports* (Hughes Report) p. 31.
49. *Australia's national competitiveness*, pp. 17–18; *The Australian*, 22 June 1992.
50. Ibid. p. 35.
51. *The global challenge*, pp. 6ff, 130ff.
52. *Australia's national competitiveness*, p. 35 and p. 30; Bureau of Industry Economics, *Impediments to manufactured exports*, Discussion paper 12, AGPS, Canberra, 1990.
53. *Australian exports*, p. 6.
54. K. Ohmae, *The borderless world: power and strategy in the interlinked economy*, Fontana, London, 1990.
55. *Innovation in Australia*, Report for the Industry Research and Development Board by Pappas Carter Evans and Koop, AGPS, Canberra, July 1991, pp. 6–9. *The Age*, 8 June 1992, reported business spending on research at 0.53 per cent of GDP, about a quarter of its main rivals.
56. EPAC Discussion Paper 91/08, 'Science, technology and industrial development', September, 1991, pp. 24–8.
57. One major example was the sale of the gene shears technology developed by the CSIRO to Limagraine and Johnson and Johnson (American pharmaceutical company) in the absence of Australian interest—although much of the research would still be done by the CSIRO. Gene shears provided a capacity to cut out unwanted genes in living organisms and had major commercial applications for combating virus infections in both plants and humans, including a possibility for destroying the AIDS virus gene. In July 1992 the CSIRO also pioneered the breeding of microscopic worms called nematodes which were harmless to humans but could eliminate pesticides from the food chain by killing the insect pests of crops and trees. It too had a multibillion dollar commercial application but appeared likely to be sold to overseas interests. The Australian inventor of a gas fuse which automatically stopped gas flowing in the event of a gas pipe being destroyed by fire, causing explosion, was forced to go to America for investment funds to develop it further. Australian car firms for long remained unenthused by the prospects of Ralph Sarich's orbital two-stroke engine.
58. From the transcript of 'Gene Shears', screened on ABC 2 on 3 June 1992. (Limagraine employs 400 research staff and devotes 7.5 per cent of its turnover to research.)
59. Ibid. But not all: Conzinc Riotinto diversified into biotechnology in 1979 and has invested $80 million in Biotech Australia which is

yet to show an overall operating profit. As Professor Gustav Nossal observed: 'We have to have more people prepared to . . . put money into a product and wait. In my area, it may take 6 or 8 years to turn the discovery into a pill but . . . if you have a success you may have a product worth sales of $1 billion a year.'

60. A survey of Australian company managers revealed a characteristic time-horizon of 6 to 9 months, while overseas firms think in terms of 5, 10 or 15 years. Kerr (ed.), *Reinventing socialism*, p. 68. *The Global challenge*, ch. 1.

61. ABS figures discussed in *The Weekend Australian*, 8–9 February 1992. An ANZ Bank report showed that national savings fell in seven successive quarters to the end of 1992. Public sector saving was especially weak. *The Age*, 3 May 1993.

62. From 1990 most employers were required to contribute an additional 3 per cent of award wages to a nominated superannuation scheme for their employees. The government wished to extend compulsory superannuation as part of a strategy to reduce the cost of old age pensions: 13 per cent of the population was already of pensionable age; by 2030 the projected figure was 25 per cent. In July 1992 the government legislated (after a deal with the Democrats) to require all employers with a payroll of less than $1 million to contribute an extra 3 per cent of each employee's wages to a super scheme. Employers with payrolls over $1 million would contribute 4 per cent. In both cases the figure would rise to 6 per cent by 1996 and to 9 per cent by 2002.

63. I am grateful to Dr Don Stammer of Bain and Co. for this information.

64. *Australia reconstructed*, ACTU/TDC Mission to Western Europe, AGPS, Canberra, 1987, pp. 22–3, suggested the government establish a National Development Fund, administered by the AIDC, to provide funds for R and D and industrial development to which super funds should contribute up to 20 per cent of their income. The Block Committee (1991) inquiring into the commercialisation of research, also suggested that super funds holding more than 10 per cent of their assets offshore should be obliged to commit 1 per cent of assets to industry development.

65. In its *Annual Report, 1989–90*, p. 15, the IC acknowledged that 'it might be possible for firms to build competitiveness in [certain] areas over time, [but] it is a high risk strategy . . .'

66. Treasury, *Economic round-up*, Autumn, 1992, p. 43: 'Manufacturing sector performance'.

67. ABS figures from *The Age*, 18 August 1992.

68. *Economic round-up*, p. 60.

69. Bob Conlon, 'Australia's sectoral trade: has manufacturing's performance declined?' *Economic Papers*, 11:1 1992.

70. The 700 companies were growing at an average real compound growth rate of 13 per cent a year. About 40 per cent of them had only recently moved into exporting. About 30 new companies a year were emerging. Although only one-quarter exported more than 75 per cent of their output, the study projected that the value of their total exports would nearly double over the next five years, independent of the state of the Australian market. *The Australian*, 16 December 1992. Also, *One Nation* (Statement by the Prime Minister, 26 February 1992) provided detail on improvements.

71. *The Australian*, 10 June 1992 (AMC advertisement).

72. See further, *Going international: export myths and strategic realities*, Report to the AMC from the Australian Graduate School of Management, AMC, Melbourne, 1992.
73. See *Australian business in Asia: climbing the mountains*, Business Council, Melbourne, 1992.
74. Brian Loton's often stated view.
75. See e.g. Evans, 'The *global challenge* report'; Stanford, 'Industrial policy'.
76. Charles, 'Common themes', p. 33: 'In the really successful countries in Europe and elsewhere, it is the development-oriented parts of the bureaucracy, the business community, the scientific community, engineers and industrial banks which set the agenda and the tone of the industry policy debate. In Anglo-Saxon countries the debate tends to be driven by people remote from industry whose interests are best served by arguing for an industry policy requiring little, or preferably no knowledge of industry.'
77. *The Bulletin*, 11 February 1992, special article on economic rationalism.
78. E.g. in mid-1992 it contemplated a 20 per cent tax on industrial design and product development work (*The Age*, 9 June 1992). It reduced funding for medical science in 1992, so that the Melbourne research team that invented the bionic ear would lose its funding from 1994, among others. The bionic ear had 85 per cent of the world market and already earned $100 million in exports. *The Age*, 6 November 1992.
79. Department of Industry, Technology and Commerce, *Annual Report 1988–89*, AGPS, Canberra, 1989, p. 23.
80. *The Global challenge*, part 4; *Going international*, ch. 5.
81. Kambrook complained that Australian governments refused to consider purchasing a computer the company exported successfully to China; Australian governments imported about $400 million of computers annually. *The Australian*, 21 May 1992.
82. The government granted a $60 million aid package to Kodak to retain it as a strategic exporter in Australia. It refused to assist Labtam, an Australian fast-growth computer hardware firm which collapsed in 1989 when the USSR defaulted on its debts to the firm.
83. R. Stewart, 'Industrial policy', p. 106.
84. Stanford, 'Industrial policy', pp. 51–2.
85. As Tony Cole said: 'Basically we will end up with more imported manufactures and we will end up with domestic production concentrated in narrower areas. It's not our job [i.e. the IC's] to predict which firms will survive, which sectors will make most profits, but people in industry are thinking about it all the time.' *The Age*, 13 December 1990.

Chapter 7: *The impact of globalisation*

1. Senator Button, quoted in *The Australian*, 28 February 1992.
2. *One Nation*, Statement by the Prime Minister, 26 February 1992, e.g. p. 33 and p. 133.
3. Ibid. p. 70. Senator Button also assured the business community of this point (note 1).
4. See *Business Review Weekly*, 1 May 1992.

5. *The Australian*, 13 May 1992. The states were also now allowed to originate references to the IC, in consultation with Canberra.
6. M. Pusey, *Economic rationalism in Canberra*, Cambridge UP, Melbourne 1991; J. Carroll and R. Manne (eds), *Shutdown: the failure of economic rationalism and how to rescue Australia*, Text Publishing, Melbourne, 1992; P. Vintila et al. (eds), *Markets, morals and manifestoes, Fightback! and the politics of economic rationalism in the 1990s*, Institute for Science and Technology Policy, Murdoch University, 1992.
7. A form of state direction over economic matters, associated especially with the French style of indicative planning.
8. C.K. Chase-Dunn, *Global formation: structures of the world economy*, Blackwell, Cambridge, Mass, 1989.
9. See esp. John M. Stopford and Susan Strange, with John S. Henley, *Rival states, rival firms; competition for world market shares*, Cambridge UP, Cambridge, 1991; P. Drucker, 'The changed world economy', *Foreign Affairs*, Vol. 64, No. 4, 1986; Robert B. Reich, *The work of nations*, Vintage Books, New York, 1992; Lester Thurow, *Head to head: the coming economic battle among Japan, Europe and America*, Allen and Unwin, Sydney, 1993; K. Ohmae, *The borderless world: power and strategy in the interlinked economy*, Fontana, London, 1990; S. Gill and D. Law, *The global political economy: perspectives, problems, policies*, Johns Hopkins UP, Baltimore, 1989; J. Camilleri and P. Falk, *The end of sovereignty? The politics of a shrinking and fragmenting world*, Edward Elgar, Aldershot, 1992.
10. Reich, *Work of nations*, p. 111. See also Tom Forester, *High-tech society: the story of the IT revolution*, Blackwell, Oxford, 1987; A. Hamilton, *The financial revolution*, Penguin, Harmondsworth, 1986.
11. K. Ohmae, *Triad power: the coming shape of global competition*, Free Press, New York, 1985.
12. Reich, *Work of nations*, ch. 7, and Thurow, *Head to head*, for a parallel argument.
13. Ibid. p. 82. See also Stopford and Strange, *Rival states, rival firms*, pp. 35–6.
14. Ibid. p. 82 and p. 84.
15. E.g. the market for computer products, worth $200 billion in 1985; or markets for the product of bio-technology: half the drugs to be approved in the US in the 1990s will be such products (the majority of modern diseases have a genetic cause). In the next 40 years, humankind will have to produce as much food as in the entire history of agriculture; new strains produced through genetic manipulation will be central.
16. See, generally, Ohmae, *Borderless world* and *Triad power*; Tom Forester, *The materials revolution: superconductors, new materials and the Japanese challenge*, Blackwell, Oxford 1988; Barry Jones, *Sleepers, wake!*, Oxford UP, Melbourne, third edition, 1990.
17. See esp. M.J. Piore and C.F. Sabel, *The new industrial divide: possibilities for prosperity*, Basic Books, New York, 1984; Stephen Cohen and John Zysman, *Manufacturing matters: the myth of the post-industrial economy*, Basic Books, New York, 1987, chs. 10 and 11; Stopford and Strange, *Rival states, rival firms*, ch. 2.
18. *Work of nations*, chs. 10 and 11; see esp. pp. 94, 113, 131.
19. Ibid. pp. 98–9.
20. Ibid. p. 104.
21. See esp. *The global challenge*, ch. 8.

22. See e.g. Don E. Kash, *Perpetual innovation: the new world of competition*, Basic Books, New York, 1989; and John M. Legge, *The competitive edge*, Allen and Unwin, Sydney, 1992; George Stalk, Jr. and T.M. Hout, *Competing against time: how time-based competition is reshaping global markets*, Free Press, New York, 1990.

23. See J. Mathews, *Age of democracy: the politics of post-Fordism*, Melbourne, Oxford UP, 1989; and James T. Womack et al., *The machine that changed the world: the story of lean production*, Harper Collins, New York, 1990.

24. R. Johnston, 'The power to change', Paper presented to the Electricity Supply Association of Australia, 20 October 1992, pp. 7–8.

25. Note also L. Thurow, *Head to head*.

26. Johnston, 'The power to change', p. 7. Ohmae, *Borderless world*, ch. 1.

27. Stopford and Strange, *Rival states, rival firms*, pp. 1, 56–64. Also, Thurow, *Head to head*, and C.V. Prestowitz Jr., *Trading places: how we allowed Japan to take the lead*, Basic Books, New York, 1988.

28. Ibid. pp. 1–2.

29. Ibid. p. 56.

30. Ibid. p. 34.

31. Johnston, 'The power to change', p. 6.

32. *Work of nations*, p. 3 (and ch. 17).

33. H. Makler, A. Martinelli and N. Smelser (eds), *The new international economy*, Sage, Beverly Hills, 1982, p. 25.

34. Stopford and Strange, *Rival states, rival firms*, chs. 2 and 3.

35. See e.g. D.C. MacCharles, *Trade among multinationals: intra-industry trade and national competitiveness*, Croom Helm, London, 1987.

36. Australian car firms have begun to penetrate this trade. Over half the $1 billion of car exports in 1991 were engines and components supplied to overseas firms. Ford now sells cylinder blocks to Mazda in Japan. Holden supplies engines to Vauxhall, a GM subsidiary in the UK.

37. *Work of nations*, p. 113 and p. 114.

38. Ibid. p. 156.

39. Ibid. p. 120. Also Ohmae, *Borderless world*, for many comparable figures.

40. Ibid. p. 122.

41. Ibid. p. 128.

42. In *The Business Australian*, 12 August 1992, G. Lehmann cited US Congressional figures which identified the percentage of manufacturing employment provided by foreign-owned companies in six of the world's seven leading economies: Canada, 34 per cent; France, 21 per cent; UK, 14 per cent; Germany, 13 per cent; US, 7 per cent; Japan, 1 per cent.

43. Paul R. Krugman, 'Is free trade *passé*?' *Journal of Economic Perspectives*, Vol. 1, 1987; also Paul R. Krugman (ed.), *Strategic trade policy and the new international economics*, The MIT Press, Cambridge, Mass., 1988.

44. Also Clive Hamilton, 'Does free trade produce the goods?' *Economic Papers*, Vol. 8, No. 2, 1989.

45. Krugman, 'Is free trade *passé*?' p. 135.

46. Neo-classical economists are also concerned, rightly, that to legitimise such intervention on broad strategic grounds will accentuate the damaging drift away from global liberalisation which has already

started. Note e.g. *World Economic Review*, Vol. 12, No. 2, 1989, 'Statement by forty economists on American trade policy', pp. 263–5.

47. Michael E. Porter, *The competitive advantage of nations*, Free Press, New York, 1990. Quotations in the following pages come from M.E. Porter, 'The competitive advantage of nations', *Harvard Business Review*, March–April 1990, pp. 73–93.

48. Porter provides abundant illustrations which space precludes reproducing here.

49. Cf. *Australian exports* (Hughes Report), p. xxii: 'It has been recognised since the mid-1960s that Australia, like other industrial countries, needs institutional support for longer-term policy perspectives. At present these become lost in the day-to-day concerns of a bureaucracy geared to parliamentary cycles.'

50. These points are clearly acknowledged by a report from the Office of Technology Assessment, *Competing economies: America, Europe and the Pacific Rim*, Congress of the US, Washington DC, 1991. Note also G.C. Lodge, *Perestroika for America*, Harvard Business School, Boston, 1990, and *Comparative business-government relations*, Prentice-Hall, Englewood Cliffs, NJ, 1990; Thurow, *Head to head*; Prestowitz, *Trading Places*. The Department of Industry, Technology and Commerce in its *Annual report, 1989–90*, ch. 2, pp. 16–17, also referred to a supporting monograph by Bucaille and Costa de Beauregard, *The states as actors in industrial competitiveness*.

51. Industry Commission, 'Strategic trade theory: the East Asian experience', Information Paper, November 1990.

52. Robert Wade, *Governing the market: economic theory and the role of government in East Asian industrialisation*, Princeton UP, Princeton NJ, 1990.

53. Ibid. p. 342.

54. Ibid. pp. 26–7.

55. Ibid. p. 343.

56. G. White, *Developmental states in East Asia*, Macmillan, London, 1988.

57. Wade, p. 334.

58. C. Johnson, 'Institutional foundations of Japanese industrial policy', in C. Barfield (ed.), *Politics of industrial policy*, American Enterprise, Washington, 1986.

59. See e.g. A. Cox (ed.), *State, finance and industry*, Wheatsheaf, Brighton, 1986; F.W. Scharpf, *Crisis and choice in European social democracy*, Cornell UP, Ithaca, 1987.

60. Note esp. 'use national policies to promote industrial investment within the national boundaries, and to channel more of this investment into industries whose growth is important for the economy's future growth'; 'use protection to help create an internationally competitive set of industries'; 'if the wider strategy calls for heavy reliance on trade, give high priority to export promotion policies'.

61. Lodge, *Perestroika*, p. 13 (esp. ch. 1).

Chapter 8: The social market model

1. G. Dow, 'The economic consequences of economists', *Australian Journal of Political Science*, 27:2 July 1992.

2. Colin White, *Mastering risk: environment, markets and politics in*

Australian economic history, Oxford University Press, Melbourne, 1992.

3. A point made consistently by G. Barker and T. Colebatch in *The Age*.

4. See e.g. C.B. Macpherson, *The life and times of liberal democracy*, Oxford UP, Oxford, 1977.

5. S. Rees, G. Rodley and F. Stilwell (eds), *Beyond the market: alternatives to economic rationalism*, Pluto Press, Sydney, 1993.

6. M. Costa and M. Easson (eds), *Australian industry: what policy?* Pluto Press, Sydney, 1991.

7. P. Kelly, *The end of certainty: the story of the 1980s*, Allen and Unwin, Sydney, 1992.

8. G.C. Lodge and E.G. Vogel (eds), *Ideology and national competitiveness: an analysis of nine countries*, Harvard Business School, Boston, 1987.

9. J.P. Nettl, 'The state as a conceptual variable', *World Politics*, 20, 1968. Note also L. Pye, *Asian power and politics: the cultural dimensions of authority*, Belknap Press, Cambridge, Mass., 1985.

10. *Ideology and national competitiveness*, p. 316.

11. Ibid. p. 306.

12. Ibid. p. 311. Also, G. Clark, 'The Japanese tribe: what makes it work?' *Quadrant*, January/February 1992.

13. Ibid. p. 319.

14. Ibid. p. 23.

15. Ibid. p. 18. Also Thurow, *Head to head*.

16. For further details and references, see H.V. Emy and O.E. Hughes, *Australian politics: realities in conflict*, Macmillan, Melbourne, second ed. 1991, pp. 555–61.

17. Dow, 'The economic consequences of economists', p. 265; W. Korpi, *The democratic class struggle*, Routledge, Kegan Paul, London, 1983.

18. See e.g. F.W. Scharpf, *Crisis and choice in European social democracy*, Cornell UP, Ithaca NY, 1987.

19. See esp. Reich, *Work of nations*, Parts 3 and 4.

20. See Wade, *Governing the market*, pp. 375–7, also 337–44.

21. The issues in this section are discussed more fully in *Australian politics: realities in conflict*, pp. 100–13. Also H.V. Emy, 'Economic development versus political development', in H.V. Emy and A. Linklater (eds), *New horizons in politics: essays with an Australian focus*, Allen and Unwin, Sydney, 1990.

22. Cf. S.P. Huntingdon and J. Nelson, *No easy choice: political participation in developing countries*, Harvard UP, Cambridge, 1976.

23. ABS figures in *The Age*, 29 May 1992.

24. *Australian politics: realities in conflict*, p. 111 for further details.

25. Ibid.

26. *The Australian*, 13 December 1991.

27. Data from *Common wealth and common good*, A (Draft) Statement on Wealth Distribution from the Catholic Bishops of Australia, Collins/Dove, Blackburn, 1991.

28. *Accommodation for people with disabilities*, Report of the Senate Standing Committee on Community Affairs, AGPS, Canberra, May 1990. *The Australian*, 5 March 1992.

29. M. Olson, 'Rapid growth as a destabilising force', *Journal of Economic History*, 23:4, 1963.

30. See Alan Peacock, Hans Willgerodt, Daniel Johnson (eds), *German*

neo-liberals and the social market economy, Macmillan, London, 1989, p. 27, original emphasis. Also by the same editors, *Germany's social market economy: origins and evolution*, Macmillan, London, 1989.

31. *German neo-liberals*, p. 21.

32. See esp. K. Dyson, *The state tradition in Western Europe*, Martin Robertson, Oxford, 1980.

33. Note H. Dessloch, 'The social market economy in Germany and in Europe—principles and perspectives', in *Religion in communist lands*, Vol. 19, Nos. 1–2, Summer 1991 (special issue of papers from the Ampleforth Conference, 1990). The social market position is in some ways an attempt to reunite classical political economy and moral philosophy in the way they were linked originally in Adam Smith's work.

34. Cf. Brian Barry, *Does society exist? The case for socialism*, London, Fabian Trust No. 536, 1989; J. Gray, *The moral foundations of markets*, The IEA Health and Welfare Unit, London, 1992.

35. See e.g. G. Smith, W.E. Paterson, P.H. Merkl (eds), *Developments in West German Politics*, Macmillan, London, 1989, p. 28. Also Dyson, *State tradition*, chs. 4 and 6.

36. K. Dyson, 'Preparing for the single European market: a new agenda for government–industry relations', *Political Quarterly*, 62:3, 1991, p. 344; also K. Dyson, 'The politics of corporate crises in West Germany', *West European Politics*, 7:1, 1984.

37. Dessloch, 'The social market economy', p. 116; Smith et al. (eds), *West German politics*, ch. 9.

38. Ibid.

39. R. Skidelsky, *The social market economy*, The Social Market Foundation, London, 1989, p. 4. (These four points are adapted from Skidelsky.)

40. See esp. D. Brack, 'David Owen and the social market economy', *Political Quarterly*, 61:4, 1990: '[the term] can mean one where the state intervenes *less*, to allow the market free rein, or *more*, to establish a genuinely free market and break up monopolies; *more* to effect a greater distribution of income and wealth, or *less*, to allow the creation of that prosperity which would allow all to benefit. The social market has meant all these things at different times to different people' (p. 472). See also Peacock et al., *German neo-liberals*, for further discussion.

41. German workers who lose their jobs can receive two-thirds of their old wage for a year plus retraining for a new job, sometimes provided by their previous company.

42. In 1990 the three levels of the German public sector spent just over 48 per cent of GNP. Germany spends around 30 per cent of GDP on social security, health, education and community services, compared with around 18 per cent in Australia. Government subsidies to industry in the mid-1980s were roughly 13 per cent of GNP, the *lowest* level in the EC. Bureau of Industry Economics, *Federal Republic of Germany*, AGPS, Canberra, 1988, ch. 4.

43. *The Whitlam phenomenon: Fabian papers*, McPhee Gribble and Penguin, Melbourne, 1986, pp. 182–3.

44. See further, H.V. Emy, 'From liberalism to conservatism? Changing political alignments in the 1990s', *Quadrant*, December 1991, and the ensuing debate, esp. the essays by C. Kukathas (April) and M. Krygier (May).

45. M. Walzer, 'The communitarian critique of liberalism', *Political Theory*, 18:1, 1990, p. 21.
46. S. Avineri and A. de-Shalit (eds), *Communitarianism and individualism*, Oxford UP, London, 1992.

Bibliography

Accommodation for people with disabilities, Report of the Senate Standing Committee on Community Affairs, Australian Government Publishing Service, Canberra, 1990

Anderson, K. and Garnaut, R. 'The political economy of manufacturing protection in Australia', in *The political economy of manufacturing protection: experiences of ASEAN and Australia*, eds C. Findlay and R. Garnaut, Allen & Unwin, Sydney, 1987

Australia and Northeast Asia in the 1990s: accelerating change, Department of Foreign Affairs and Trade, Canberra, 1992

Australia and the Northeast Asian ascendancy (The Garnaut Report), Australian Government Publishing Service, Canberra, 1989

Australia reconstructed, ACTU/TDC Mission to Western Europe, Australian Government Publishing Service, Canberra, 1987

Australian business in Asia: climbing the mountains, Business Council of Australia, Melbourne, 1992

Australian exports: performance obstacles and issues of assistance, Report of the (Hughes) Committee for Review of Export Market Development Assistance, Australian Government Publishing Service, Canberra, 1989

Australian manufacturing and industry development: policies and prospects for the 1990s and into the twenty-first century, ACTU, Melbourne, 1990

Australia's foreign debt: choices for the future, National Summit on Debt, Business Council of Australia, Melbourne, 1990

Avineri, S. and de-Shalit, A. eds *Communitarianism and individualism*, Oxford University Press, London, 1992

Barfield, C. ed. *Politics of industrial policy*, American Enterprise Institute, Washington DC, 1986

Barry, B. *Does society exist? The case for socialism*, Fabian Trust Pamphlet No. 536, London 1989

Bell, S. 'The travails of industry policy in Australia', *Australian Quarterly*, Autumn, 1991

Blandy, R. and Niland, J. eds *Alternatives to arbitration*, Allen & Unwin, Sydney, 1986

Brack, D. 'David Owen and the social market economy', *Political Quarterly*, vol. 61, no. 4, 1990

Brett, J. 'The end of the parties', *Arena Magazine*, no. 1, October–November, 1992

Bureau of Industry Economics, 'Manufacturing enterprises and other strategies for growth', Discussion Paper 8, Canberra 1990

——'Impediments to manufactured exports', Discussion Paper 12, Canberra, 1990

Camilleri, J. and Falk, P. *The end of sovereignty? The politics of a shrinking and fragmenting world*, Edward Elgar, Aldershot, 1992

Carroll, J. and Manne, R. eds *Shutdown: the failure of economic rationalism and how to rescue Australia*, Text Publishing, Melbourne, 1992

Castles, F.G. *Australian public policy and economic vulnerability*, Allen & Unwin, Sydney, 1988

——ed. *Australia compared: people, policies and politics*, Allen & Unwin, Sydney, 1991

——'Australia and Sweden: the politics of economic vulnerability', *Thesis XI*, no. 16, 1987

Caves, R.E. and Krause, L.B. eds *The Australian economy: a view from the North*, Allen & Unwin, Sydney, 1984

Charles, D.T. 'Common themes between Australian and European industrial policy', in *Industrial policy in Australia and Europe*, ed. J. Stanford, Australian Government Publishing Service, Canberra, 1992

Chase-Dunn, C.K. *Global formation: structures of the world economy*, Blackwell, Cambridge, Mass., 1989

Clark, D. *Student economic briefs 1991/92* (annual), *Australian Financial Review*, Sydney, 1991

Clark, G. 'The Japanese tribe: what makes it work?' *Quadrant*, January/February, 1992

Cohen, S. and Zysman, J. *Manufacturing matters: the myth of the post-industrial economy*, Basic Books, New York, 1987

Common wealth and common good, Draft Statement on Wealth Distribution from the Catholic Bishops of Australia, Collins/Dove, Melbourne, 1991

Conlon, B. 'Australia's sectoral trade: has manufacturing's performance declined?, *Economic Papers*, vol. 11, no. 1, 1992

Conway, R. *The great Australian stupor*, Sun Books, Melbourne, 1971

Costa, M. and Easson, M. eds *Australian industry: what policy?*, Pluto Press, Sydney, 1991

Cox, A. ed. *State, finance and industry*, Wheatsheaf, Brighton, 1986

Daly, M.T. and Logan, M.I. *The brittle rim: finance, business and the Pacific region*, Penguin Books, Melbourne, 1989

Daniels, P. L. 'Australia's foreign debt: searching for the benefits', *Economic Papers*, vol. 11, no. 1, 1992

Dawkins, J.S. 'Privatisation and deregulation: myths and practicalities', *Journal of Australian Political Economy*, 20, October, 1986

Denemark, D. 'Social democracy and the politics of crisis in New Zealand, Britain and Sweden', in *The fourth Labour government*, eds M. Holland and J. Boston, Oxford University Press, Auckland, 2nd edn, 1990

Department of Industry, Technology and Commerce, *Annual Report 1988–89*, Australian Government Publishing Service, Canberra, 1989

Dessloch, H. 'The social market economy in Germany and in Europe—principles and perspectives', *Religion in Communist Lands*, vol. 19, nos. 1–2, Summer, 1991

Developing Australia's national competitiveness, Business Council of Australia, Melbourne, 1991

Dow, G. 'The economic consequences of economists', *Australian Journal of Political Science*, vol. 27, no. 2, 1992

Drake, P. J. and Nieuwenhuysen, J. P. *Economic Growth for Australia: agenda for action*, Oxford University Press and CEDA, Melbourne, 1988

Drucker, P. 'The changed world economy,' *Foreign Affairs*, vol. 64, no. 4, 1986

Duncan, T. and Fogarty, J. *Australia and Argentina: on parallel paths*, Melbourne University Press, Melbourne, 1984

Dyson, K. *The state tradition in western Europe*, Martin Robertson, Oxford, 1980

——'Preparing for the single European market: a new agenda for government–industry relations', *Political Quarterly*, vol. 62, no. 3, 1991

——'The politics of corporate crises in West Germany', *West European Politics*, vol. 7, no. 1, 1984

Dyster, B. and Meredith, D. *Australia in the international economy*, Cambridge University Press, Melbourne, 1990

Economic Planning Advisory Council (EPAC), Micro-economic reform, Council Paper No. 42, Canberra, 1990

——Improving Australia's international competitiveness, Council Paper No. 45, Canberra, 1991

Current account adjustment: options for the 1990s, Council Paper No. 50, Canberra, 1992

——Competing on world markets, Discussion Paper 90/08, Canberra, 1990

——Science, technology and industrial development, Discussion Paper 91/08, Canberra, 1991

Emy, H.V. 'From liberalism to conservatism? Changing political alignments in the 1990s', *Quadrant*, December, 1991

Emy, H.V. and Hughes, O.E. *Australian politics: realities in conflict*, Macmillan, Melbourne, 2nd edn, 1991

Emy, H.V. and Linklater, A. eds *New horizons in politics: essays with an Australian focus*, Allen & Unwin, Sydney, 1991

Enterprise-based bargaining units: a better way of working, Business Council of Australia, Melbourne, 1989

Evans, R. 'The global challenge report and the clash of paradigms', in *Australian industry: what policy?* eds M. Costa, and M. Easson, Pluto Press, Sydney, 1991

Ewer, P. et al. *Politics and the Accord*, Pluto Press, Sydney, 1991

Ewer, P., Higgins, W. and Stevens, A. *Unions and the future of Australian manufacturing*, Allen & Unwin, Sydney, 1987

Fightback! Taxation and expenditure reform for jobs and growth, Liberal Party of Australia, Melbourne, 1991

Forester, T. *High-tech society: the story of the IT revolution*, Blackwell, Oxford, 1987

——*The materials revolution: superconductors, new materials and the Japanese challenge*, Blackwell, Oxford, 1988

Forsyth, P. ed. *Microeconomic reform in Australia*, Allen & Unwin, Sydney, 1992

Foundations for the 'clever country', Australian Vice-Chancellors' Committee, Report for the 1992–94 Triennium, Canberra, 1991

Frankel, B. *From the prophets deserts come: the struggle to reshape Australian political culture*, Arena Publishing, Melbourne, 1992

Galligan, B. and Capling, A. *Beyond the protective state: the political economy of Australia's manufacturing industry policy*, Cambridge University Press, Sydney, 1992

Galligan, B. and Singleton, G. eds *Business and government under Labor*, Longman Cheshire, Melbourne, 1991

Garnaut, R. 'The end of protection and the beginnings of a modern industrial economy', *Australian Quarterly*, Autumn, 1991

Gerritsen, R. 'Authority, persuasion and exchange (revisited): the public policy of internationalising the Australian economy', IPSA Working Paper, Canberra, September 1922

Gill, S. and Law, D. *The global political economy: perspectives, problems, policies*, Johns Hopkins University Press, Baltimore, 1989

Going international: export myths and strategic realities, Report to the Australian Manufacturing Council from the Australian Graduate School of Management, Australian Manufacturing Council, Melbourne, 1992

Gordon, M. *A question of leadership: Paul Keating, political fighter*, University of Queensland Press, St Lucia, 1993

Graetz, B. and McAllister, I. *Dimensions of Australian society*, Macmillan, Melbourne, 1988

Gray, J. *The moral foundations of markets*, The IEA Health and Welfare Unit, London, 1992

Gruen, F. 'How bad is Australia's economic performance and why?' Discussion Paper, 127, Centre for Economic Policy Research at the ANU, Canberra, 1985

Haddad, L. 'The rise and fall of planning: a global perspective', *Australian Journal of Public Administration*, vol. 49, no. 2, 1990

Hamilton, A. *The financial revolution*, Penguin Books, Harmondsworth, 1986

Hamilton, C. 'Does free trade produce the goods?', *Economic Papers*, vol. 8, no. 2, 1989

Hamilton, F.E.I. ed. *Industrialisation in developing and peripheral regions*, Croom Helm, London, 1986

Higgott, R. 'The politics of Australia's international economic relations', *Australian Journal of Political Science*, vol. 26, no. 1, 1991

Higher education, a policy statement, Australian Government Publishing Service, Canberra, 1988

Higher education: quality and diversity in the 1990s, Australian Government Publishing Service, Canberra, 1991

Hilmer, F. *When the luck runs out*, Harper & Row, Sydney, 1985

Horne, D. *The lucky country*, Penguin Books, Melbourne, 1964

——*Money made us*, Penguin Books, Melbourne, 1976

Huntingdon, S. and Nelson, J. *No easy choice: political participation in developing countries*, Harvard University Press, Cambridge Mass., 1976

Hyde, J. and Nurick, J. eds *Wages wasteland*, Hale and Iremonger, Sydney, 1985

INDECS, *State of play 6: the Australian economic policy debate*, Allen & Unwin, Sydney, 1990

Industrial Relations and Management Newsletter, vol. 8, issue 11, December 1991

Industry Commission, *Annual report for 1989–90*, Canberra, 1990

——*Annual report for 1990–91*, Canberra, 1991

——*Strategic trade theory: the East Asian experience*, Information Paper, Canberra, November 1990

——*Export of education services*, Report No. 12, Canberra, 1991

Innovation in Australia, Report for the Industry Research and Development Board by Pappas Carter Evans and Koop, Australian Government Publishing Service, Canberra, 1991

Intergovernmental News, various issues

Interstate Commission, *Waterfront investigation: preliminary findings and discussion papers*, Australian Government Publishing Service, Canberra, 1989

Jennett, C. and Stewart, R.G. eds *Hawke and Australian public policy: consensus and restructuring*, Macmillan, Melbourne, 1990

Johnson, C. 'Institutional foundations of Japanese industrial policy', in *Politics of industrial policy*, ed. C. Barfield, American Enterprise, Washington, 1986

Johnston, R. 'The power to change', Paper presented to the Electricity Supply Association of Australia, 20 October 1992

Jones, B. *Sleepers, Wake!*, Oxford University Press, Melbourne, 3rd edn, 1990

Junankar, P.N. and Kapuscinki, C.A. *The cost of unemployment in Australia*, EPAC Background Paper No. 24, Canberra, 1992

Kahn, H. and Pepper, T. *Will She Be Right? The future of Australia*, University of Queensland Press, St Lucia, 1980

Kash, D.E. *Perpetual innovation: the new world of competition*, Basic Books, New York, 1989

Keating, M.A. 'The nature and significance of overloaded government', *Australian Journal of Public Administration*, vol.43, no. 1, 1984

Kelly, P. *The end of certainty: the story of the 1980s*, Allen & Unwin, Sydney, 1992

Kerr, D. ed. *Reinventing socialism*, Pluto Press, Sydney, 1992

Korpi, W. *The democratic class struggle*, Routledge & Kegan Paul, London, 1983

Krugman, P.R. ed. *Strategic trade policy and the new international economics*, The MIT Press, Cambridge, Mass., 1988

——'Is free trade passé?', *Journal of Economic Perspectives*, vol. 1, no. 1, 1987

Legge, J.M. *The competitive edge*, Allen & Unwin, Sydney, 1992

Levitas, R. ed. *The ideology of the New Right*, Polity Press, Cambridge, 1986

Lodge G.C. *Perestroika for America*, Harvard Business School, Boston, 1990

——*Comparative business–government relations*, Prentice-Hall, Englewood Cliffs, New Jersey, 1990

Lodge, G.C. and Vogel, E.G. eds *Ideology and national competitiveness: an analysis of nine countries*, Harvard Business School, Boston, 1987

Loton, B. 'Advance Australia—where?', *Australian Journal of Public Administration*, vol. 49, no. 3, 1990

Lougheed, A.L. *Australia in the world economy*, McPhee-Gribble, Melbourne, 1988

Luard, E. *The management of the world economy*, Macmillan, London, 1983

MacCharles, D.C. *Trade among multinationals: intra-industry trade and national competitiveness*, Croom Helm, London, 1987

McGregor, C. *Profile of Australia*, Penguin Books, Melbourne, 1968

Macpherson, C.B. *The life and times of liberal democracy*, Oxford University Press, Oxford, 1977

Makler, H., Martinelli, A. and Smelser, N. eds *The new international economy*, Sage, Beverly Hills, 1982

Mathews, J. *Age of democracy: the politics of post-Fordism*, Oxford University Press, Melbourne, 1989

Office of Technology Assessment, United States Congress, *Competing economies: America, Europe and the Pacific Rim*, Washington DC, 1991

Ohmae, K. *Triad power: the coming shape of global competition*, Free Press, New York, 1985

——*The borderless world: power and strategy in the interlinked economy*, Fontana, London, 1990

Olson, M. 'Rapid growth as a destabilizing force', *Journal of Economic History*, vol. 23, no. 4, 1963

——'Australia in the perspective of *The rise and fall of nations*', Centre for Economic Policy and Research, Discussion Paper 109, ANU, Canberra, 1984

One Nation, Statement by the Prime Minister, 26 February 1992, Australian Government Publishing Service, Canberra, 1992

Parbo, Sir A. 'Snake oils and bears in the cave', *Australia and World Affairs*, No. 11, Summer 1991

Peacock, A., Willgerodt, H. and Johnson, D. eds *German neo-liberals and the social market economy*, Macmillan, London, 1989

——eds *Germany's social market economy: origins and evolution*, Macmillan, London, 1989

Piore, M.J. and Sabel, C.F. *The second industrial divide: possibilities for prosperity*, Basic Books, New York, 1984

Porter, M.E. *The competitive advantage of nations*, Free Press, New York, 1990

——'The competitive advantage of nations', *Harvard Business Review*, March–April 1990

Prestowitz, C.V. Jr. *Trading places: how we allowed Japan to take the lead*, Basic Books, New York, 1988

Proceedings of the H.R. Nicholls Society: Arbitration in contempt, The H.R. Nicholls Society, Melbourne, 1986

Pusey, M. *Economic rationalism in Canberra: a nation-building state changes its mind*, Cambridge University Press, Melbourne, 1991

Pye, L. *Asian power and politics: the cultural dimensions of authority*, Belknap Press, Cambridge, Mass., 1985

Rees, S., Rodley, G. and Stilwell, F. eds *Beyond the market: alternatives to economic rationalism*, Pluto Press, Sydney, 1993

Reich, R. *The work of nations*, Vintage Books, New York, 1992

Santamaria, B.A. 'Whither Australia?', *Australia and World Affairs*, No. 11, Summer 1991

Sawer, M. ed. *Australia and the New Right*, Allen & Unwin, Sydney, 1982

Scharpf, F.W. *Crisis and choice in European social democracy*, Cornell University Press, Ithaca, 1987

Schedvin, B. 'The Australian economy on the hinge of history', *The Australian Economic Review*, First Quarter, 1987

Scutt, J. ed. *Poor nation of the Pacific: Australia's future*, Allen & Unwin, Sydney, 1985

Sheridan, K. ed. *The Australian economy in the Japanese mirror*, University of Queensland Press, St Lucia, 1992

Skidelsky, R. *The social market economy*, The Social Market Foundation, London, 1989

Smith, G., Paterson, W.E. and Merkl, P.H. eds *Developments in West German politics*, Macmillan, London, 1989

Stalk, G. Jr. and Hout, T.M. *Competing against time: how time-based competition is reshaping global markets*, Free Press, New York, 1990

Stanford, J. ed. *Industrial policy in Australia and Europe*, Australian Government Publishing Service, Canberra, 1992

Steward, J. 'Industry policy and why Australia needs one', *Canberra Bulletin of Public Administration*, No. 59, August 1989

Stilwell, F. *The Accord . . . and beyond*, Pluto Press, Sydney, 1986

Stopford J. and Strange, S. with Henly, J. *Rival states, rival firms; competition for world market shares*, Cambridge University Press, Cambridge, 1991

Strange, S. *States and markets*, Pinter, London, 1988

Stretton, H. 'The quality of leading Australians', *Daedalus*, vol. 114, Winter 1985

The Australian vocational certificate training system, Report by the Employment and Skills Formation Council under Mr Laurie Carmichael, Australian Government Publishing Service, Canberra, 1992

The global challenge: Australian manufacturing in the 1990s, Final Report of the Pappas Carter Evans and Koop/Telesis Study, Australian Manufacturing Council, Melbourne, 1990

The Whitlam phenomenon: Fabian papers, McPhee-Gribble/Penguin, Melbourne, 1986

Thurow, L. *Dangerous currents: the state of economics*, Oxford University Press, Oxford, 1983

——*Head to head: the coming economic battle among Japan, Europe and America*, Allen & Unwin, Sydney, 1993

Treasury, *Economic round-up* (Quarterly)

Vintila, P., Phillimore, J. and Newman, P. eds *Markets, morals and manifestos. Fightback! and the politics of economic rationalism in the 1990s*, Institute for Science and Technology Policy, Murdoch University, 1992

Vision 10: a ten year vision statement, Manufacturing Council of Victoria, Melbourne, 1992

Wade, R. *Governing the market: economic theory and the role of government in East Asian industrialisation*, Princeton University Press, New Jersey, 1990

Walsh, M. *Poor little rich country*, Penguin Books, Melbourne, 1990

Walzer, M. 'The communitarian critique of liberalism', *Political Theory*, vol. 18, no. 1, 1990

Waterfront Industry Reform Authority, *Final Report*, Melbourne, October 1992

White, C. *Mastering risk: environment, markets and politics in Australian economic history*, Oxford University Press, Melbourne, 1992

White, G. *Developmental states in East Asia*, Macmillan, London 1988

Whitwell, G. 'The triumph of economic rationalism: the Treasury and the market economy', *Australian Journal of Public Administration*, vol. 49, no. 2, 1990

Womack, J.P., Jones, D.T. and Roos, D. *The machine that changed the world: the story of lean production*, Harper Perennial, New York, 1991

Young people's participation in post-compulsory education and training, Report of the Australian Education Council Review under Mr Brian Finn, Australian Government Publishing Service, Canberra, 1991

Index

Aboriginal people, 4, 11
absenteeism, 143
Accord, the, 90, 91, 93, 131
ACOSS, 20, 27
ACTU, 25–6, 84, 92, 93, 94,
    96–8, 99
agricultural industry, 13, 138
Alston, Senator, 117–18
Arbitration Commission, 87–8,
    90; *see also* Industrial
    Relations Commission
Asia, integration with, 63–8
Asia–Pacific Economic
    Cooperation (APEC), 66
AUSSAT, 83
AUSTRAIN, 118
Australian Airlines, 83, 115
Australian Council of Social
    Services (ACOSS), 20, 27
Australian Industries
    Development Corporation
    (AIDC), 37, 150

Australian Manufacturing
    Council (AMC), 37, 153
Australian National Training
    Authority, 106, 107
Australian Technology Group
    (ATG), 162–3
Australian Trade Commission,
    134
Australian Traineeship System,
    107
Australian Vocational Certificate,
    107
Australian Wool Corporation, 51
aviation, domestic, 77
award restructuring, 91, 97,
    100, 104

balance of payments, 24, 27,
    68, 74, 75
banana republics, 71, 73
Barker, Geoffrey, 119
Better Cities program, 87

BHP, 57, 63, 145
Brereton, Laurie, 163
broadbanding, 100
budget deficit, 75
Bureau of Industry Economics, 145
Business Council of Australia, 20, 21, 79, 91, 96
Business Regulation Review Unit, 78
Button, Senator, 66, 161

cabotage, 85
capital account, 68
capitalism, 7, 17, 38, 40; free market, 34, 35
Career Start Traineeship Program, 107
Carter, Colin, 156
Catholic Social Welfare Commission, 27
centralism, 98, 99
Chamber of Commerce, Australian, 79
civil offsets program, 133
Clark, Manning, 4
Cleary, Phil, 26
collective responsibility, 2, 29, 38, 112, 160, 217, 220
Collins, Senator, 85
commodities, exports of, 60; prices of, 51–4; primary, 135–6; value-added, 136
Commonwealth Bank, 82
communitarianism, 41, 202–3, 220
company mergers, 78
competitiveness, 176, 186–95, 203
Confederation of Australian Industry (CAI), 78, 96
consumer price index (CPI), 90, 91, 92, 93
Cook, Senator, 95
corporatisation, 19, 80–3, 216
corporatism, social, 204–5
Council of the Australian Federation, 87
Crean, Simon, 96, 164

current account deficit, 20, 21, 46, 51, 68–71, 73, 74, 76

Dawkins, John, 75, 161
debt, external, 72, 76; foreign, 20, 21, 45, 46, 68, 69, 74; ratio, 153; repayment of, 72–3; *see also* current account deficit
decentralisation, 91, 96, 99
democracies, liberal, 205; social, 39, 40, 196–201
Department of Employment, Education and Training (DEET), 102
Department of Industry, 132, 156
Department of Social Security, 118
deregulation, 18, 21, 36, 76, 77–9; financial, 17–18, 69; of the labour market, 90
development, economic, 205–8; social, 205–8
dirigisme, 166

Economic Planning and Advisory Council (EPAC), 37
economic rationalism, 7, 8, 9, 10, 13, 16, 17, 20, 25, 29–35, 129, 130, 165
education, 19, 102–7, 175; social, 47
egalitarianism, 3
Elaborately Transformed Manufactures (ETMs), 23, 24, 55, 56, 62, 63, 70, 136, 137, 147, 151, 154, 156
enterprise bargaining, 22, 40, 90, 92–4, 95, 96, 97, 100–1, 122–3
environmentalism, 4, 11, 127
European Community (EC), 52
exchange rate, 74
Export Access program, 163
export assistance, 133, 157
Export Market Development Grant Scheme, 133
exports, 65, 153; agricultural, 50; Australian, 19;

commodity, 47, 50, 51, 53, 73, 153; ore and mineral, 50; service, 137

federal spending, 117
federalism, 78, 85–7
Ferguson, Mr, 96
Fightback!, 4, 109–21, 125, 140, 150, 163, 219
Fightback Mark 2, 120, 121
Finn Review, 104–5, 107
foreign ownership, 72
free market policies, 8, 9, 10, 16, 30, 31–4, 110
free market theory *see* economic rationalism
free trade, 25, 26, 183

Garnaut, Professor Ross, 59, 65, 70
Garnaut Report, 65, 66
General Agreement on Tariffs and Trade (GATT), 25
Global Challenge, The, 24, 136, 137, 141, 152, 157
globalisation, 13, 15, 18, 23, 24–5, 36, 44, 48, 61, 114, 134, 156, 161–95, 197, 198, 201, 203, 216
Goods and Services Tax (GST), 2, 4–5, 22, 27, 108, 116–17, 120, 121
government business enterprises (GBEs), 81, 82
Grants for Industrial Research and Development (GIRD), 132
Griffiths, Mr, 164
Gross Domestic Product (GDP), 13, 44, 71, 74
growth rate, 74–5

Hawke, Bob, 59, 85–6
Hewson, Carolyn, 3
Hewson, Dr John, 5, 23, 47, 112; flexibility and, 127; GST and, 120–1; speeches of, 119; structural reform and, 126; unions and, 123
high-value enterprise, 175
Horne, Donald, 43–4, 47

Howard, John, 121–2, 123

immigration, 44
imports, 24, 153, 158
individualism, 112, 220; possessive, 114
industrial relations, 87, 99, 191
Industrial Relations Commission (IRC), 90, 93–5, 97–9, 101, 121
Industries Assistance Commission (IAC), 30, 31, 79
Industry Commission (IC), 23, 25, 56, 57, 59, 79, 81, 83, 115, 129, 130, 134, 135, 140, 142, 151, 152, 163–4, 193
industry policy, 129–60, 155, 162, 169
infrastructure assistance, 27, 189
Institute of Company Directors, 101
International Monetary Fund (IMF), 54
intervention, 165, 185, 186, 193; government, 130, 132; selective, 28
intra-industry trade, 179–82
Investing in the Nation, 164
investment, in manufacturing, 72; sustained, 189
Investment Promotion Program, 132

Job Search Allowance (JSA), 118
Jones, Barry, 35, 148–9, 156, 161
Joseph, Sir Keith, 215

Keating, Paul, Asia and, 67; business leaders and, 161; enterprise bargaining and, 101; policies of, 7, 29, 40–1, 86, 196, 198; political judgment of, 2, 3; promises to lower tariffs, 163; speeches of, 3–4, 77, 101
Kelly, Paul, 11
Kelty, Bill, 93, 96, 97, 100
Kennett, Jeff, 3, 126
Kerin, Mr, 161

Kinnock, Neil, 215
Kirner, Joan, 106

Labor Party, election victory of, 1–2; policies of, 2–3, 4, 7, 8–9, 10, 19–20
Liberal Party, policies of, 4–5
liberalisation, 22; economic, 24, 25, 40–1, 56, 111, 216; of trade, 66
liberalism, 6, 109, 215, 220; free market, 29
Lucky Country, The, 43

Mabo decision, 4
Management and Investment Companies (MIC) program, 132
Manufacturing Council of Victoria, 159
manufacturing industry, 22, 23–4, 25, 28, 47, 48, 54–6, 58, 62–3, 129, 131, 134–53, 171–2, 180
market economies, 16, 20–30, 35–42, 47; social, 208–15
market failure, 165
market forces, 28
McLachlan, Ian, 23
Medicare, 2
Menzies, Robert, 6
Metal Trades Industry Association, 92–3, 96
mining industry, 13, 47, 48
modernisation, 24, 25
Moore, Des, 21
motor vehicle industry, 57, 58, 140–1, 172
Muller-Armack, Alfred, 209
Multi-National Corporations (MNCs), 179, 193
multi-skilling, 92, 100, 104
multiculturalism, 4, 6

National Industry Extension Service (NIES), 132–3
national strategic plan, 40
national wage case, 94, 98, 123
nationalism, 6
negative gearing, 150

neo-classical theory, 154, 155, 158, 159, 165, 167, 176, 178, 183, 186, 190, 192, 195, 197, 206, 207, 219–20
net debt servicing ratio, 74

OECD, 27, 46
One Nation, 21, 87, 106, 125, 134, 157, 162, 163, 164
Ordo-Liberals, 208, 209–10
Organisation for Economic Cooperation and Development (OECD), 13
original equipment maker (OEM), 141
OTC, 82
Owen, David, 215

paternalism, 30
Pooled Development Funds, 162
Porter, Michael, 186–7
poverty, 28, 45, 119, 196, 206–7
price mechanism, 110
privatisation, 19, 80–3, 115, 117, 216
productivity, bargaining, 97, 98, 99, 101; levels, 142–4
protectionism, 25, 30, 58, 59–61, 134, 154, 186, 198; *see also* tariff protection

Qantas, 83, 115

recession, 1, 5, 20, 27
reform, labour market, 20, 87–90, 121–5; macro-economic, 130, 158–9; micro-economic, 11, 20, 21, 46, 59, 76, 79–80, 115, 131, 153, 156, 159, 216; structural, 8, 9, 76–107, 125–6, 196, 199, 216; tax, 115, 116–17; waterfront, 93–4; workplace, 90, 91, 94, 125–6
Reich, Robert B., 170, 172, 175, 180, 181
republic, Australia as a, 4, 5
research and development, 132, 133, 145–9, 151, 156, 162, 174, 185

resource allocation, 30, 216
restructuring, 39, 45, 46–7;
arguments about, 20–6;
importance of, 14–20; society
and, 26–9
Richardson, Graham, 164

savings, 157; lack of, 149–50
Schiller, Karl, 210
science, developments in, 171–2
Smith, Adam, 219
social policy, 6–7, 8, 11
social security, 117–18, 119
solidarity, 211, 212
Special Premiers' Conferences
(SPCs), 86
standards, 189–90
statism, 29–30, 111
Stone, John, 21
strategic trade theory, 182–6,
189, 195
subsidiarity, 212
superannuation funds, 150, 157

tariffs, 56–9, 60; protection of,
15, 16, 18, 22–3; reductions
in, 140–1; reform of, 22, 131
tax, company, 75, 164;
consumption, 116;
depreciation scheme, 21, 162;
payroll, 116; reform of, 115,
116–17
Technical and Further
Education (TAFE), 103–4, 106
technology, 180; biotechnology,
156; developments in, 171–2,
173; information, 156–7
Telecom, 82–3, 115, 133
textiles, clothing and footwear
(TCF) industry, 57, 58–9,
141, 143–4, 163, 164
trade, international, 61–3, 66,
136
Trade Practices Commission, 78
transnational corporation
(TNC), 133

Triad, 180–1; economic,
169–70, 171, 174
Tricontinental Holdings, 82
two-airline agreement, 77

unemployment, 1, 5, 8, 11, 13,
26–7, 28, 29, 33, 45, 46, 74,
75, 90, 106–7, 118–19, 161,
165, 196, 206, 214
unions, 88–9, 91, 92, 97, 123,
124, 125

value-added goods, 55, 62, 136,
154
value-system, 201, 215
venture capital, 149
Vision 10, 159

Wade, R., 194–5
wages, fixation of, 19, 40, 101,
123, 124; increases in, 88, 90,
95, 123; indexation of, 91, 97
waterfront, the, 83–5
Waterfront Industry Reform
Authority, 85
Waterside Workers Federation,
84, 115
Watson, Don, 4
wealth, 169, 191, 198, 200,
202, 206, 207–8, 218–19;
creation of, 113–14
welfare, 109, 117, 127
wheat, 51, 52, 78
Whitlam, Gough, 218
workplace, agreements, 101;
bargaining, 122–3; reform, 21,
22, 94, 124, 156
World Competitiveness Report,
144
World Economic Forum, 46
world systems theory, 168

Young Liberals, 6
youth labour market, 104